Whyte in his prime, cigar at the ready,
in Moscow, about 1968

Champagne and Meatballs

Working Canadians: Books from the CCLH

Series editors: Alvin Finkel and Greg Kealey

The Canadian Committee on Labour History is Canada's organization of historians and other scholars interested in the study of the lives and struggles of working people throughout Canada's past. Since 1976, the CCLH has published *Labour/Le travail,* Canada's pre-eminent scholarly journal of labour studies. It also publishes books, now in conjunction with AU Press, that focus on the history of Canada's working people and their organizations. The emphasis in this series is on materials that are accessible to labour audiences as well as university audiences rather than simply on scholarly studies in the labour area. This includes documentary collections, oral histories, autobiographies, biographies, and provincial and local labour movement histories with a popular bent.

Series Titles

Champagne and Meatballs: Adventures of a Canadian Communist
by Bert Whyte, edited and with an introduction by Larry Hannant

Champagne and MEATBALLS

ADVENTURES of a CANADIAN COMMUNIST

Bert Whyte

edited and with an introduction by
Larry Hannant

AU PRESS

Canadian Committee
on Labour History

Published by AU Press, Athabasca University
1200, 10011–109 Street Edmonton, AB T5J 3S8

Library and Archives Canada Cataloguing in Publication

Whyte, Bert, 1909–1984

Champagne and meatballs : adventures of a Canadian communist
/ Bert Whyte ; edited and with an introduction by Larry Hannant.

(Working Canadians, ISSN 1925-1831)
Includes index.
Also issued in electronic format (ISBN 978-1-926836-09-6).
ISBN 978-1-926836-08-9

1. Whyte, Bert, 1909–1984.
2. Communists — Canada — Biography.
3. Communist Party of Canada — Biography.
4. Journalists — Canada — Biography.
5. Soldiers — Canada — Biography.
I. Hannant, Larry, 1950–
II. Title.
III. Series: Working Canadians

HX104.7.W59A3 2011   335.43092   C2010-907657-5

Cover and book design by Natalie Olsen, Kisscut Design.
All photographs courtesy of the Whyte family.
Printed and bound in Canada by Marquis Book Printing.

We acknowledge the financial support of the Government
of Canada through the Canada Book Fund (CBF) for our
publishing activities. ▮◆▮ Canadian   Patrimoine
                              Heritage   canadien

A volume in the Working Canadians: Books from the CCLH series
ISSN 1925-1831 (Print) ISSN 1925-184X (Online)

 Canadian Committee on Labour History

Dedicated to Bert's son, Rick Whyte,
and grandsons, Kevin Albert and Dylan Albert

Acknowledgements

In my ongoing quest to interview communists of a certain age, in 2006 I made the acquaintance in Toronto of John Boyd. How I had missed him before that year is one of life's oddities. Then over ninety years of age, John sat with me for three hours answering my questions and engaging in a lively discussion about the inner politics of the Communist Party of Canada, which he knew intimately for decades. Towards the close of the conversation, he said to me, "You should look up Monica Whyte in Victoria. She has the manuscript memoir of her husband, Bert Whyte." With that, I came — to my pleasure and instruction — to know Monica and to gain access, indirectly, to Bert Whyte. John has continued to offer assistance that has helped turn *Champagne and Meatballs* from a manuscript into a book. Numerous other people have also contributed in many ways. Monica Whyte's input is too comprehensive to begin to describe. Jon Rathbone transformed Whyte's original typescript into clean computer copy ready for editing; he scanned photos, transcribed a lengthy interview with Monica, and has retained an enduring interest in the Whytes and their story. Bryan Palmer's assistance has been invaluable. He will disagree — perhaps quite strongly — with some aspects of the introduction. But the fact that, despite his objections, he read both the introduction and the manuscript carefully and made numerous insightful comments speaks to his dedication not just to scholarship but to Left politics in Canada and beyond. Others have read the introduction in various manifestations and offered important suggestions. Jim Hamm, Franca Iacovetta, David Lethbridge, Reg Whitaker, and an anonymous reader for Athabasca University Press are among them. Kim Willoughby encouraged me to persist in the project. All errors, of course, are my own.

— LARRY HANNANT

In addition to John Boyd, I would like to thank Lori Boittiaux for her assistance in organizing and copying the many letters that Bert wrote to Rick and to me, excerpts from which now form a final chapter to *Champagne and Meatballs*.

If not for Larry's driving force, this book would still be a manuscript sitting in a drawer.

— MONICA WHYTE

Champagne and Meatballs

ℓℓℓℓℓℓ

Introduction

Champagne and Meatballs is Bert Whyte's account of how he navigated half a century of historical upheaval, mayhem, and catastrophe. Historians call it the twentieth century. Whyte cut a merry path through the Roaring Twenties, bummed across Canada like countless others during the Depression of the 1930s, battled fascism in the Second World War, and held fast to communism throughout the 1950s, despite the Cold War. Communism and anti-communism marked much of his life. He lived through decades when people worldwide were expected to choose between being Red or White. Always the rebel, Whyte dared to be Red. Yet while his choice imposed a burden on him, Whyte was never weighed down by it, and his writing displays this ebullience. *Champagne and Meatballs* is by turns funny, irreverent, and revealing. Whyte considered it to be an "autobiography of sorts." He thought it presumptuous to claim to write a formal autobiography, so he assembled a collection of engaging stories about a life of adventure.

As we're swept into *Champagne and Meatballs* we discover a man of action with considerable writing talent. True, it's untutored. Whyte never spent so much as an hour in journalism school. But even the first articles he wrote for the Communist Party of Canada (CPC) press — "What I Know About Relief Camps," "A Worker Is Dead," and "Night Freight" — illustrate a capacity to use first-hand observation to vividly sketch the reality of life for common folk. Whyte began writing for the communist press in 1936 and continued to do so for almost forty years. Not only did he cover events across a good part of Canada, he also filed articles from Europe during World War II, and, as official *Canadian Tribune* correspondent, from Beijing, Moscow, and other parts of Asia and Europe.

Like all of us, James Albert Whyte — known simply as "Bert" — was blessed and cursed by his birth and upbringing. Both his mother and father could trace their ancestry to Scots United Empire Loyalist settlers in eastern Ontario. In 1784, when the Loyalists came to what would become Canada, being Scottish was no special advantage in life, and might in fact have been the mark of McCain. But by 1909, the year of Whyte's birth, Scottish ancestry had come to be a badge of honour. That didn't pay the grocery bill, of course. Whyte's father, Jack, was a skilled worker, but ill health and the vagaries of the boom-and-bust mining economy in northern Ontario, where his folks found their livelihood, cast a net over the family. It let them imagine prosperity but kept them from seizing it.

Yet Whyte's family also favoured him with a stable and nurturing nest. Despite — yet also in part because of — the stern Christianity of his mother, Edith, there was space for reading, inquiry, and the development of social consciousness. The last was sometimes abstract to the youthful Whyte. Where was Armenia, and why exactly would him finishing the food on his dinner plate help the starving Armenians? Nevertheless, as a boy he learned the simple fact that "there" and "here" are part of a dialectical whole.

Whyte had relatively little formal education, completing school just to grade eight. Still, he became and remained an avid and eclectic reader. In 1950, for instance, he gave a lecture at the Vancouver Book Fair comparing Soviet and Western novelists of the mid-twentieth century, then published the lecture. In 1954 he wrote articles on the Doukhobors, a group of Russian cultural and religious dissidents living in Canada. The series included excerpts from works by the Russian novelist Leo Tolstoy, who had helped the Doukhobors escape from tsarist persecution and emigrate to Canada. He introduced his second wife, Monica, to the nineteenth-century French poet Charles Baudelaire. But Whyte's learning was not confined to books. He showed an endless curiosity about the world and the people in it. He could glean the makings of a newspaper story from a bar stool or at the rail of the racetrack as well as in a formal interview with notepad in hand. He drew inspiration for columns based on both the terrifying "hurry up" aspects of army life and the tedious "wait" phases. Characteristically, in 1950, when he interviewed Mary Kardash, a CPC activist just returned from a Moscow conference of the World Federation of Democratic Women, he told her to spare him the formal conference report. "I want to ask you about other things. The people you met. The stores you shopped in. The children. Your impressions of Moscow." [1]

Whyte's determination to savour life's experiences is never far from the surface in *Champagne and Meatballs*. He's a storyteller fascinated by people in all their forms and peculiarities. And he's intent on making the most of life's opportunities. As a youth hitchhiking and riding the rods across North America in the 1920s and 1930s, his greatest joy is in his fellow travellers and the folk he encounters en route. Intrinsically he sides with the underdog. But this bias emerges out of action and observation, not study and ideology. Indeed, ideology seems to him almost an after-thought. In this way *Champagne and Meatballs* contradicts the common image of a communist. Communists are frequently presented in Western culture as ideologically dogmatic, narrowly political, austere, and humourless. Novelist Earle Birney offers up the usual stereotype in *Down the Long Table*, which depicts the 1930s in Toronto. Among the characters is Kay, a fictional alter ego of communist Jean Watts, who was a contemporary of Whyte's. Birney has his protagonist, Gordon, describing Kay as a "long, thin-breasted, humourless pedantic wildcat." [2] By contrast, the Whyte we observe in *Champagne and Meatballs* seems to embrace Karl Marx's favourite phrase — "Nothing human is foreign to me." [3] Whyte revels in the sensual experience of the pool hall, the boxing ring, the race track, the burlesque theatre. Life for Whyte is a multi-hued kaleidoscope, even if red is the dominant colour in it.

If we take our cue only from the Royal Canadian Mounted Police, communism defined Whyte's life, from his decision to join the CPC, when he was twenty-seven, to his death in 1984, at the age of seventy-four. Relentlessly bureaucratic, the RCMP built up a 3,400-page file on Whyte that is pre-occupied with the superficial details of Whyte's communism. Who did he associate with? What was his position in the party? Where were the meetings he attended? When did he become the *Canadian Tribune* correspondent in Beijing? But we must ask more penetrating questions. Why did Whyte, the good-humoured sensualist, throw in his lot with this little band of outcasts? Why did he show lifelong loyalty to a party that was saddled with controversy, watched and harassed constantly by the RCMP, and damned for its allegiance, some say subservience, to the Soviet Union?

How did the free-spirited Whyte endure party discipline and routine? What kind of communist was Whyte? Whyte's decision to take up with the CPC was based on a very practical assessment of which political force in 1930s' Canada was on the front lines of change. In 1934, when he found himself in Vancouver after riding freight trains and thumbing rides across Canada, he was briefly intrigued by the Industrial Workers of the World. The IWW, or Wobblies, was a long-standing collection of militants who had waged epic free-speech battles on the west coast in the first decade of the twentieth century. But, as Whyte observes in his memoir, "for all the fiery speeches, everyone [in the IWW] was either gray-headed or bald." As for the other left-wing political contender in that volatile decade, J.S. Woodsworth's Co-operative Commonwealth Federation (CCF), Whyte had an equally utilitarian objection: "All they seemed to want was my vote, with a promise that by 1955 they would be elected to power federally. I couldn't see that outfit doing anything very revolutionary." Conditions cried out for fundamental change; if that was what you wanted, the CPC was your choice.

Whyte's account of throwing in his lot with the Reds is a droll scene like so many in his memoir. Working at the copper smelter in Noranda, Quebec, in the sixth year of the Great Depression, Whyte is trying to organize a union. He's advised that "someone from Toronto" wants to meet him at midnight. At an all-night diner after his 3:00-to-11:00 p.m. shift he's indulging in a plate of ham and eggs. He notices a small fellow sidle into the café. The stranger sits down beside him. There's no intellectual foreplay. The recruiter gets right to business: "You wanna join party?" "Which party?" "Communist Party!" "Sure." Through this delightfully commonplace exchange, James Albert Whyte set himself on a path that took him into a life of activist journalism, underground organizing, a world war, years of political persecution, and travel across half the world.

There were doubtless many other angry young Canadians in the 1930s who joined the CPC in a similar way. But while he was typical in that sense, Whyte was different in another. Whyte remained in the party, while most quit. One detailed study of rank and file members of the Communist Party of the United States of America (CPUSA) in Chicago from 1928 to 1935, for example, reveals that half of those who joined left within a year.[4] The desertion rate from the Canadian party was likely similar. Political disenchantment, boredom, and just plain overwork drove out many. Not Whyte. He stuck with the party through events that led others to see it as The God That Failed — the 1939 German-Soviet Non-Aggression Pact, the reversal of the party's stand on World War II, the anti-communist hysteria of the late 1940s, Nikita Khrushchev's 1956 attack on Joseph Stalin's leadership, and the Soviet military interventions in the Hungarian political conflict in 1956 and in Czechoslovakia in 1968. If these crises caused Whyte to doubt the party, he did not confide this to his memoir. Virtually to the end of his life he devoted his verve and his verbs to writing for what he must well have understood were fringe newspapers and audiences.[5]

Perhaps Whyte weathered all these trials because communism was merely one part of his life. At times, in fact, politics seemed to be mere sideshow. His 1938 political statement in the files of the Communist International, for instance, reads like an early version of *On the Road*. He recounted adventures and peccadilloes with a breezy frankness: "In 1926 I went on my first . . . tramping trip down to Kentucky. . . . I worked at Noranda from fall 1931 to spring of 1934. . . . I made good money, did plenty of drinking and didn't save much."[6] What Communist International functionaries in Moscow thought of this is not hard to imagine. Doubtless it confirmed an already well-established Comintern disdain for the political backwardness of leftist Canadians. International commissars' criticism of the lack of political discipline of Norman Bethune and other Canadians who joined the Mackenzie-Papineau Battalion to fight fascism in the Spanish Civil War, for example, is well documented.[7] Although Whyte stuck with the CPC, he remained a dissident Red until his death. This is well illustrated by a penetrating assessment of the woes of the Communist Party leadership recorded by the RCMP in March 1970. The report was written as communism worldwide struggled to deal with the great blow it suffered with the events in Czechoslovakia of 1968. In April 1968 the Czechoslovakian Communist Party adopted a reform program that promised the country "socialism with a human face." But when the Communist Party of the Soviet Union, led by Leonid Brezhnev, crushed the Czech initiative by military invasion in August 1968, communist parties worldwide, including the CPC, were thrown into what historian Norman Penner described as "a state of utter confusion."[8] Divisions in the CPC were marked, and the party leadership itself changed its stand on the issue several times. (Whyte was the *Canadian Tribune* correspondent in Moscow at the time; this distance from internal debates within the CPC allowed him to avoid having to take sides on the matter directly.) The RCMP assessment of March 1970, based on the observations of an informer who was extremely well placed in the CPC, detected a profound malaise in the party. The five-page report surveyed the outlook of CPC leaders and offered trenchant judgments of their strengths and weaknesses and the difficulties each faced in the power struggle within what the source considered to be an ailing, stagnant organization.

Whyte's position and outlook were succinctly summarized when the RCMP informer turned to the problem of how the party would memorialize Leslie Morris, the longtime editor of the *Canadian Tribune* and, from 1961 to his death in 1964, the general secretary of the CPC. Whyte had worked with Morris for several years and was approached by the party elite to write a biography of him. "Source referred to WHYTE as an opportunistic rather than a dogmatic Communist," the RCMP report noted. Whyte agreed to write the biography but insisted that he be free to portray Morris "as a man and a Communist. He wanted to write a biography that could be sold as a pocket book on the newsstands which would tell ordinary Canadians what a leading Canadian Communist was like." This was too radical for the leadership, the RCMP source reported, and they turned to another party insider, John Weir, who wrote an ideological tract whose analysis irritated the Morris family and set off inner-party squabbles. As a result, it was never published.[9] So Whyte was denied the chance to present Morris "as a man and a Communist." But, when it came to an account of his own life, he put up with no such restrictions. The memoir likely benefited from being written in Moscow, where he was living at a safe distance from CPC oversight. *Champagne and Meatballs* is his unvarnished declaration of independence, a statement of self-affirmation in the face of authorities from right and left.

Why, despite being a dissident in his own party, Whyte remained in it is never openly addressed in the memoir. This is at once its weakness and its strength. *Champagne and Meatballs* is not a chronicle of self-reflection but a recollection of events and action. As the narrative of an engaging rogue, especially in its account of life on the bum in the 1930s, it joins a long list of picaresques from the legions who were made into drifters by the Great Depression.[10] But Whyte's experience differs in one key way from that of most of his fellow hobos. He quit a good job to join thousands of young men who had no work. And when he tired of tramping, when the daily toil of not working finally wore him out, Whyte returned to the hard-rock smelter he had left earlier. Giving up a job in 1934 was a brave, some might say foolhardy, act. Many working people were putting up with wage cuts, speedups, and other daily humiliations just to *keep* jobs. It was an act that displayed Whyte's sense of class solidarity, his independent spirit, and his determination to chronicle life's experiences. Choosing to *leave* a job and becoming a blanket-stiff put him among the hundreds of thousands of men his age for whom the open road was not a choice. Equally important, the Depression and World War II were the singular events of his generation. Whyte could no more miss that train than Émile Zola could fail to descend into the satanic mines of nineteenth-century France to chart the agonizing birth of the industrial world.

Not only in recounting his experiences on the road but throughout *Champagne and Meatballs*, Whyte portrays humanity affectionately but not romantically. He presents a host of engaging characters — the small businessman who gives Whyte his first job, his hobo pals, his workmates in the smelting plant, his comrades in the Communist Party. Although Whyte is political, these vignettes are often not politicized. Even the magistrate in Sioux Lookout, in northern Ontario — who would represent, for most leftists, an instrument of class-based capitalist injustice — shares a laugh with Whyte and his co-accused at the expense of the dumb cops who believe they've snared a cell of international revolutionaries rather than five mouthy youths fed up with the indignities of life at a federal slave labour camp. For Whyte, experience came first, ideology second. Humanity was primary for him, communism secondary.

Like many young Canadians who in the 1930s rode the freights to a leftist political consciousness, Whyte was ready to make the next logical step and fight fascism in the Spanish Civil War. In 1936, Adolf Hitler and Benito Mussolini armed and aided General Francisco Franco's military rebellion against the elected republican government in Spain, hoping to add another country to the fascist bloc. Tens of thousands of people worldwide saw it as their duty to fight this fascist threat. Close to 1,700 of them were from Canada. Whyte desperately wanted to join them, but internal Communist Party dynamics ruled this out. Party leaders saw Whyte as a relative rarity among party activists — a native-born, articulate Canadian with a knack for organizing. They were not prepared to let this promising activist, whose roots went back to the United Empire Loyalists, run the risk of dying in Spain. So Whyte was kept at home, while his long-time friend and travelling buddy, Jimmy Black, volunteered and went overseas with the Mackenzie-Papineau Battalion. In Spain, Black earned commendations for his bravery in battle and, at the age of only twenty-six, an untimely death.[11] No one can enumerate all the factors, from the global to the personal, that may lead people to act, but the memory of Black's death was no doubt part of what sent Whyte into the Canadian army in January 1942 to fight in the next round of the world war against fascism. This time the party did not stop him.

The RCMP began tracking Whyte in 1936, when it noticed his articles in the communist paper the *Daily Clarion*.[12] The

RCMP's file on him would continue to grow, so that by the time of his death it would contain (complete with military records) over 3,400 pages. (Most of the retrieved pages have, unfortunately, been severely redacted by the Canadian Security Intelligence Service, which has the authority to vet RCMP Security Service files now in Library and Archives Canada.)[13] The frequency of the RCMP's reports would increase during World War II. One police document, from the period when the party was banned, suggests that although Whyte was "underground," he had not totally escaped the attention of the RCMP. It notes that "Bert Whyte, a member of the CP, who is organizing in small country towns where he is not well known, is trying [to] cause trouble wherever possible."[14] Even though he was under surveillance, Whyte avoided arrest, unlike many communists who tried to disappear. Ben Swankey, another CPC organizer who was instructed by the party to vanish and organize secretly, was not so lucky. Swankey, who admits that he "knew nothing about underground work" and apparently received no instruction in it from party leaders, decided that avoiding arrest meant that "I never appeared anywhere in daytime." As a result he "felt isolated . . . and out of touch with the CPC leadership." Even this didn't stop him from being picked up by the RCMP and interned in 1940. Swankey concluded that "this 'underground' activity was as amateurish as it was ill-advised."[15]

No doubt it was poorly carried out. Despite repression in the 1930s, the Communist Party of Canada had little experience in this kind of politics. But, had the two men conferred, Whyte might have taught Swankey a few lessons. Whyte positively thrived during his days underground in Ottawa. He sketches the time with a delicious humour that also reveals how different was his strategy from Swankey's.

Whyte decided that avoiding arrest required being open and looking as conventional as possible. His cover was that he sold picture frames, which justified him travelling in and around Ottawa. And, to complete the image, some well-deserved luxury: "When I needed a haircut I went to the expensive barber shop in the Chateau Laurier. I avoided eating in cheap cafes and often conferred with the chain store manager [a covert CPC member] over a good dinner at a respectable hotel dining room — letting him settle the tab. I dressed conservatively and wore a blue homburg." Once Whyte was in an elevator in the parliament buildings when Prime Minister William Lyon Mackenzie King, no doubt wearing a similar three-piece suit, joined him.[16] One suspects that Whyte might just have enjoyed playing the bourgeois.

Another aspect of his strategy for survival underground involved hobnobbing with people who could never be accused of radicalism. Whyte joined a bridge club at the YMCA, for instance, where he frequently found himself in a foursome with the editor of a Roman Catholic newspaper that was "known for its anti-communist views." Although he later admitted to his wife, Monica, that from time to time he feared his cover had been blown, he continued to play his hand as a respectable member of Ottawa society.

When he was in character as a Red, Whyte's underground party work in early World War II involved writing, reproducing, and distributing the clandestine *Ottawa Clarion* and other CPC leaflets. They were simple mimeographed productions, but for the better part of six months, as the party struggled under illegality, these publications tweaked the noses of the establishment. Indeed, living under the threat of arrest didn't deny Whyte and the other CPC activists in Ottawa their fun. Just to show that the arrest and jailing of party members like Harry Binder in 1940 had not entirely stifled opposition, in January 1941 Whyte and his comrades mailed a copy of the *Clarion* to the editor of the *Globe and Mail.* Alarmed, a *Globe* editorial writer lamented that "there is published in Ottawa, right under the Government's nose, *The Clarion*, boldly announced as 'organ of the Ottawa District of the Communist Party of Canada'. There is a defiant ignoring of the fact that the Communist Party is declared an unlawful organization in this country." The *Ottawa Citizen* then took up the case and asked the local RCMP where the *Clarion* was being printed. The resulting article gave Whyte and his comrades still more grist for humour. As the *Clarion* summed it up: "In other words, no paper is printed here but the police are actively searching for the printing shop where it isn't being printed. Simple, isn't it? Perhaps the RCMP sleuths lack only a starting clue — a whiff of perfume, a broken comb, a soiled handkerchief, or something. The editor of *The Clarion*, anxious to be of help, is herewith enclosing a lock of his hair with this issue of *The Clarion* going to the *Globe and Mail.*"[17]

The first two years of World War II, however, were not all spy-vs.-spy thrills for the Communist Party. It was not just a matter of being outlawed. The CPC also found itself losing support because of dramatic shifts in its political position. After the outbreak of hostilities on September 1, 1939, the CPC leadership initially thought that Canada should join the war, viewing it as a campaign against fascism. Yet on September 20 it reversed direction, calling the war a fight between rival imperialists that people should reject.[18] In his memoir, Whyte skated around the switch, explaining only that "after a period of indecision, the CPC declared that it was an imperialist war, between imperialist powers, for imperialist aims on both sides." Assessing the reversal, historian Norman Penner asked why communist parties worldwide made such an about-face. "The answer is that . . . Joseph Stalin issued [a] directive through the Communist International to all Communist Parties" declaring the war to be imperialist and unjust.[19] In his memoir, Ben Swankey declared that the party's "uncritical acceptance of the [Communist International's stand on the war] was a major error." On June 22, 1941, when Nazi Germany attacked the Soviet Union, the Canadian party, following the Comintern's decree, reversed itself again and declared the war to be a general struggle against fascism and urged an all-out Canadian war effort.

The "Stalin-as-master-manipulator" argument has come to be widely accepted as an explanation for the peregrinations of the CPC during World War II and for a broad range of flaws in the party's political line and practice. But it's important to recognize that conditions from 1933 to 1941 worldwide were extremely complex and rapidly fluctuating. The reason was the political volatility of the Great Depression and the terrifying advance of fascism, which was an aggressive, anti-democratic bid to preserve capitalism in what appeared to be its hour of final crisis. The intense political manoeuvring inside Germany that led to Hitler being appointed chancellor of Germany in January 1933 soon turned into an even more complicated international contention over the political future of the world. In this time of heightened conflict, the consequences of error could be catastrophic — witness the destruction of the sizable Communist Party of Germany after Hitler took power.

In response to these explosive changes, international communism was forced to shift its tactics more than once. But to claim that communists alone changed their tactics in this complex situation is to ignore the facts. The British elite, for example, reversed course frequently between 1938 and 1941. In September 1938 Neville Chamberlain, a prime minister whom historians Clement Leibovitz and Alvin Finkel describe as colluding with Hitler, signed the Munich deal with Germany. Chamberlain hoped that sacrificing part of Czechoslovakia in this way would guarantee peace between Britain and Germany. Hitler, however, upped the ante in the spring of 1939, seizing the rest of Czechoslovakia. As a tactical response, the British elite shifted to threats of war. When, on September 1, 1939, Germany invaded Poland, which Britain had pledged to defend, Britain declared war. But it did nothing to help Poland; for eight months the conflict remained strictly the "Phoney War." In May 1940, when what the British press had taken to calling the "sitzkrieg" became a German blitzkrieg throughout western Europe, Hitler-colluder Chamberlain was replaced by Hitler-antagonist Winston Churchill. In June 1941, Britain did another about-face after Germany turned its military forces on the Soviet Union. The fiercely anti-communist Churchill contradicted his own political stand and embraced the USSR as an ally. Thus, in a bid to live on, from 1938 to 1941 the British elite acted like nothing more than a child's top, constantly spinning.[20] Virtually *every* world political party and leader of any significance shifted to and fro in a similar fashion as concrete conditions changed. The international communist movement, centred in the Soviet Union, well understood Western capitalism's hostility to it. If communism had not adjusted its tactics to keep abreast of the new developments that emerged daily, it would have been doomed to oblivion. Instead communism not only survived this period of contention but emerged considerably strengthened from the dozen years of struggle against fascism.

If they were mindlessly following Stalin's decrees, Whyte and his comrades at the *Ottawa Clarion* displayed some considerable political panache in their subservience. On February 1, 1941, the *Clarion* laid out an impressive synopsis of the war under the headline "Communists and the War." The article noted that after seventeen months of war, its character in Canada was clear. Civil liberties had been suppressed, national registration and conscription legislation had been passed and the screws of state control tightened. "War profiteers are having a field day.... The rich grow richer, the poor grow poorer." The Communist Party, the *Ottawa Clarion* added, had anticipated this, and at its Eighth Dominion Convention in October 1937 it had urged Canadians to fight for peace. However, the CPC had declared at the time that "should imperialist war none the less break out despite the struggle for peace," communists would follow the plan of the Communist International, which called on progressive people "to work for [the war's] speedy termination" and use the opportunity to "hasten the downfall of capitalist class domination." With considerable foresight the Communist International also anticipated the German invasion of the USSR, advising communists worldwide that in the event of "a counter-revolutionary attack on the Soviet Union," it would be the duty of all progressives "to do everything possible for the defeat of the imperialist and fascist forces."[21] This points out that what is commonly referred to as the Second World War was not one war but a series of wars with different characteristics at different moments. Different tactics, therefore, were required at each unique moment. Was fascism such a scourge that its opponents should never contemplate any tactical shifts? To argue that is to believe that all wars must be fought by an unrelenting offensive — surely a recipe for failure.

In 1942, world events reshaped Whyte's personal path. When the Grand Alliance of Britain, the USSR, and the USA temporarily fell into place in January 1942, Bert Whyte faced a new future. We don't know how much of his action was due to his consciousness of an international political trajectory and how much to his personal regret that he had missed an earlier battle against fascism in Spain. But his resolve was clear. On January 26, 1942, Whyte joined the Canadian military to fight fascism in Europe. He served in uniform for the next four years, ending the conflict with the rank of corporal. When he signed up with the Toronto Scottish Regiment at the age of thirty-three, he was an older-than-average soldier. His attestation papers recorded only that he was a reporter in civilian life and mentioned no political activism. The Communist Party had ended its opposition to the war when the USSR was invaded on June 22, 1941, and was now urging the government and all Canadians to exert every effort to defeat fascism. Still, the Canadian military was resistant to allowing communists to enlist, so prudence no doubt contributed to Whyte keeping quiet about his political practice.[22]

Before throwing himself into the military, Whyte arranged his personal affairs. This included formalizing his first marriage. He wed fellow communist activist Rita on January 9, 1942, just over two weeks before enlistment.[23] Although an active western European front was not yet established, and would not exist until June 1944, his assessment of the war up to that point had led Whyte to conclude that quite possibly he would not survive, so it was only fair that Rita should have whatever benefits would be given to war widows.[24]

More than simply a good soldier, Whyte was a principled one. Being older and having professional skills of a higher level than most recruits, he could easily have negotiated his way out of front-line service. But eradicating fascism from the world required everyone to make sacrifices, and Whyte saw no reason why he should hide behind some less advantaged buddy. So from June 1944 to the end of the war he was part of the Canadian Army's Second Infantry Division, at the sharp end of the fighting in western Europe.

Just because his life was in danger, of course, didn't mean that he couldn't have fun. Indeed, it made a good case for enjoying what life there was. Whyte's account of the years from 1942 to 1945 in Europe suggests that he didn't let war get in the way of meeting people, sharing drinks, and writing about his experience for the new communist paper, the *Canadian Tribune*. On his discharge, Canadian army Captain E.B. Morgan wrote favourably about Whyte and the prospects for him in civilian life, apparently having no difficulty with Whyte's communist affiliations. "He has maintained his contacts with this work while overseas and is now coming back as political organizer for his party in Toronto.... From personal experience, this counsellor is ready to vouch for Whyte's exceptional ability in this type of work. He is a hard [and] conscientious worker, a good organizer and an able speaker. His newspaper experience will be very handy in coordinating the party paper's effort with the general policy."[25] Such praise would have fit well into the report of a counterpart in the Soviet military.

Morgan's optimism notwithstanding, prospects for the Toronto organizer of the Communist Party, which Whyte became in 1946, were not bright. The world popularity of communism that developed as a result of the Soviet Union playing the primary role in crushing fascism did spill over into Canada, but only briefly. The high tide began to ebb as early as September 5, 1945, when the agitated Soviet defector Igor Gouzenko entered the editorial office of the *Ottawa Journal*. With his heavy Russian accent, no one could understand much of the Soviet spy's plea for refuge. But one phrase was clear. "It's war," he insisted. "It's war." War it was. Not the bloody combat that had just engulfed half the world, but a Cold War that would embrace the entire planet.

Toronto was one front in the global anti-communist crusade that Gouzenko helped to launch. In the elections of 1945 and 1946, communist candidates had been elected both to the City Council and to the Board of Control (the predecessor of the Executive Committee). Stewart Smith, the son of the grand old man of Canadian communism, A.E. Smith, had carved out a place for himself on the Board of Control and won respect even in Tory Toronto as an able administrator. But 1947 was different. One of the candidates for the board, M.A. Sanderson, who in his advertisements proclaimed his pride in being a veteran of the First World War, insisted there was only one issue — "no meddling by Moscow in Toronto's Civil Affairs." Stewart, apparently, was Moscow's Man in Maple Leaf Land. The Communists replied with Bert Whyte. Pictured in his Toronto Scottish uniform over the caption "A Vet? You Bet!" Whyte implored voters to keep Smith on the board. Whyte's appeal failed. A triumphant front page *Globe and Mail* headline of January 2, 1947 told the story: "Smith Ousted from Board of Control." [26]

Despite the defeat, Whyte was seen as a rising figure in the party (which, because the Communist Party had been outlawed, in 1943 rechristened itself as the Labour-Progressive Party). In a report to the second annual convention of the Toronto and York Labour-Progressive Party, leader Charles Sims declared that among the two thousand members in the city and region, young ones like Bert Whyte were the force of the future and could expect to take on new roles. Accordingly, in June 1946 Whyte was chosen as an Ontario representative on the National Committee of the party — colloquially known as the Central Committee — and went on to attend the party's leadership training school.[27] In 1947, as part of a plan to strengthen the *Canadian Tribune*, Whyte was urged to take up his neglected journalism career. He likely needed little convincing. However, the anticommunist tenor of the times made it difficult for a daily *Tribune* to survive, and when, after six months as a daily, it returned to being a weekly, Whyte's thoughts turned to relocating to British Columbia. From 1948 to 1960 he would be a feature of the left wing in Vancouver and southern BC, writing for the communist *Pacific Tribune*.

With the move to the west coast, Whyte lost his celebrity status within the party. But he might not, in fact, have seen this as a drawback. At the *Pacific Tribune* he was far removed from petty political sparring at party headquarters, and he could engage other facets of his character and intellectual interests. Literature, sports, politics — he would write on all these topics and more in Vancouver.

Not everything was idyllic on the coast. Whyte had an independent streak that landed him in trouble with both capitalist authorities and his own comrades. Tormenting the former was, of course, a communist's very raison d'être. Still, it could be traumatic. In 1952, for instance, Whyte broke a story in the *Pacific Tribune* that exposed Vancouver cops' racist violence against the city's black citizens. Beatings of blacks by the police, systemic bias against them in the city's Hogan's Alley bars, and anti-black job discrimination were all common in Vancouver of the early 1950s. The beating of fifty-two-year-old black longshoreman Clarence Clemons on July 19, 1952, might have been another instance that was ignored by the media and politicians except for two factors:

Clemons was battered so severely that he died five months later, and the *Pacific Tribune* featured the story. After Clemons was assaulted by Constable Dan Brown, whom local blacks called "a Negro-hating cop," Clemons's family and supporters went to the *Vancouver Sun*. The *Sun* refused to run an article. Whyte, however, picked up the case and, beginning on August 8, 1952, for the next several months wrote articles that kept the issue prominent in the city.[28] In January 1953 the matter took a new turn when Brown initiated a libel suit against the *Pacific Tribune* and two of its editors. Whyte managed to avoid being included in the court case because the paper did not make frequent use of bylines then, so the key articles about Clemons and Brown did not appear under Whyte's name. But the financial pressure of a libel case weighed heavily on a struggling weekly paper, and editor Tom McEwen confided to a friend in Toronto that the legal action promised to be "loaded with ... headaches."[29] The paper emerged, however, with a victory of sorts — an out-of-court settlement that required no apology and a payment to Constable Brown of just $750.

A story that Whyte was not so happy to have explode in his hands was the controversy over the March 17, 1955, riot by Montreal Canadiens' fans over the suspension of their hero, Maurice "Rocket" Richard, by National Hockey League President Clarence Campbell. The fans were infuriated over Campbell's decision that Richard could not play out the balance of the season or in the playoffs because he had violently attacked both an opposing player and a referee. Joined by other Montrealers, who were stirred by a rising national and class militancy in Quebec, fans trashed downtown Montreal, causing $500,000 damage. Whyte weighed into the donnybrook in his column, Sportlight, and in a news article about the events. The article — more column than reportage — blamed Richard for the trouble, saying it was "high time such temperamental outbursts were ended." As for the fans and the "punk hoodlums" involved in the riot, "well, they deserve the full penalty of the law." This was a continuation of Whyte's ongoing campaign against excessive violence in NHL hockey, which he contrasted to the cleaner, quicker game played in the Soviet Union. Still, coming from a communist, it sounded curiously conservative. In an accompanying column, Whyte made matters worse by skating with the class enemy, arguing that "NHL president Campbell was right." [30] The Communist Party's National Executive Committee was not impressed. Party brass wanted Whyte to write a column to recant, but he refused. [31] That shot the puck back behind Toronto's blue line. In the next issue of *Pacific Tribune*, headquarters sent in the party line: the issue in the dispute was national and class bias. Campbell's suspension of Richard was "unwarranted . . . and a clear case of discrimination against French Canada's Mr. Hockey." Richard was merely doing what others taught him, and "why should the Rocket take the rap" for Anglophone hockey club owners and coaches such as "the Smythes, the Adams and yes, the Irvins too?" [32] The issue likely confirmed an important fact to party leaders: just as war is too important to be left to the generals, reporting on the politics of sport is too delicate to be left to the sports reporter. Whyte was furious about being overruled, but he kept his mouth shut and remained on the team. [33]

Aside from favourite hobbies like horse racing, Whyte could and did pursue in Vancouver another interest — women. To say that Whyte was a handsome man would be an understatement. Boxing in his youth and an early life of roughing it had given him a broad set of shoulders that was topped by a well-crafted face. Even the RCMP remarked on his dapper appearance. And his physical good looks were augmented by an appealing wit and intelligence. His attractiveness to women was matched by his interest in them. His marriage to Rita was marked by occasional dalliances. Aside from what he no doubt heard about this at home, his appreciation for the finely etched shape of a woman got him into political trouble more than once. In a 1951 Sportlight column that featured a photo of a Soviet female gymnast wearing shorts, he slyly referred to what he regarded as excessive Communist Party puritanism: "The last time this column printed a picture of a pretty girl in a bathing suit it resulted in a deluge of protests (2) against exhibiting a gal's l-gs."[34] Victorian furniture had to have its legs covered, lest they prove suggestive. In the 1950s' Communist press, females had to have the very mention of theirs abbreviated in order to purge impure thoughts. But the "protests (2)" against Whyte did not teach this clever reprobate a lesson. In 1965, briefly back in Toronto, he wrote a review of a show titled "This Was Burlesque" at the Royal Alexandra Theatre, calling this celebration of a passing era "a trip down mammary lane." The *Canadian Tribune* editor, John Boyd, took momentary leave of his political sanity and published it. Then he compounded his infraction by including a photo of burlesque artist Ann Corio. Feminists in the party did not appreciate the article.[35]

While from time to time some women were a curse to Whyte, one particular woman turned out to be a blessing. In Vancouver Whyte met a woman as fetching, charismatic, and politically engaged as he was. Monica Roberts, ironically, came from a family of White Russian gentry who had fled the revolutionary changes in their homeland after 1917 and ended up on the west coast of Canada. Given this traumatic history, the family held deep-seated political sentiments — not all of them progressive. Monica, however, benefited from her family's attention to politics and from being raised by an emancipated, free-thinking grandmother. Ever the rebel, by age seventeen she was a member of the Communist Party of Canada, and, beginning in 1957, was the BC leader of the National Federation of Labour Youth, the CPC organization whose goal was to bring young people into the party. She cut a fine figure in left-wing circles in BC, and it was little surprise that in 1951 she married fellow activist Roy Samuelson. She was just seventeen, he a decade older. She was reluctant to marry, but, paradoxically, was also seduced by the exciting prospect of "wearing a long white dress to my wedding." [36]

In 1953 she and Whyte began a relationship that, she said, "started on a light note, with the tacit understanding that it was an affair, nothing more." Several times a week they enjoyed an adventure together — mini-golf at Stanley Park, a horse race, or the poolroom, where women were rarely seen. All the while, the two couples continued to socialize, celebrate birthdays, and even vacation together. In the midst of this, Monica became pregnant, and late in 1954 Eric (Ricky) was born. After that, Monica later recalled, she grew increasingly unhappy. [37]

Another complication in their relationship was the Communist Party itself. Most of the party leaders and members were fully aware that, like human organizations of all kinds, theirs was one built of mismatched timber. Party members were not always paragons of bourgeois morality. Many of the leaders — Fred Rose, Harvey Murphy, and Dewar Ferguson, among others — were well acquainted with the bottle. And Tim Buck, the CPC general secretary from 1929 to 1964, carried on a three-decade-long intimate relationship with Bess Mascolo, apparently without the knowledge of his wife, Alice.[38] Aside from a wish to avoid scandal that might harm the party, why should communists accept monogamy? Hadn't communists going back to Friedrich Engels dismissed bourgeois marriage as an extension of capitalist property relations? Ideology aside, however, the Communist Party of Canada was a small subculture, and Whyte and Monica found little privacy within it. For whatever reason — perhaps it was the twenty-five-year difference in age between the two — an anonymous party insider inundated CPC leaders with letters condemning their ongoing affair. Party headquarters in Toronto agreed with Whyte and Monica that this was a personal matter, but the whisper campaign did increase the pressure on the illicit couple. Finally, in 1959, after much anguish, Whyte and Monica broke with their spouses and, together with their son, established a household.

Fate, or opportunity, gave them no time to rest. Late in 1959 Whyte was offered the position of *Canadian Tribune* correspondent in Beijing, covering events in the People's Republic of China. Since a small weekly paper could never afford such an extravagance, the Chinese government paid the correspondent's salary and expenses. (This was a comparatively small financial inducement to the *Canadian Tribune*; a far more substantial subsidy came from the USSR, which ordered and paid for many copies of the Canadian paper to distribute in a country where almost no one read English.) Whyte accepted the offer, but he was uncertain how the Chinese might react if he brought along a woman to whom he was not married, to say nothing of their child. And so Monica and Ricky temporarily stayed behind. Soon after his arrival in Beijing, however, Whyte spoke with a fellow correspondent, Alan Winnington from the British *Daily Worker*, who advised him that the Chinese would in fact have no objection. Perhaps the CPC would also be no barrier.

On July 4, Whyte exulted in a letter to Monica that Nelson Clarke at the *Tribune* had advised him that "we consider this to be a personal, family matter" and saw no reason why all three could not be reunited in Beijing. In September 1960, they were.

To arrive in China in 1960 was a superb opportunity to assess the wisdom of the well-known Chinese proverb/curse: "May you live in interesting times." By March 1960, when Whyte took up his posting, "interesting times" were beginning to be evident in China in the growing rift between the Soviets and the Chinese. Tensions within the international communist system were already becoming public, even if the communists themselves were not prepared to admit to any significant discord. The Chinese revolutionary upheaval had been a challenge to the leadership of the Communist Party of the Soviet Union right from the 1920s. Although Joseph Stalin had welcomed the Communist victory in China in 1949, astute political observers elsewhere in the world were alert to possible contention between him and Mao Zedong. After Stalin's death in 1953, Nikita Khrushchev set out a new foreign policy strategy that called for peaceful coexistence with the United States. Having fought the US military in the Korean War and seen that part of the country's elite was ready to seize any pretext to attack China and even use nuclear weapons to do so, Mao Zedong was understandably skeptical that US imperialism was capable of "peaceful coexistence." [39] (Sixty-five years after the end of World War II, people worldwide have considerable evidence that supports Mao's view of US imperialism.) Disagreements between the USSR and China on other matters of international communist strategy followed. Encouraging that rivalry was a plan set out in the bible of the ultra-conservative wing of the American elite, *U.S. News and World Report*, in January 1950, just three months after the birth of the People's Republic of China. The magazine suggested the following strategic attitude: "*Good Commies* are Commies who do not knuckle under to Russia. . . . *Bad Commies* are Commies who bow to Russia, and they'll be opposed" (by the US administration)."[40] Arguments over the very notion that there could be "good commies" and "bad commies" would consume the US elite for the next two decades. Only in 1972 would the dispute be resolved by President Richard Nixon. Having won his reputation in the 1950s by being a consummate anti-communist, Nixon opted to ally with the "good commies" in Beijing and isolate the "bad commies" in Moscow.[41] But in 1960 many in the world communist movement still hoped that the Sino-Soviet dispute was mostly the invention of a hostile Western media. Monica still remembers that, before leaving Canada, Whyte was briefed on the split and was told that the "so-called divisions in the socialist camp were just a matter of cultural differences and approaches between East and West — they weren't fundamental."

Experience on the ground in Beijing, however, proved to the Whytes that the stresses that would ultimately lead to military clashes along the border and an international battle between the communist rivals were only too evident in China itself. "Gradually it percolated through that the Russian experts had all left," Monica recalled.[42] The foreign press corps — mostly composed of reporters from communist papers that adhered to the Soviet line — was alive with rumour, speculation, and low-key disrespect for the Chinese. Chinese nationals that the Whytes met and befriended soon found themselves dissidents in their own country. For political and personal reasons, the Whytes also grew apart from Dorise Nielsen, the pioneering feminist who had been, in 1940, the first communist (although nominally United Front) candidate to be elected to the Canadian House of Commons. Nielsen had moved to China in 1957, and she adhered to its worldview. In the study group they formed, the Whytes resented Nielsen's persistent advocacy of the Chinese view on the international communist strategy. As Monica observed, "she tried to push the Chinese line down everybody's throats."[43]

By 1963, the political conflict between China and the USSR was undeniable and had become a matter of intense debate in the international communist movement. The question of imperialist war was one of the key contentious points. The Soviet view was succinctly summarized by Leslie Morris in the *Canadian Tribune*: "War . . . now has a fundamentally different character than formerly." In this new, nuclear era, war had become "all-pervasive, all-destructive." Thus "the ability of the imperialists to intervene in the 'classical' way has been curbed by the modern nature of war."[44] By contrast, Mao continued to adhere to the long-standing communist policy that imperialism constantly generated and gravitated towards war. In his view the Soviet policy of "peaceful coexistence" was a dangerous retreat before US imperialism, which had not moderated its ambitions for world hegemony. Concessions, compromise, and conciliation, Mao believed, did nothing but blunt "the revolutionary struggles of the people" against imperialism. Unsheathed, this revolutionary impulse would indeed show that both imperialism and atom bombs were paper tigers that could be defeated. "It is people and not weapons, of whatever kind, that decide the outcome of war," the Chinese insisted.[45] In the late summer of 1963, with the *Canadian Tribune* featuring headlines such as "Chinese Communists Harming Cause of Peace," Chinese party officials must have concluded that it was futile to continue to pay to have a *Tribune* correspondent in their midst.[46] In November 1963 the Whytes packed up and left Beijing. They were not replaced. Back in Canada, Whyte made public where he stood on the global political conflict between China and the USSR, speaking critically of the Chinese.[47]

Even before the Sino-Soviet dispute became heated, life in Beijing contained plenty of pitfalls for a Western journalist. Indeed, Whyte's predecessor as Beijing correspondent for the *Tribune*, Sydney Gordon, had landed in some of them. By 1959 the Chinese were trying to ease out Gordon, the first *Canadian Tribune* correspondent. They didn't like his outlook and practices; for his part, Gordon didn't hide his dissatisfaction with a host of inconveniences in Beijing. He objected to living in a hotel room and had arranged that he and his wife move to a small house with a courtyard. The two of them also seemed to be caught up in a bourgeois buying spree of inexpensive Chinese clothing, jewellery, and curios, perhaps with the idea of setting up a shop once they had left the country. Rose Kastner in distant Toronto got wind of this Chinese dissatisfaction with Gordon and triumphantly spilled the tale to Ted Allan, Gordon's co-author of the book *The Scalpel, the Sword: The Story of Doctor Norman Bethune*. Gordon and Allan had remained cordial with one another until the book was published in 1952, but by 1959 the enmity between the two was clear. Kastner wrote to Allan that the inebriated wife of a CPC executive member had asked "what I thought of the boy. Well, needless to say I didn't spare the horses."[48]

Gordon's personality aside, it would be easy to see why a Western journalist in Beijing could become a cynical souse. In his letters back to Monica, Whyte made it clear how insular was life for the handful of Westerners in China. Most

Western countries obeyed the dictates of the United States, which refused to recognize the People's Republic, so Beijing was scarcely a desired diplomatic destination. Western media were unwilling to brook the displeasure of the world's most powerful military, economic, and political power just to report on the one-fifth of humanity who lived in the PRC.[49] As a result, life for the correspondents from communist party papers in Italy, France, Australia, and Britain was a boring round of seeing the same tired faces, of wining and whining.

Whyte griped more than once in letters to Monica about another frustration: "channels." "You can't just visit a factory, or a gymnasium — it takes days or weeks of negotiations. Even a movie, tickets have to be arranged beforehand, an interpreter assigned to you, etc." Whyte tried to, and to an extent did, get around the formalities using "a bit of brash Canadianism," but the restrictions were sometimes irritating. Journalists in the West came to call jobs at mainstream newspapers "the velvet rut" — comfortable but dull. Life in the early 1960s in a Beijing that the West was still determined to keep behind a "Bamboo Curtain" was likewise something of a rut. To describe it as a "silk rut," however, would not have done justice to the Spartan character of life just a decade after the Chinese revolution.

Back in Canada in 1964, Whyte returned to the *Canadian Tribune*, but his Canadian sojourn was brief. In 1966 he was appointed the Moscow correspondent for the paper. His first article from Moscow was classic Whyte, quoting Marx — "Groucho, not Karl" — about the USSR being a state of mind, and an immense one at that.[50] While there, he also did English-language radio broadcasts for Radio Moscow. Whyte finally began to disagree with the Communist Party of Canada over the issue of the Soviet decision to militarily snuff out the "Prague Spring" reform in the Communist Party of Czechoslovakia. His dissent, although mild, might have been part of the reason that in 1974 he lost his position as the *Canadian Tribune*'s Moscow correspondent. Whyte told Monica that he would not have minded being replaced by a younger correspondent, but when the man who got the nod turned out to be long-time party loyalist John Weir, Whyte saw it as nothing short of insulting. He had not been paying dues to the Canadian Communist Party since he had moved to the USSR, so he was saved the task of formally cutting his ties to the party that he had stuck fast to for almost four decades. He moved to *Sputnik* magazine, a new publication that was intended to be the Russian equivalent of the American mass-circulation monthly, *Reader's Digest*. It aimed at having an international appeal, so was brightly written, filled with photos, and published in English, Italian, French, German, and Spanish. Whyte transformed the original Russian articles into colloquial English. Monica also translated for and helped edit *Sputnik*.[51]

Curiously, however, although Whyte criticized the Soviets over Czechoslovakia, he and Monica continued to live in the USSR and to promote it abroad through *Sputnik*. "We didn't see anything wrong with presenting the Soviet Union positively," Monica later explained. "Bert always said that it was unfortunate that the first socialist country in the world was in a backward peasant country without any tradition of democracy.... If it [had] happened in France it would have been very different, but because it happened in Russia, it's not really very surprising that it's from the top down instead of from the bottom up."[52] In any case, by the mid-1970s it appeared that warm breezes like those of the "Prague Spring" were drifting onto the Russian steppes and that some democratization was coming to the socialist motherland.

Being in Moscow from 1966 until 1984 was perhaps a god-send to Whyte. Effectively it allowed him to escape the malaise of and infighting within the Communist Party of Canada and avoid seeing and coming to grips with its degeneration and its increasing isolation in a rapidly changing Canada.[53] Even in Moscow, however, he was not immune to inner-party intrigue. The March 6, 1967, edition of the *Canadian Tribune* contained a remarkably candid and lengthy letter to the editor from Nicholas Balan of Toronto criticizing an earlier article by Whyte concerning crime in the USSR. Balan contradicted Whyte's claim that there was no economically motivated crime in the Soviet Union. The RCMP considered the letter significant. At the bottom of the clipping in the RCMP's file an anonymous officer wrote "possibly printed to discredit WHYTE."[54] But there did not need to be a great effort to harm his reputation; increasingly Whyte became irrelevant to the CPC. His articles written from Moscow retained their flair and humour but covered little that was deeply politically contentious. One of them, printed in the *Tribune* on February 9, 1973, dealt with the pragmatic issue of the cost of living, a matter of growing political controversy worldwide. Whyte pointed out that prices for many basic necessities in the Soviet Union had not increased in decades. A ticket for the Moscow subway was five kopeks, the same as it was when the system opened in 1935. How far did five cents take one on the Toronto subway? he asked rhetorically.[55]

Towards the end of his time in Moscow, Whyte wrote *Champagne and Meatballs*. Ending his account in 1959 seemed appropriate. It took him through half a century of his life. And 1959 was also a significant demarcation point. Going to China catapulted him into an international arena, where he would live for the last twenty-five years of his life. No less important, once Monica and Ricky joined him in Beijing, life became defined by domesticity, so different from the spontaneous gallivanting of his youth. After he completed *Champagne and Meatballs*, he thought, it would make sense to write a separate book on life in China and the USSR. But he fell ill before he had a chance to write the second work.[56]

No doubt it was less the influence of Marxist philosophy than Whyte's innate grasp of life's contradictions that led him to the title of his memoir. *Champagne and Meatballs* aptly summarizes the highs and lows of his eventful, dynamic, and complex life. Monica remembers that, lying in a Moscow hospital in May 1984, as he slipped in and out of consciousness, at one point he lucidly declared, "I've had a wonderful, wonderful life, and there's nothing I regret."[57]

The book you hold is substantially the manuscript that Whyte completed in the early 1980s. It has been edited and reordered in relatively minor ways, guided by respect for Whyte's vision and intention. Additions of my own appear inside square brackets. Some brief passages in the original manuscript — such as lists of books that Whyte was reading in his youth — have been deleted. Chapter 5, "Letters from China," was not part of Whyte's original manuscript. It has been pieced together from over two hundred letters, some of them very lengthy, that Whyte sent to Monica and Ricky between March and August 1960. Selections were made among the letters with several goals in mind. One was to employ the letters to describe the People's Republic of China, then barely one decade old and still a mystery unfolding. The letters were also chosen and edited in an effort to capture Whyte's enthusiastic first encounter, as well as his frustration, with the new China. Because of a US-led boycott of the People's Republic, Western diplomats, journalists, and visitors were rare in China, so Whyte found himself, to an extent, in uncharted waters, and his reaction to the situation is intriguing. Another aim was to introduce the small group of Western correspondents and Western residents then residing in Beijing, as well as the few Chinese they interacted with. Monica Whyte has written a foreword to the chapter that provides essential background to the letters and thus a context in which to understand them.

Champagne and Meatballs is an addition to a growing body of memoirs and biographies by and about people who have been active on the political left in Canada.[58] Given the faint imprint of the radical left on Canadian politics over the twentieth century, an objective observer might be tempted to dismiss the literature as little more than an extended lament of losers. Whyte's more than forty years of activism with the Communist Party of Canada were, from that perspective, a wasted effort. Even at the height of its influence at the end of World War II, the CPC was weak, and as the Cold War raged it was more and more driven to the sidelines. Whyte saw all this, even if he conceded little of it in the pages of his memoir. But politics aside, *Champagne and Meatballs* is the record of a life lived to the full. It comes out of and addresses an era of human struggle that was by turns promising and appalling. True, its point of view is that of a political ideal that has been ravaged by time and events. Yet *Champagne and Meatballs* is no dirge. It's a brash, funny, irreverent, and always entertaining log of one man's journey. It is history and autobiography, accompanied by a wink of Bert Whyte's eye — the left one, of course.

— LARRY HANNANT

CHAPTER ONE

Mother

"Your MNX," said the waitress in a greasy spoon cafe, plonking down a plate in front of me. The eggs were runny, the french fries limp and soggy, the ham almost non-existent. My impulse was to push away the mess, but my whole training and background prevented me from doing so.

How many times, in 1917–18, had my mother told me: "You can't leave the table until you clean up your plate. Remember the starving Armenians!" At the age of eight or nine I couldn't figure out how cleaning up my plate would help the starving Armenians (I still can't), but the habit has stuck with me.

During the Depression we hungry road kids would often say, "If I had some ham I'd have some ham and eggs if I had some eggs." So I ate my MNX and paid the bill, thought again of the starving Armenians, and in a rush came memories of my mother.

My mother was born Edith McDermid in Martintown, Ontario, in 1878. She was of United Empire Loyalist stock. So was my dad, John K. Whyte, born in Alice County, Ontario, in 1872. Both of Scots descent.

Go back far enough and we're all smorgasbords, but I can't trace beyond the United Empire Loyalists, and since then I can find only Scots.

So my mother met my father on a train. He was seated opposite her in the restaurant car. They got to talking, exchanged addresses. From this followed a series of letters. My dad proposed. She accepted. They married. At an early age my dad had gone to work in the mines, taken a correspondence course, and earned third-class engineer's papers. My brother, Clinton, was born in Copper Cliff in 1906 and I was born in Cobalt in 1909. A few years later the family moved to Haileybury, a pretty little town on the shores of Lake Timiskaming.

My mother was a devout Christian. Every Sunday she attended both morning and evening service in the Presbyterian Church. My brother and I went to Sunday school, each carrying a small two-section church envelope containing 10 cents for local work and 10 cents for foreign missions, that is, to save the souls of the "heathen Chinese" who lived upside down on the other side of the world. There were a few times when I stole the missionaries' dime to buy candy, though my conscience bothered me a bit — was I condemning some "Chinaman" to hellfire?

My mother gave a dollar a week to the church, regardless of the state of family finances. I remember Dad complaining about this on one occasion. He had been off work for two months with a case of shingles and we were broke and in debt. But Mother calmly replied, "The Lord will provide."

Actually, it was not the Lord but Daddy Adshead, the grocer, who provided. At one point our food bill reached $127, an enormous sum in those days. I was in the store with Mother. The grocery store was in fact a general store, with a bit of everything, including a meat department on one side.

Mother was buying a pound of hamburger, about 15 cents, and said in a trembling voice, "I'll have to charge it."

Although I was very young, I remember clearly how big, fat Daddy Adshead told my mother, "Mrs. Whyte, stop worrying about your bill. Your credit is good for any amount and for any length of time." When we got home my mother broke down and cried.

There was one Chinese laundry and one Chinese cafe in Haileybury. The cafe owner was Harry Lee Tong — obviously a Westernized version of his original name. One summer he closed his cafe and took a trip to China. When he returned he brought along a very young, plump wife. She was the only female Chinese in our town, and when the word got around that she was "expecting," the women in Mother's church sewing circle decided it was their Christian duty to visit her. But no one wanted to risk their virtuous reputations by going into Harry's cafe and climbing the stairs to his living quarters. Everyone knew that "Chinamen" smoked opium and threatened the lives of heroic missionaries and ate strange foods and did God-knows-what else.

Finally, my mother volunteered. To protect her good name she took my brother and me along with her. We sat at the cafe counter and ate huge wedges of coconut cream pie while mother visited the pregnant wife upstairs. These visits became weekly events, with the good churchwomen sending along knitted baby clothes, booties, diapers, and so on. How Mother and Mrs. Lee Tong managed to communicate with each other remains a mystery.

The baby was born, fat and healthy, and a few days later mother and daughter appeared downstairs in the cafe. Business boomed and gaggles of curious women dropped in for a cup of tea and a look at the first Chinese child born in Haileybury.

Harry Lee Tong, flushed with prosperity, bought a car. The horse-and-buggy era was coming to an end, but automobiles were still something of a novelty in 1918. I'm not sure whether a driver's licence was required at that time or not.

One afternoon Harry drove proudly up to our house, with wife and baby in the back seat of the Ford, and invited Mother and Clint and me for a drive. Mother was embarrassed, but could hardly refuse. We travelled exactly one block and then Harry stepped on the gas to climb a steep incline to get onto the main gravelled road. He almost took us into a ravine on the far side, but applied the brakes, shifted into reverse, and came back too far, the car beginning to slide down our side of the road into the ravine. This time the brakes didn't save us. Slowly the car tilted, slowly it rolled over and came to rest upside down at the bottom of the galley. Somehow we all managed to get out, and miraculously no one was hurt — except that the baby lost a toenail on one little toe. Harry Lee Tong sold his wrecked car the next day and to the best of my knowledge never drove again.

Sunday was a dull day around our house. Mother knew exactly what God intended us to do on Sunday. All reading material except the Bible was put up on a high shelf and not to be touched. My brother and I were forbidden to go to the schoolyard and play baseball with the other kids, though we were allowed to have a quiet game of catch alongside the house, after our return from Sunday school.

In any case there wasn't really so much to read in our home. Mother's tastes ran to books like Gene Stratton-Porter's *A Girl of the Limberlost*, Booth Tarkington's *Seventeen*, Kate Douglas Wiggin's *Rebecca of Sunnybrook Farm*, Harold Bell Wright's *The Shepherd of the Hills*, Zane Grey's *Riders of the Purple Sage*, Alice Hegan Rice's *Mrs. Wiggs of the Cabbage*

Patch, Louisa May Alcott's *Little Women* and John W. Fox's *The Little Shepherd of Kingdom Come.*

By the time I reached the age of nine I had set my course in life — I was going to become the world heavyweight boxing champion and also a famous writer. I spent most of my spare time either boxing or writing. One story I wrote got me into trouble. I had fallen in love with a beautiful little redhead, Eva Murray, who became a victim that same year of the 1918 flu epidemic, which killed some twenty million people throughout the world [contemporary estimates place the mortality at a minimum of fifty million and as high as one hundred million]. There had been a quilting bee at our house (half a dozen women sat around a big wooden frame and gossiped and created a patchwork quilt). When they were relaxing over tea and cookies I announced that I had written a story and would read it. The women all smiled and encouraged me to begin.

Now, at the age of nine I was not one of those authors who disguise their characters and state that both places and people are entirely imaginary. My hero was named Bert and he was a boxer, my heroine was named Eva and had red hair. I can't recall the whole plot, but I do recall the closing punch line, which I delivered with gusto: "Then Bert threw Eva down on the floor and kissed her and she had a baby."

I waited for the applause. There was none. Then my mother said firmly, "Go to your room. I'll speak to you later."

My mother had some strong prejudices. She loved the Chinese on the other side of the world, but shrank from close contact with Catholics, Jews, and Native Indians who happened to swim within our ken. Catholics were Christians, of course, but still...

The war against the Catholics was carried on enthusiastically by the small fry. The Catholic and public schools were only a block apart, and we daily watched a crocodile of Catholic children pass our schools, with nuns in black fore and aft. It was rumoured that if you got too close a nun might throw her skirt over your head and then take you away and turn you into a Catholic.

On July 1 every year the Orange Order in our town celebrated the Battle of the Boyne, when William went to Ireland in 1690 and defeated James. "King Billie" led the straggling parade on a white horse. This was a day when feelings rose to fever pitch. We taunted the Catholic kids:

Up the long ladder
And down the short rope
Hurrah for King Billie!
To hell with the Pope!

Our enemies were not slow to respond:

Catholic, Catholic
Ring the bell,
Protestant, Protestant,
Go to hell!

After which we would clash in mortal combat, though I don't recall anyone really getting hurt.

It was during one of these scuffles that I developed a close friendship with a Catholic boy my own age. We were evenly matched: I would pin him down, but just as often he would have me flat on my back. Now the Catholic Cathedral in Haileybury had a set of bells which would produce chimes. Our Protestant Churches — Presbyterian, Methodist, Baptist — weren't even in the running. The bells had to be hand-pulled: a priest made the chimes ring by pointing to each boy hanging onto a rope and ordering him to pull. My Catholic chum was one of the lads selected for this exciting task every day. Once the big bells got really going, he told me, they would hoist you way up in the air. "Come along," he invited me. So I went, and wonder of wonders, one boy was missing and I was allowed to fill the gap. Sure enough I found myself soaring into the air — well, at least a couple of feet.

But the next day, when I turned up, the priest drew me aside and said, "My son, you are not a Catholic, are you?" I confessed that I wasn't. "Then I'm afraid you can't be a bellringer." "Even if I'm not a Catholic, I believe in God," I said hopefully. But the priest only smiled and shook his head.

Imagine the excitement at our house when my Aunt Belle from Pembroke came to visit us and announced that she was engaged — to a Catholic! There were grave misgivings and long solemn talks from which I was excluded. I listened at keyholes but couldn't make much of what was said. Then the young man arrived for inspection, and everybody took to him. He was handsome and had curly hair and a wonderful smile and a fund of clean jokes that had everyone laughing so hard you forgot he was a Catholic. He returned to Pembroke with the wedding date all set — and four days later came a wire saying he had caught the Spanish flu and was dead.

My mother's attitude towards Jews was a contradictory one. She said yes, she knew they were God's Chosen People. But why did they have such big noses? Many years later, when she was in her sixties, I visited her after a long absence and said I was married to a Jewish girl. "Has she got a crooked nose?" was mother's first concern. "No, a snub nose," I assured her.

As for Native Indians, we met members of one tribe when Dad was working at the Tough-Oakes Mine in Kirkland Lake and we spent a whole summer camping in a small cabin near the mine. Mother worried that the Indians would sneak up at night and steal something. They never did. Am I drawing an unflattering picture of my mother? Prejudiced in many ways she undoubtedly was. But there was the other side. She was a kind and unselfish woman, honest as the day is long, always willing to share what she had with those less fortunate, fierce in her loyalty to friends, ignoring the danger of the terrible flu epidemic to nurse sick acquaintances, and facing death with a quiet courage when the scourge of cancer brought her own life to an end on November 12, 1940.

Dad

My first memory of Dad is him looming over the horizon on his way to our rented Cobalt shack. A huge figure, he seemed to me (he was five feet ten and weighed 220 pounds). I was sitting pulling the ears of Ponto, my water spaniel, to our mutual enjoyment. But I left Ponto when I saw my Dad had a present for me — a saw made out of wood. It wouldn't cut anything but I loved playing with it, pretending I was sawing wood.

Shortly afterwards we moved to Haileybury, five miles away. Ponto disappeared — what had happened to him? Did he die of old age — as I was told — or did he get lost, or was he done away with? I shed bitter childish tears, and well I might have, for I was not to own another dog until fifty years had passed.

I remember the start of the World War in 1914. I was five years old. We lived only a block away from the armoury. Shepherded by my older brother, I watched recruits marching — "left right left right left wheel right wheel halt form fours." We collected cigarette cards on which our gallant soldiers sloped arms, fixed bayonets, and did other things necessary to defeat the Kaiser.

When I was six or seven the war was brought home to me. Jim Murray, the sixteen-year-old son of our neighbour, had falsified his age and joined the army. He went overseas and a few months later a telegram arrived — he had been wounded. My mother and Mrs. Murray cried together, but then came the news that the wound was not serious.

Time passed. The war ended. Kaiser Bill was hanged in effigy and then burned in a giant bonfire, like Guy Fawkes. I was nine years old and marched my squad of kids around the block, blowing horns and banging on tin drums. Jim Murray returned home in a blaze of glory. The war to end all wars was over and we were to have a world fit for heroes to live in.

Came the 1921 depression and my dad was out of work. He was a good third-class engineer, accustomed to making $200 a month. Now he refused to work for $150. The engineers had no union, but he said, "If we stick together, the bosses will have to give in." They didn't stick together and Dad eventually was forced to take a job, far from home, at $180.

Far from home. That's the story of my father's life. At Cobalt we had lived together as a family, but for the next twenty years, never, except on a couple of occasions when he was ill.

The farther back in the bush you go, the bigger the money. Dad in his active lifetime worked at fifteen or twenty mines, nearly always far away from home. He had a family of three to support. When we moved south to Kingston, where my brother Clint was studying medicine at Queen's University, Dad was working at the Howey mine in Red Lake, hundreds of miles away. But the job paid $350 a month — of which Dad kept only tobacco money. He smoked a pipe, bought leaf tobacco, and chopped it into shreds with a homemade cutter.

What kind of life did he lead? Was he lonely, or did he like it? When I was eighteen, I went north and got a job at the Conroyal Mine, near Kirkland Lake, where Dad was hoistman. After a few weeks underground as a mucker I was transferred to firing a 125-hp. boiler, working a ten-hour night shift, seven days a week, 45 cents an hour. In the bunkhouse I had a cot and clothes chest next to Dad's. For eight months we lived side by side, and every second week worked together, with him running the hoist and looking after the compressor, me shovelling coal. On alternate weeks the night shift hoistman was Fred Windsor, a stern, religious man. Dad was the better hoistman, Fred the better mechanic (he had second-class papers).

During those long nights we talked a lot, drew water from the boiler and washed our work clothes, and became very close. Dad taught me to run the hoist, though this was illegal. We recalled the good times we had had when I was very young and Dad came home to Haileybury from Kirkland Lake on a long weekend once a month. On Sunday we would all troop down to the livery stable and Dad would hire a fine carriage drawn by a spanking pair of bays, or perhaps a pair of dapple greys, young and frisky. And I would sit up front with him, and sometimes hold the reins for a minute or two, or be allowed to flick the whip over the horses. We would take the gravelled road leading to Cobalt, and go at a good clip, though the team would shy at the occasional Ford we met. Sometimes an automobile would be parked on the side of the road, with a gauntleted driver changing a flat tire, and Dad would jokingly call out, "Get a horse!" But a mile or so later the car would usually pass us in a cloud of dust.

Sometimes in the fire-hole we talked boxing, for Dad knew

Jack Monroe, the former Mayor of Elk Lake, a silver mining town that had sprung up in 1909 during the Gowganda rush. Monroe's fame rested on the fact that he had decked the world heavyweight champion, Jim Jeffries, for a count of nine in an exhibition bout at San Francisco a few years earlier. Many miners referred to him as "the man who beat Jeffries." Well, not quite. When they met in a title bout on August 26, 1904, Jeff knocked Jack into the middle of next week. But Monroe was quite a man, well liked by everyone. He went overseas in 1914 with the Princess Pats. Only a handful of that regiment returned alive, and Jack was one of them.

There were several young fellows of my own age or thereabouts working at the Conroyal, and some evenings they would drop around to my fire-hole for a gabfest. We talked about hockey and women and baseball and women and religion and women and war and women and women and women. When I was switched to day shift three of us — Miles McMillan, Cliff Hines, and I — often walked the four miles to Kirkland Lake in the evening to shoot pool, eat in the Royal Cafe, or have a couple of drinks in a blind pig. Once or twice we went to the Finnish steam bath and then took a quick roll in the snow.

One evening Dad and I walked to town, ate in a restaurant, and went to a poolroom, where he watched me take on some of the local talent. I played a good money game, the result of hundreds of hours bent over pool tables in Kingston. Half a dozen miners from the Conroyal turned up around closing time, and one of them suggested we pay a visit to Dolly's before heading home. "I need to get my ashes hauled," he explained. Another miner laughed and said, "You're crazy. You won't get old Jack Whyte going to a whorehouse." Thus indirectly challenged, Dad said to me, "You want to go to Dolly's and have a drink?" "Sure," I said.

Dolly ran a famous house. If she had ever been in the profession, she had long ago given it up to practise a more lucrative side of the game. She was a handsome woman, but a strict madam who demanded that her customers act with decorum. While we sat and talked and drank gin rickeys (at 50 cents a shot) her four girls appeared, and two of the miners selected a partner and retired upstairs. Pat Gologolly, a little black Irishman, suddenly turned to Dolly and said, "And will ye no be doing a bit yerself, Dolly?" Dolly laughed and replied, "No, Pat, but thank you for your kind invitation." After my third gin rickey Dad leaned over and whispered, "You feel all right, son?" I drank very little in those days. I told Dad I was feeling fine, just fine, and to prove it burst into song on the way back to the mine.

I quit the Conroyal in April 1928 and took to the road, hitchhiking my way across half a dozen US states and the Canadian prairie provinces.

When I next saw my Dad in 1931 he was a changed man. He had suffered a minor stroke and also lost the sight of one eye. No longer able to work at his trade, he had been given the job of caretaker of the closed-down Green-Stabell Mine near Val d'Or, Quebec. After my brother graduated from Queen's in 1929, Mother had moved north to be with her husband. She seemed quite happy to be living in the bush, wore breeks [trousers] and would go for long walks, accompanied by her dog. The Siscoe Mine, situated on an island in nearby Lake Kenowesky, was working at the time, and occasionally a miner would drop in for a meal and a chat with my parents, but mostly Dad and my mother lived a life without visitors. I stayed with them for a few weeks and picked up three or four days' work with a surveying crew.

One evening there was a knock at the door. Our visitors turned out to be W.B. Boggs, superintendent of the Noranda smelter, and an engineer named Vaughan. They were paddling up the Colombo River to look over some property, but had gone off course at dusk, traversed the length of narrow Lake Blouin, and ended up at our landing. So they beached their canoe, and reasoning that our narrow-gauge wooden railway must lead to some habitation, followed it for a mile to the mine and our living quarters.

Mother fed them sausages and mash and coffee, and before they bedded down in one of the bunkhouses we had a long discussion on many subjects, but mainly centring on the Depression. Boggs turned out to be a chauvinist (I wasn't familiar with the word then, but that's how I'd label him today). "There's always a job for a white man in my plant, even if I have to fire a foreigner to make room for him," he declared.

He followed this by offering me a job in "his" smelter. "I'll either make you or break you. You'll learn all about copper, and if you work hard you'll get ahead.... The coming copper country of the world is Rhodesia, and if I were a younger man I'd head for there tomorrow. You get to know copper, young fellow, and then go to Rhodesia, a country where a white man who knows copper has a great future."

(I took him up on his offer, and worked for several years at Noranda, but that's another part of my story. As for Rhodesia, in the long run Boggs turned out to be a poor prophet).

I saw Dad for the last time in 1940, in Ottawa. It was a sad occasion. My brother, who had joined the RCAF, was stationed somewhere out west. My mother was entering the hospital for a second cancer operation. That night I was called to the hospital to give her a blood transfusion. I was at her bedside when she died a few hours later. When I returned to the apartment to break the news to Dad, he sat up in bed and asked, "How is Mother?"

I put my arms around him and said, "Mother is gone."

"Oh, Edith, Edith, Edith, Edith," said Dad, rocking in my arms, "Edith, Edith, Edith, Edith, Edith ..."

He fell asleep at dawn, still murmuring, "Edith, Edith ..."

Dad died in a nursing home in Ottawa on December 27, 1944. At that time I was overseas, a corporal in the Toronto Scottish Regiment, fighting somewhere in Holland, and the news of Dad's death reached me much later. It seemed that his mind had gone, but he was calm and happy in his last months, believing that mother visited him every day, and that they reminisced about their courtship and early married life and their two sons: one a Communist and one an anti-Communist.

Me

I appeared on the scene in Cobalt on July 27, 1909. Had I been born a Chinese, that day would have marked my first birthday, which would make me a year older than I am today. Cobalt, Ontario, now has a population of less than two thousand, but in 1909 it was a roaring mining camp, the scene of a silver rush which brought prospectors and adventurers from the four corners of the earth.

Legend has it that Alfred LaRose, the blacksmith of the railway construction crew pushing the Timiskaming and Northern Ontario Railway north in 1903 to link up with the transcontinental line in Cochrane, saw a silver fox, flung his hammer at it, and chipped off a hunk of native silver from a cutting. A more prosaic version has him hacking off a bit of cobalt bloom, for its pretty pink colour, and sending it to the Director of the Bureau of Mines. That brought the Provincial Geologist, Dr. W.G. Miller, hotfooting it to the scene of the find. Pick-up samples showed native silver running $4,000 to the ton.

LaRose sold his claims for $30,000, a mere bagatelle. Some smart operators (Duncan McMartin and John Mc-Martin of Montreal, Noah and Henry Timmins and David A. Dunlop of Mattawa) formed the LaRose Mining Company and became the first "Silver Kings" of the Cobalt camp. "In the early days Cobalt was a poor man's hunting ground," wrote J.B. MacDougall, in his chronicle of the northland, *Building the North* [Toronto: McClelland Stewart, 1919]. "It might have been a prospector's paradise. With silver cropping up at every turn, and almost flowing over the surface, it called for neither science nor capital to do business. The plant might comprise only a two-hand drill, a sledge hammer, a hand-winch and bucket, and a few sticks of dynamite. A two-man company could handle the plant. A government customs concentrator on the plan of the old grist mill on a toll basis would have rounded out the pattern; but it was lacking. Big business held the fort, and the poor prospector had to forfeit his claim for a pittance or be frozen out and take to the trail for another chance, for he had no means and no chance to refine the ore in bag lots."

For a few years Cobalt was a town of tents, pitched anywhere. By the time I was born it was the fastest growing centre in Canada, with a population of 10,000, and a motley collection of shacks and wooden houses and hotels. The mines in the first decade produced some $400 million, and the "Cobalt song," written in 1910, was heard everywhere. One verse ran:

We've got the only Lang Street; there's blind pigs every where
Old Cobalt Lake's a dirty place, there's mud all over the Square,
We've got the darndest railroad, that never runs on time —
But it's hob-nail boots and flannel shirt in Cobalt town for mine.

Though the Cobalt of that period had its blind pigs, gambling dens, whorehouses, claim-jumpers, and con men, it was still, in the main, a law-abiding camp.

Naturally, men with families looked for a quieter place to live, and found it in Haileybury, just five miles to the north. The town, built on a slope overlooking Lake Timiskaming, had been founded a few years earlier by an Englishman, C.C. Farr, who had named it after his public school in Herts. When Cobalt hit its full stride, Haileybury mushroomed too, and soon had a population of over three thousand. Its poshest street, running parallel to the lake front, became known as Millionaires' Row.

The Whytes moved to Haileybury, but didn't live on Millionaires' Row. Dad rented a small, two-storey wooden house close to the public school. My brother was already going to school but I was still too young.

Those were good years, as I remember them. Dad had a job in Kirkland Lake, some sixty miles north, and would come home for a weekend every month. At Christmas we always had a tree and a turkey, and Clint and I would receive marvellous presents — skates and skis, a toboggan, boxing gloves, a bound volume of *Chum's Annual*, plus mundane things such as sweaters, mitts, woollen stockings, and fleece-lined underwear. In winter we skated, skied, and played street hockey using frozen road-apples for pucks. We wore Indian moccasins all winter.

The Great War was raging somewhere overseas, so of course we played war games, winter and summer. In winter we built snow forts, made snowballs which we soaked in water and let freeze before the battle. In summer we used broomsticks for guns and drilled endlessly in the schoolyard. We also played Duck on the Rock, I'm the King of the Castle, Blind Man's Buff, and Pom, Pom, Pullaway.

At the age of nine or ten I became acquainted with parlour games like Post Office and Spin the Bottle. And this marked, more or less, the beginning of my sex life. Long before puberty little boys can develop rigid digits, and an older girl introduced me and my coevals to a game called Doctor. We played it in her house whenever her mother went downtown to shop. Marian was invariably the doctor, and whatever imaginary complaint we suffered from ("I broke my arm") she decided that a complete examination was called for. Her bedside manner was impeccable, and her soothing fingers quickly produced nugatory erections.

Garnett and I first heard of masturbation from Norman, who lived in the next block. He had seen an elder boy pulling his pud, and a stream of milk had shot out. We all promptly tried it, and yanked and yanked like a trio of demented milkmaids. Absolutely nothing happened. Garnett and I accused Norman of telling us an enormous fib.

Then there was the love letter which Alan, Garnett's teenage brother, sent to Marian. We were entrusted to act as couriers, and warned on pain of death not to peek at the contents of the note. So naturally we did. It was a one-line love message: "Are you bleeding much this month?" This completely mystified us. Was Marian sick? Had she cut herself?

I had long discussions with Herb, who lived just across the street, about the differences between boys and girls. Herb said he had seen his sister naked once and she was kind of funny-looking. How? He wasn't sure, he'd not had a good look and she wouldn't let him see her again. We worked out a plan. He would bring his sister over to play when my mother was out and we'd wrestle and then hold her down and pull off her panties and satisfy our curiosity. We knew that girls had holes below their belly buttons, where the babies came out. We proceeded with the project, everything went according to plan, his sister struggled a bit but we finally managed to get her panties down around her knees, looked for a hole — and there wasn't any. Just a plain little crack between her legs. Herb told her to beat it, and he and I sat down to talk things over. We agreed that girls had been shortchanged and that boys were a lot better equipped.

Looking back, it seems to me that we were a very ordinary, if sometimes rather nasty, bunch of small-town boys. Once we made a little girl swallow a live worm before we would let her join our game of Hide and Seek. I dimly recall a visit from outraged parents and being punished by having my weekly 10 cents pocket money cut off.

None of our gang ever showed a touch of genius, like Mozart playing the piano at three months and writing a symphony at six months, or whatever. On the contrary, our cultural level was rather low. We had a gramophone in our house — you wound it up by hand — and played records like "When Father Papered the Parlour" and "Cohen on the Telephone." We also had several Harry Lauder records.

In those days before radio and television, folk often sat in rocking chairs on their verandas in the evening, neighbours would drop by, and sometimes we would all join in singing popular songs. They made songs to last then, not like today. Aside from the war songs, "It's a Long Way to Tipperary," etc., we sang golden oldies from the days of Stephen Foster ("Jeannie with the Light Brown Hair") down to the latest hits from the Ziegfeld Follies ("Shine on Harvest Moon," "Peg o' My Heart") and popular vaudeville songs ("Melancholy Baby," "Take Me Out to the Ball Game," "School Days").

Another cultural event was the Saturday afternoon matinee at the Bijou Theatre. Admission fee for kids was 5 cents or two potatoes. You dropped the spuds into a barrel near the box office.

Pearl White in *The Perils of Pauline!* How many times in that never-ending serial did we see her tied across the railway track while the train came thundering round the bend? "Continued next week." You just HAD to be there next week to find out what happened.

And *The Mysterious Rider*, who sat on his motorcycle at the very top of a mountain, waiting for a message to rescue someone. Down he would rush on his bike, and try to cross a canyon on a single strand of rope, but just before he reached the other side the bad guy cut the rope with an axe and..."Continued next week"...I think the hero of that epic was Elmo Lincoln.

Then there were the comedians, Fatty Arbuckle, Chester Conklin, Harold Lloyd, Buster Keaton, Charlie Chaplin. I was a bit older when I saw Chaplin in his classic war movie, *Shoulder Arms*. Who can forget the scene where he brings in a group of German prisoners and when he's asked how he captured so many single-handed, his reply flashes on the silent screen, "I surrounded them!"

The film industry created a one-way time machine, the fountain of youth. It is possible to return to our youth by simply watching motion pictures made half a century or more ago. For age cannot change the figures on the screen: they remain eternally young.

Two big events in the lives of me and my peers were the annual visits of the circus and Chautauqua. The former gave us our first exposure to such unlikely animals as giraffes and elephants. And we split our sides laughing at the antics of the clowns. How could they think up so many funny things to do on the spur of the moment?

Chautauqua (a sort of road show) brought "culture" to

the backwoods towns of the USA and Canada. We found it sometimes exciting and sometimes a bore. The big tent, set up behind the armouries, presented "educational" programs — rousing talks by Billy Sunday evangelists, rejoinders by Bob Ingersoll skeptics, health lectures by medical "experts" on the evil of smoking, drinking, masturbation, and consorting with women of the streets. One evening the classic *Broken Blossoms* was shown on the screen, but it was too strong stuff for my mother, who dragged my brother and me out in the middle of the film.

At the age of eleven or twelve, I was a going concern. In addition to my physical activities I was also drawing a war comic strip, featuring Canadian airplanes battling German balloonists who were bombing London. I had absolutely no talent for drawing (my brother, on the other hand, was quite a good cartoonist) but I dauntlessly carried on. At the same time I was turning out short stories, and producing a handwritten sports magazine, mostly about boxing.

I was badly bitten by the boxing bug when the French war ace, Georges Carpentier, kayoed glass-jawed British heavyweight champion Joe Beckett in seventy-four seconds of the first round on December 4, 1919. That put Carpentier in line for a shot at the world title, held by Jack Dempsey.

I resolved that when I grew up I would become the heavyweight champion. Though I was only a flyweight at the time, I was confident that someday I'd grow into a heavyweight (and strangely enough I did, though more flab than muscle. But as a friend of mine once remarked, "Muscle deteriorates — flab lasts!")

Georges Carpentier remained my ring idol for many years. The debonair Frenchman, who started boxing professionally as a teenager and fought in every division from flyweight to heavyweight (winning the French lightweight title at fifteen years of age) became known to the world as "le gentleman boxeur." When he flattened Joe Beckett a spectator named George Bernard Shaw described him as "an amazing apparition, nothing less than Charles XII, The Madman of the North, striding along in a Japanese dressing gown as gallantly as if he had not been killed exactly 201 years before."

Carpentier met Jack Dempsey on July 2, 1921, in what was billed as "The Battle of the Century." Most fight fans wanted "Gorgeous Georges" to win. Weighing only 168 pounds, he didn't have a hope against the Manassa Mauler, and was smashed to the canvas for the count in the fourth round. Nevertheless, the *New York Times* gave most of page one and its sports section to a description of the fight, as did other metropolitan papers.

Irvin S. Cobb, in a multi-column story, wrote: "The arts, the sciences, the drama, commerce, politics, the bench, the bar, the great newly-risen bootlegging industry — all these have sent their pink, their pick and their perfection to grace this great occasion." Heywood Broun, not usually a gusher, described the challenger as "one of the most beautiful bodies the prize ring has known." A woman reporter for the *Morning Telegraph* went into raptures over the son of *la belle France*: "A Greek athlete statue of Parian marble warmed to life." And Neysa McMein, the illustrator, wrote that "Michelangelo would have fainted for joy with the beauty of his profile."

They were just as effusive on the other side of the Atlantic. Arnold Bennett said of Carpentier: "He might have been a barrister, poet, musician, Foreign Office attaché, or Fellow of All Souls, but not a boxer." François Mauriac described Carpentier as "this kind of man so dear to Pascal." And after the fight was over, Lloyd George sent Carpentier a cable from London: "I admire you all the more."

Reading all this glamorous prose, it is little wonder that the French boxer, a hero who had won the Croix de Guerre and Médaille Militaire while serving in the French Air Force, fired my young imagination. I was determined to emulate him. Every day after school I rounded up my coevals (some of whom were reluctant sparring partners) and cajoled them into donning boxing gloves and going a few rounds with me in our backyard. And every morning I spent half an hour shadowboxing in front of a mirror.

My "ring career" began at the age of fourteen and included a few bouts held in the Cobalt YMCA (all of which I won) and a draw with an older opponent at a smoker in Haileybury. Then, when we moved to Kingston, I continued training at the YMCA, and my biggest moment came when I defeated Stan Brennan of Gananoque in the main bout of a yearly boxing card staged by the Y.

The Kingston press was more than kind to me. "Fine Bouts Seen in Annual Assault at 'Y' Last Night" said the head, and a deck (decks [subheadings] and bars were common in newspapers of those days) reported that "Boxers from Queen's and Gananoque Helped Make Card Complete One." After reporting on the preliminary bouts, the account continued:

The big feature of the card was the final bout, between Stan Brennan of Gananoque and Bert Whyte, Kingston. Both boxers entered the ring tipping the scales at 135 pounds, and were about the same build and height. Dancing away after the hand-clasp in the first round, Brennan came in with a rush, and mixed things right at the start. Both exchanged blows freely and it appeared to be about even, when the gong sounded. With the opening of the second round,

Whyte released a terrific left punch which rocked his opponent from head to foot. Following the advantage, the local youth delivered another left uppercut, putting his whole weight into the blow, and floored the visitor for a count of seven. At seven, however, Brennan rose to his feet, still a little bit dazed, but managed to deliver some punishing blows before the close of the round. In the third round the Gananoque man, probably in order to avoid a knock-out, adopted wrestling tactics and went into clinches repeatedly. The round as a result lacked any great excitement, and very few blows were exchanged. The decision was awarded to Whyte.

Following the performance of last night, Phil Brockel, physical director of the YMCA, stated that there is a possibility of sending Whyte to Toronto to compete in the championship bouts which will be held at the Central "Y" there. Whyte certainly has the condition, and spectators of last night's performance were loud in their praise of the manner in which he put every ounce of weight behind his punches, outclassing and outboxing his opponent in every way.

Heady stuff for a teenager. But I was taken down a peg when Brennan outpointed me in a return bout held in Gananoque. It wasn't a home decision, either. He swarmed all over me from the first bell, kept crowding me into the ropes, and won by a mile. That wasn't the worst of it. A doctor warned me that I must give up boxing because of the many internal mouth cuts I suffered frequently.

So I switched my goal: if I could not become a boxing champion, I would at least become a great fight reporter. I began to write articles on boxing for the *Whig* and the

Standard (later they amalgamated and became the *Kingston Whig-Standard*). I set my own terms — 60 cents a column; later I raised it to a dollar (that's per column, not per column inch). Every couple of weeks I'd visit the two papers with my clipped-out stories and the cashiers would measure them and pay me, I suppose out of petty cash.

For the *Whig* I did a series on World Heavyweight Champions, from John L. Sullivan to Jack Dempsey. And for the *Standard* I did fifty articles called Fifty Famous Fights. I conducted my research work at Queen's University, having received special permission from one of the university heads, whose title I can't remember. It might have been the chief librarian. In any case, he was a bearded, gentle-speaking man, who received me in his home one evening and listened carefully to my impassioned appeal. I intended, I said, to study newspapers files over a period of forty years, to find and copy out the original accounts of famous fights, such as John L. Sullivan's win over Jake Kilrain in seventy-five rounds on July 8, 1889 — the last championship bare-knuckles bout. "I see you have an aim in life, and that is a good thing," said the beard. "Of course I'll give you permission to use our files. But don't you think that as you grow older your ideas may change somewhat, that is, you may decide to aim for something that is, well, shall we say, somewhat higher than becoming a writer on boxing?" "There is nothing higher," I told him firmly. He smiled, let it go at that and gave me the written permission I sought. For the next several months I spent most of my days ploughing through newspaper files. As a result, I accumulated a vast amount of material and submitted a few stories under the byline "Old Timer" (I was sixteen) to various sports journals. Great was my joy when *Ring* magazine of New York, the bible of boxing, accepted an article and sent me a cheque for $10.

Then a weekly pink sheet publication, the *Minneapolis Boxing Blade*, bought a series of articles at $4 per article. My star was again in the ascendancy. But then something happened to change my direction in life. Before going into that phase, however, let us return to Haileybury.

Haileybury, 1922

That was the year I became a caddy at the new six-hole (later nine-hole) golf links near the baseball park, out past Millionaires' Row. Caddies were supposed to be paid 25 cents a round, though a few of the stingier golfers would go around the six-hole course twice and then hand you 35 cents. We dozen or so caddies were also supposed to be hired in turn, but as we gained experience we tried to avoid the stingy types and foist them onto the newest recruits in our ranks.

Some of the cheapies also turned nasty if you lost balls. The practice at that time was for the caddy to hand his player the required club, then march a hundred yards or so down the fairway and turn to face the ball as it was driven towards him. If you were looking into the sun it was easy to lose sight of the ball. The Haileybury course was rather a rough one, with plenty of gullies and bunkers and clumps of trees, so to lose a ball was not uncommon. Naturally, the green caddies were prone to lose more than the "old hands" who had several weeks of experience under their belts. The players soon learned who the better caddies were, and would ask for them by name. This also upset the unwritten rule that we be chosen by turn.

Some of the wealthiest players, from Millionaires' Row, were also the most miserly. The best to caddy for were the small businessmen, doctors, and lawyers. No workers belonged to the Golf Club, for the annual dues were $500. My favourite "customer" was a real estate agent of about thirty-five. He often turned up rather late in the evening, paid me 50 cents for six holes, and gave me a lift back to the centre of town in his small sports car.

Sometimes the resident professional would call me to caddy for him while he was going round the course with a member — usually a girl. I hated this, not only because the pro never paid us, but also because I was forced to follow the drill. If the pro's ball landed in a rut, or up against a tree, his caddy (on pain of being fired) had to unobtrusively kick it into a better playing position. In this way the pro always shot a round well under par and preserved his high reputation.

As usual, I was a slow learner, but gradually improved, lost few balls, and could hand my player the right club before he asked for it. I even learned to play a little, with old broken and discarded clubs which I patched up. Like all the caddies, I became ambidextrous, for I had a right-handed putter and driver, a left-handed mashie and niblick. (Clubs were not numbered in those days.)

It had been a long and hot summer, and autumn brought no relief. Lack of rain meant numerous small forest fires, and the wind would carry smoke from thirty miles away south to our town. Everyone talked about the distant forest fires, but no one believed Haileybury was in any danger, though people remembered the Porcupine Fire of 1911 which wiped that mining town off the map, and the Matheson Fire five years later which blotted out the prosperous little farming town.

October 4, 1922, began like any other day. After breakfast my brother and I set off for Haileybury High School carrying our books and sandwiches. Clint was in the fourth form, I was in the first. One dreary class succeeded another, the day dragged on. At 2 p.m., however, the principal, Mr. Tooke, paid an unexpected visit to my classroom. The smoke from the forest fires had grown heavier, he said, and some parents had been phoning and asking that their children be sent home. Now, there was absolutely no danger and no cause for alarm. We had all seen the farmers and their teams ploughing up a wide strip of ground on the far side of the T & N.O. railway tracks, so that even if the forest fire approached the town, it could not leap across that protection belt. Nevertheless, as some parents were worried, he had decided that school would close for the day, and we were all to return directly to our homes. Class dismissed.

Our house was at least a mile away from the school, on the other side of town. Dad had bought it two years before for $1,800, and had just made the final payment. He was planning to insure it, but had not done so yet. It was a two-storey wooden house, five rooms in all. We had a good-sized garden and grew our own vegetables — potatoes, cucumbers, carrots, tomatoes, peas. We also had some blackberry bushes. Mother made jars of preserves, jams and jellies, and shelves in the cellar were loaded with these goodies. Our winter supply of coal had also been delivered and filled a big bin in one corner of the cellar.

As Clint and I hurried home, the sky suddenly turned black with smoke, and sometimes tongues of flame darted out. Before we had gone more than three blocks the fire had jumped the railway tracks and set some houses aflame. The wind was strong, a gale, almost a hurricane. Flaming treetops flew through the air and landed on houses around us. When we rushed into our house Mother said quietly, "we will go to the lake." She was by no means calm, but she did not give way to hysteria. Some of our neighbours were rushing around, trying to get lifts in cars which were already jammed with people fleeing to Cobalt. But Dad had warned us time and again never to attempt to run away from a forest fire, but always to head for a lake if there was one handy. Lake Timiskaming, six miles wide at this point, was only three blocks away. Yet by the time we reached it houses were burning all around us, and the smoke was making it difficult to breathe. Mother sat down by the water's edge, and Clint and I, following the example of some men, broke into a lakeside house and collected armloads of blankets. We saw some panic-stricken people do odd things. One man was carrying half a dozen light bulbs; another was dragging a rocking chair to the waterfront.

The heat was becoming unbearable, and the hundreds of people along our section of the shoreline began moving into the water, dipping blankets and pulling them over their heads. Every couple of minutes we would have to soak our blankets again. Gusts churned up the lake, flaming embers hissed as they struck the water.

This went on for hours. Night came. There was a terrific explosion half a mile away, as the gasoline depot on the dock blew up, sending flames shooting high into the sky.

Sometime during the night the wind changed, blowing the flames inland away from us, and we were safe. Then it started to snow, and we became desperately cold. People began to hunt for bits of driftwood and lit little fires! We stood on some huge boulders near the shore; they were so hot that the rubber heels on my boots sizzled down to the leather.

Some men came along, and told everybody, "Follow us. There are still some houses at the other end of town, where you can take shelter." We stumbled along the pebbly shore for what seemed ages, and found ourselves on Millionaires' Row. The shift in the wind had saved a few dozen homes of the rich, while the rest of Haileybury was levelled to the ground. Scores of us, utterly exhausted, crowded into the nearest house and slept on the floor.

Morning. Our town had vanished. All gone. Nothing left of the massive stone cathedral and hospital. Not a wall standing. The railway tracks were tangled up like spaghetti. No sign of the biggest hotels — the Matabanic, Vendome, Maple Leaf, and others.

We three — Mother, Clint, and I — set out to try to find where our home had been. We passed a few bodies here and there, burned to a crisp. Men were laying blankets over them. We finally located our cellar. The coal pile was still burning, and in one corner we spied an unbroken cup. That was all.

We learned something of the extent of the tragedy only later. Four thousand people left homeless. Other towns and villages had been wiped out: Charlton, Engelhart, Earlton, Thorntoe, Uno Park, a section of New Liskeard, North Cobalt. Two thousand square miles of ruin. Some fifty people dead. For days a pall of smoke that had drifted southward hung over Ottawa, four hundred miles away.

A makeshift registry office was opened in one of the houses on Millionaires' Row. Free tickets to anywhere in Canada. Relief trains were already backing into the outskirts of the town, where railway gangs were laying down temporary tracks. We asked for passage to Pembroke, as we had relatives there. By nightfall, packed into an old-fashioned passenger car, we were on our way.

When the news of the Haileybury Fire reached Kirkland Lake, Dad and another miner whose family lived in Haileybury rushed to the railway in their work clothes, commandeered a handcar and pedalled it without rest the sixty miles to the edge of our town. Plunging through the queue at the registry office — people waiting for train tickets — he asked about his family. "A Mrs. Edith Whyte and two sons entrained last night, destination Pembroke," he was told. Dad relaxed, lay down on a bench, and fell into a sound sleep.

Time effaces many memories. The year we lived in Pembroke was largely uneventful. I have long forgotten the names of my schoolmates. I do recall, however, a strike that a few of us staged against the principal, a German named Ulysses Jacob Flock. He was a puffed-up little martinet who had a nasty habit of sneaking up behind your desk and giving you a clip on the ear with two stiffened fingers. A born sadist. We called him "Useless Jacob" and planned our revenge. On the day when spring examinations were due to start, six or seven of us stood up, yelled "Down with the Kaiser!" and rushed out the door. I never went back and consequently had to repeat my first year in Haileybury High when we returned north.

Haileybury was rebuilding itself, slowly and painfully, and there were no houses for rent. Many families were still living in antique Toronto streetcars, minus the undercarriages, which had been shipped in after the fire. All that was left of the original town was Millionaires' Row and the high school, the only large building that escaped the flames.

Dad bought a one-storey, three-room wooden shack in Cobalt's slum district, just off Lang Street. The roof leaked and the floors sagged. Nearby was a Catholic church, simply a cellar boarded over and covered with tarpaper. Steps led below ground level to the church door. The congregation had been too optimistic and started to build when the Cobalt boom was already over, mines were closing down, and miners were leaving town to find work elsewhere.

There was no high school in Cobalt, so we rode the five miles to Haileybury on electric trolleys, which ran on a half-hour schedule. These trolleys were actually remodelled railway cars, and each had a smoking compartment. The fare was 5 cents, collected by a conductor with a little box. We kids from Cobalt loved that twice-a-day trip.

The year was 1923, and in October our school held its annual athletic championships, for junior, middle, and senior awards. Events included the high jump, broad jump, shot put, hundred-yard dash, plus a couple of unorthodox contests — the baseball pitch and running the bases. I won the junior gold medal, though I only came first in the baseball pitch. But in most events I finished second or third and gained some points.

I joined the Cobalt YMCA and learned to swim in its dismal little pool. But I've remained a poor swimmer all my life, and retain a certain fear of water. To me, the sailors in the Second World War seemed far braver than the soldiers or airmen. I once met a British seaman who had had five ships go down under him. Twice he had been rescued from the icy waters of the North Sea, while on the Murmansk run. I simply couldn't understand how he found the courage to go right back to sea.

At the Y I also learned the rudiments of billiards, pool, and snooker. I say the rudiments because we juniors were only allowed to play on tables smaller than regulation size. And under the keen eye of Sandy Hall, our gym instructor, I boxed and punched the bag, swung from the rings, and did exercises on the parallel bars and horse. Sandy was a fine instructor, though he showed a fondness for giving his young charges a playful slap on the bottom.

Masturbation and wet dreams comprised my sex life in that period. In my dreams and fantasies I screwed every girl in every class, including the young female teacher. I had the most fantastic dreams ... well, not so fantastic, I suppose, for they are common to all young adolescents.

There was one recurring dream, which I could some-how call up at will. A girl was completely bound in tape, which wound around her body from head to foot. I began walking around her, unwinding it. When her face was un-covered, there would be a brief pause in my dream while I decided which girl I desired that night — Betty? Marion? Helen? Or our French teacher, Mlle. Belanger? Having de-cided, I would resume walking around her, until presently her breasts, with their pink nipples standing at attention, would be revealed. (I sometimes chose globular breasts, at other times bomb-shaped, but whatever type, the nipples were always bright pink, which was odd, because I had a preference for brunettes.) And now we reached the navel, that carved jewel. And because it was Marion who was my lover, Marion with her glorious blue-black hair and heavy black eyebrows, which meant a thick bush ... and yes, her bush was coming into sight ... and I was coming too.

Kingston: The Limestone City

My mother, my brother, and I moved to Kingston from Co-balt in the summer of 1924. Clint was entering the faculty of medicine at Queen's University. He graduated in 1929, took a postgraduate course in Edinburgh, set up practice as a gynecologist in Ottawa, served in the RCAF during the Second World War, and retired in the 1970s.

We lived in Kingston for about seven years, and it was there that I "grew up." The first year saw little change in my living habits. I joined the YMCA, boxed, played pool, read Westerns. In 1925 I became a school dropout, got a job as a clerk, and began to earn my own living, at least partly. I was paid $8 a week and gave my mother $5. Every week-day morning I turned up at W.T. Mills's hat and fur store on

Princess Street, scattered Dustbane and swept the floors, then took my place behind the cap counter. Not yet sixteen, I was nevertheless always addressed as "Mr. Whyte" by other members of the staff. Discipline was strict. Even when the store was empty of customers, one could not sit down or relax. I had to fuss around, rearrange stock, etc.

I remember my first sale. A mother came in with a small boy in tow. I eagerly produced one cap after another, but the little brat spurned them all. He would look at himself in the mirror, say "Don't like it," and throw the cap back on the counter. The boss was keeping a sharp eye on me from his office, and Jim Lindsay, my senior in the hat department, hovered nearby, ready to enter the fray if needed, but giving me every opportunity to make my own sale. I was becoming desperate, until finally the dear child exclaimed, "I like this one!" Adoring mother agreed. I made out the bill, took the money to the cashier, popped the receipt into a paper bag with the cap, warmly invited the mother to visit us again when sonny needed winter headgear. They left. Jim said, "you did fine," and I was as happy as a dog with two tails. I had made my first sale! I would work hard and become the best clerk in Kingston! I would climb the business ladder and someday own my own store! I would become a financial tycoon!

A representative of the Dale Carnegie outfit (*How to Win Friends and Influence People*) came to town and started classes at the YMCA. I attended the first, free session to sample the menu. Some fifteen people, mostly young businessmen, turned up. We sat around an oval table, then were told to stand up in pairs, turn to your partner, and with a wall-to-wall grin say clearly, "I'm Bert" (or Jack, or Bob), while giving him a firm, manly handshake. Remember to speak up, speak slowly, never lose that friendly smile. So

we practised, and teeth gleamed at teeth for the next hour
... and I walked away from the class, never to return.

At the store I advanced from caps to hats. Lindsay, a nice
guy, married, one child, earning $13 a week, taught me how
to estimate a potential customer's head size. It improved
chances of a sale if you could greet him by saying, "A hat?
Yes, sir, about 7 1/8th is your size, I believe?" After a few
months I rarely made a mistake.

Working hours were 8:30 a.m. to 6:00 p.m., except on Sat-
urdays, when we worked till 9:00 p.m., and one night a week
we had to stay late, window dressing, under the supervision
of the boss, "Billy" Mills, son of the founder of the establishment. Actually, the fur department, occupying half the
store, was the big money maker, but the men's and women's
hat departments, in the front parts of the building, drew in
a lot of customers off the street.

Our most expensive hats were Christies and Borsalinos.
Spring was by far our busiest season, for in those days all
men wore straw skimmers and we would sell dozens a day.
That year Yeddo straw hats were in style. The tightly wo-
ven rim, with an elastic quality, made it possible for young
blades to impress girlfriends by casually doffing their lid,
bouncing it on the pavement, catching it smoothly and donning it nonchalantly. Needless to say, whenever Mills was
out of the store I practised this bit of legerdemain until I
had it taped. A few girls were amused by this caper, but still
found me resistible.

As the dogsbody of the place, I sometimes had to take fur
coats from storage into a small enclosed backyard and beat
the moths out of them. The moth invasion had to be kept
secret from customers, of course. If the damage to coats,
either those in storage or in stock, was too great, they were
taken upstairs to the fur cutting and repair department,

presided over by a dour little man who had been with the firm for forty years. He had started working for the founder at $5 a week, and his wages had been increased by a dollar every year. Now he was drawing down a cool $45 weekly, which seemed to me a fabulous sum. He also had the privilege of reporting for work fifteen minutes later than the rest of the staff.

Around this period the Ku Klux Klan came to Kingston. There were few Negroes in the Limestone City, and only a very small Jewish community, so the Klan concentrated their venom on the Roman Catholic minority. One of our sales clerks in the women's hat department was a Catholic, and she was terrified when four crosses were burned in various parts of the city one night. Each cross was supposed to represent a thousand Klansmen, though I doubt if there were ever four thousand members in Kingston. As far as I can recall, there was no active violence during the two-year period when the Klan flourished. On one occasion they held an evening rally on a farm just outside city limits. The night before they had painted white arrows on the streets and highway, pointing the way to the grounds. Hoping for a bit of excitement, a few of us young lads piled into someone's old Model T Ford and headed for the farm. We were stopped at the gate by white-sheeted figures. "You all Protestants? Canadian citizens? All right, drive through, park on the left." As darkness fell, torches were lit. About half the crowd of some two thousand wore sheets. Someone introduced a King Kleagle (I think that was the title) who mounted a farm wagon and began his harangue: Keep Canada Canadian, loyal, God-fearing, Protestant, down with the Pope, the Jews, niggers, defend our heritage, let the heathen tremble, the Vatican crumble . . .

The KKK faded away almost as rapidly as it had appeared.

At the height of its "power" it had attracted a certain number of Orangemen and received the blessings of an obscure Baptist preacher, whose church benefited financially. On the other hand, most Kingstonians, basically conservative (and Conservative) tried to ignore the whole affair. One United Church minister, though threatened by the Klan, preached a series of powerful anti-Klan sermons.

I was approached to join the Klan by a plumber who was fixing some pipes in the bowels of the store. "Young fellow like you, good Canadian, should do something to get rid of the kikes and left-footers we got around here," he said. "How about coming to a meeting with me and you'll learn what it's all about?" I said I wasn't a joiner, and I thought the KKK was a nut organization.

It was about this time that I turned against religion. Shortly after arriving in Kingston a minister had called at our house to persuade my elder brother to join the United Church and take communion. Clint had agreed; my mother was pleased. Then the cleric turned his guns on me. At fifteen, he said, I was not too young to make a decision. Let us kneel and pray, shall we? And now Bert, do you not feel . . .

I felt I had been tricked. I didn't believe in Holy Communion mumbo-jumbo. It struck me as being far too close to cannibalism. And also, I was angry because it was the second time I had been conned. In Pembroke, a couple of years before, I had voluntarily gone to hear an Australian evangelist when he had advertised his tent revival meeting with a blown-up photo of Bob Fitzsimmons, former world heavyweight boxing champion. Fitz, said the preacher, knelt in his corner of the ring before every fight, and exchanged a few words with God. When the service was over I lingered behind and asked for more information. Yes, he said, Bob Fitzsimmons was a great champion and a fine Christian.

"Did you ever see him fight?" I wanted to know. The evangelist ducked that one. "He was a fighter for the Lord, as we all should be." "He won the title in 1897 by knocking out Gentleman Jim Corbett with a solar plexus punch," I volunteered. "It was the power the Lord gave him," he replied. "Still, Jim Jeffries knocked him out two years later," I argued. "Let us not question the workings of the Lord. Come, let us kneel and pray together. O Lord, let this young soul turn to Thee..."

And somehow he got me down on my knees and Fitzsimmons was shoved into the background.

The Scopes Trial in Dayton, Tennessee, in the summer of 1925, provided me with some anti-religious ammunition. Scopes was found guilty of having taught evolution in a local high school and was fined $100 and costs by a redneck jury. It was a test case: William Jennings Bryan, a three-time loser in the US presidential race, was chief counsel for the prosecution and Clarence Darrow was the chief defence counsel. Newspapers found some of the exchanges at the trial good copy:

Darrow: You have never felt any interest in the ages of the various races and people and civilization and animals that exist upon the earth today? Is that right?

Bryan: I have never felt a great deal of interest in the efforts that have been made to dispute the Bible by the speculations of men, or the investigations of men.

Darrow: Don't you know that the ancient civilizations of China are six or seven thousand years old, at the very least?

Bryan: No, but they could not run back beyond the creation, according to the Bible, six thousand years ago.

Bryan also declared that "it is better to trust in the Rock of Ages than to know the ages of the rocks." And when Darrow questioned him on the tower of Babel, Bryan stated that he believed all the languages of the earth dated from the time of the tower.

Darrow: Do you believe that the first woman was Eve?

Bryan: Yes.

Darrow: Do you believe she was literally made of Adam's rib?

Bryan: Yes.

Darrow: Did you ever discover where Cain got his wife?

Bryan: No, sir; I leave the agnostics to hunt for her.

And again:

Darrow: Do you think the sun was made on the fourth day?

Bryan: Yes.

Darrow: And they had evening and morning without the sun?

Bryan: I am simply saying it is a period.

Finally Bryan blew up at Darrow's literal interpretation of the Bible:

Bryan: Your Honour, I think I can shorten this testimony. The only purpose Mr. Darrow has is to slur the Bible... I want the world to know that this man who does not believe in God is trying to use a court in Tennessee...

Darrow: I object to your statement. I am examining you on your fool ideas that no intelligent Christian on earth believes.

And it was about this time that I stumbled across Thomas Paine's *The Age of Reason*. Paine, a Deist, sought to debunk the Bible, and I used some of his arguments as weapons in my arsenal: "Whenever we read the obscene stories, the voluptuous debaucheries, the cruel and tortuous executions, the unrelenting vindictiveness, with which more than half the Bible is filled, it would be more consistent that we called it the word of a demon, than the Word of God," wrote Paine. "It is a history of wickedness, that has served to corrupt and brutalize mankind; and, for my part, I sincerely detest it, as I detest everything that is cruel."

Turning to the New Testament, Paine saw no reason for not believing that such a woman as Mary, and such a man as Joseph, and Jesus existed. But, he continued, "it is not the existence, or non-existence of the persons that I trouble myself about; it is the fable of Jesus Christ and the wild and visionary doctrine based thereon. The story, taking it as it is told is blasphemously obscene. It gives an account of a young woman engaged to be married, and while under this engagement she is, to speak plain language, debauched by a ghost, under the impious pretence (Luke, chap. 1, ver. 35) 'the Holy Ghost shall come upon thee, and the power of the highest shall overshadow thee.' Notwithstanding which, Joseph afterwards marries her, cohabits with her as his wife, and in his turn rivals the ghost. (Mary, the supposed virgin-mother of Jesus, had several other children, sons and daughters. See Matthew, chap. XIII, verses 55, 56.)"

I was full of quotations in those days.

Remy de Gourmont: "The idea of God is only the shadow of man projected in the infinite." Winwood Reade: "Martyrs and persecutors resemble one another; their minds are composed of the same materials. The man who will suffer death for his religious faith, will endeavour to force it even unto death. . . . Jesus was not able to display the spirit of a prosecutor in his deeds, but he displayed it in his words. Believing that it was in his power to condemn his fellow-creatures to eternal torture, he did so condemn by anticipation all the rich and almost all the learned men among the Jews." Somehow I missed Marx and his "Religion is the Opium of the People." I was to enjoy Harpo, Groucho, and Chico before I became acquainted with Karl.

My belligerent anti-religious campaign shocked some of my close friends, and we had many a hot argument in all-night cafes. Youth can only argue, not discuss. Jim McLaughlin had a young Anglican clergyman plucking at his sleeve, and one night he brought him along as backup man. The sky pilot used Paley's watch and the "divine push-off" theories with some effect. I counter-punched with Paine and some pamphlets sent me by the American Association for the Advancement of Atheism. We drank innumerable cups of coffee and talked until 4 a.m.

Nothing was settled, of course. No agreement on anything. The arrogance of youth: everything is black or white, no in-between shades. No tolerance. But as William Pitt said in the British House of Commons in 1741: "The atrocious crime of being a young man . . . I shall neither attempt to palliate nor deny." In any case, it was all good intellectual exercise, and it was high time that I developed beyond my physical adolescence, time to grasp the nettle of life.

I had no guidelines, but poked around in the library, and somehow abandoned Zane Grey and plunged straight into Baudelaire, who became my revered guru for several years. I discovered Gautier, Verlaine, Zola, Balzac, Flaubert, Daudet, Maupassant, Coppée, Murger, Mendes, and other nineteenth-century French writers. Among the Russians — Turgenev, Dostoyevsky, and Gorky. But Tolstoy's *War and*

Peace defeated me — I got lost in a maze of names, patronymics, surnames, and diminutives. It was twenty years later, while a patient in Toronto's Chorley Park military hospital after the Second World War, that I finally became engrossed in this masterpiece and read it from cover to cover. The French and Russian writers in translation, of course. As for English and American fiction, at that period it failed to grab me, though in another decade I was into Meredith, Poe, Whitman, and early Hemingway.

I still boxed and played pool, as my diaries of those years show: "Boxed a fast three rounds with Jim McLaughlin last night."

"In a game of snooker tonight all the red balls were down and I was trailing by 47 points. I snookered my opponent four times, ran every coloured ball and won by a point. Hah!"

"After gym four of us went to Wheelock's Cafe and had chocolate peanut floats — our special invention. Two scoops of ice cream, chocolate syrup and a scoopful of unhusked salted peanuts. Marvellous."

"Went to the football game, Queen's vs Edmonton. Harry Batstone and Pep Leadley superb. We won easily."

"Met Bobbie, smitten, walked her home, sat on veranda, fooled around a bit but she wouldn't let me kiss her, said she was saving her lips for Rudy Vallee! Stupid bitch!"

Selling hats no longer interested me. In January 1926 I quit my job at Mills and spent the next few months studying old newspaper files at Queen's University.

Girls
He sang of lifetime's yellowed page —
When not quite eighteen years of age.
PUSHKIN, *Eugene Onegin*

In my early teens, as a result of reading Baudelaire, I adopted a jaded attitude towards sex, though I hadn't yet actually experienced any. Needless to say, there were no skin magazines in those days, no bush, beaver, split beaver and wet split beaver camera shots. There were a few nudist magazines, with the sex carefully brushed out.

Once I persuaded a young girl to come to my room and take off her clothes. Aping a scene I had read about in an article on Baudelaire, I turned away, affecting indifference, and said coldly, "Dress up." The trouble was, my dong hadn't been indifferent, nor had my thoughts been. Had someone split open my head with an axe, he would have found it full of little cunts.

In George Moore's *Lewis Seymour and Some Women* I came across a love scene that impressed me as being a sophisticated approach to sex.

"Your breasts are small," Lewis tells Lucy.

"Too small?"

"Breasts are never too small. Your breasts are good."

Then he goes on to praise her belly: "The low vault rising imperceptibly and in such exact architecture that I think of Euclid.... Your navel a gem carved inward with cunning hand, and finely set ..."

I decided to try out this approach on one of three sisters who lived in Portsmouth, and who had all shown willingness to smooch a bit on several occasions when a group of us would pay a social call. Their mother also liked flirting with growing boys.

So one night I found myself sitting on a staircase with Betty, a buxom fourteen-year-old. Her lips were soft and tender, and when I slipped an arm around her shoulder and inside her dress until I had a firm grip on a breast the size of a grapefruit, she made no protest, simply snuggled up closer.

"Your breasts are small," I said.

"They are not!" she said.

I was not to be deterred from my lines.

"Breasts are never too small."

"You're crazy! I have the biggest boobs of all the girls in grade eight!"

"And you have a beautiful belly," I continued. "The low vault rising imperceptibly and in such exact architecture..."

"Hey, Johnny, Jim! Come and rescue me from this nutty friend of yours! Take him away to the booby-hatch!"

"Your navel... a gem..."

"Go play with your own belly-button," she said, and sprang up and left me sitting there with an erection.

The other sisters wouldn't have anything to do with me, either.

The next day I called on Johnny, who told me he had scored. He was a tall, handsome lad, with rosy cheeks which made him look much younger than he really was (he was actually seventeen). Girls were always bowled over by him.

"Johnny, please tell me how you get a girl to do it," I pleaded.

"It's really very simple," said Johnny. "I just open my fly, put my Little Brother in her hand, and start to cry. It works every time."

Travelling Rough

Shortly before my sixteenth birthday I was bitten by the travel bug. Hitchhiking was easier in the twenties, for there were few superhighways and the speed limit was usually forty to fifty miles per hour. This gave the motorist a chance to size up the person trying to thumb a lift, and to brake to a halt within a reasonable distance.

With $25 in my pocket and a small rucksack over my shoulder I set off from Kingston one sunny morning, and a series of lifts took me through Belleville and Toronto. By nightfall I was in Hamilton, showing a YMCA official my Kingston membership card and persuading him to let me sleep in the gym.

Crossing into the United States at Niagara Falls, I caught a lift to Buffalo, slept in a country schoolhouse between that city and Erie. At Toledo I turned south, with the vague intention of going to New Orleans.

When I reached Lima, Ohio, half my capital had been spent, so I found my way to the Rescue Home, was handed a hymnbook and had to sing for my supper, along with a bunch of old tramps. After a meagre meal of spaghetti and one meatball, a preacher harangued us for an hour or so about the wages of sin. We slept on camp cots and in the morning were turned out without breakfast.

I had only been a week on the road, but with no one to talk to except the people who gave me lifts I was beginning to feel lonesome for the company of someone in my own age group. Then, on the outskirts of Lexington, Kentucky, I passed a private swimming pool behind a rich mansion. Three girls were splashing about, and I stopped for a moment to watch them. They waved at me and one girl said teasingly, "Why don't you join us for a swim?" She was just kidding, of course, but my spirits bounded. And suddenly I thought of Catulle Mendès's young beggar, in his ragged cloak, asking for alms, saying he had eaten nothing for two days. Three girls took pity on him. The first gave him a coin, and he thanked her. The second gave him a smaller coin, and he said, "May God reward you." The third, the poorest and prettiest, had no money, but she gave him a kiss. The hungry beggar said nothing, but a flower-seller chancing to come by, he spent the two coins on a bunch of roses and presented it to the pretty girl.

I had a sandwich and coffee in a Lexington cafe, but when I tried to change my last $10 bill the cashier wouldn't accept Canadian money. Luckily I had some US change. So I found a bank and asked a teller to change my ten-spot. He looked at me shrewdly: "You claim this is Canadian money, son? Oh no, this is Nova Scotian money." True enough, this was long before the Bank of Canada was set up, and my bill was issued by the Bank of Nova Scotia. My argument that it was good Canadian currency fell on deaf ears.

Discouraged, I decided to turn north and head for home. Just outside the city I hitched a lift in a Chevvie and told my story to the driver. "Let me see your money," he said. After glancing at it, he handed me an American ten. "But if the bank wouldn't change it, how can you be sure?" I asked. He grinned and said, "I do a lot of business with a firm an Alberta, so I know a Canadian bill when I see one." Anxious not to cheat my benefactor, I hastened to explain that the Canadian dollar was only worth about 97 cents US, or thereabouts. "'S'all right, lad, you can buy yourself an extra coffee and a couple of sinkers."

I returned home via Cincinnati, Dayton, Toledo, Detroit, and Hamilton, and finished my first journey in a blaze of glory, riding into Kingston in a Cadillac. Seeing Johnny Stephens walking down Princess Street, I asked the driver to let me out, thanked him warmly for the lift, strolled up to Johnny and said, "How are you all?"

Johnny burst into a peal of laughter. "Two weeks in the States, and you've acquired a Deep South accent!"

ꙅꙅꙅꙅꙅ

My nightlife revolved around the YMCA, poolrooms, ice cream parlours, movies, and cafes. After a gym session at the YMCA a few of us would head for the Ward and Hamilton drugstore, which had a milk bar, and splurge on huge 15-cent milkshakes and three Dad's cookies (a dime). Other nights would find us eating Western sandwiches and arguing far into the night in one of the many downtown cafes: the Capital, Crown, Princess, Mandarin, Three Castles, Kent, Frisco. Or even the One Minute Lunch or the Greasy Sleeve — which had a sign in the window, "Come In and Eat Before We Both Starve!"

Most nights I spent a couple of hours in Princess Street poolrooms — Ernie Caine's, Cotter & Cliff, Pappas Brothers. Even the Army and Navy, where the roughnecks hung out and fights were frequent.

My companions in these nocturnal wanderings (which sometimes lasted till dawn) were usually lads from the Y crowd — the three McLaughlins, Art Stafford, Vern Coe, George Ashby, Rusty Upton, Ken Robinson; Queen's University students — Johnny Stephens, Jock Kent, Scotty Mc-Gowan; or pool players — Duke Richardson, Jack Gilbert; or Jimmy Black, teenage Lothario.

Hitchhiking to Kentucky had given me a taste for the open road. In August I hiked to Ottawa for the capital's centennial celebrations. A few months later Ken Robinson and I thumbed our way to Toronto to see Red Grange, the famous American "Galloping Ghost" of football. He had made his name and his number (77) immortal in college and was now playing for the New York Yankees. The *Whig*, which faithfully reported my hiking experiences, gave Ken and I a half-column. It said, in part: "Whyte and Robinson left on Sunday morning, picking up an auto ride which gave them a lift all the way to Oshawa. Here they stayed over till Monday morning and continued their excursion. The two of them had only three dollars and the tickets to the game cost one dollar each. The return trip was made with but one cent between them. They spent Monday night in Port Hope and got many lifts from autoists who all proved very friendly. Red Grange played brilliantly, the boys say, and his one 70-yard run for a touchdown was the high spot of the whole game. The New York Yankees won from the Californians in a league game by 28 to 0."

The year 1927 rolled round, and my itchy feet kept taking me various places. In June, with 60 cents in my pocket, I set out for Brandon, Manitoba, where I had a pen pal, Lew McKenzie, who was as crazy about boxing as I was. I was selling a few articles to the *Minneapolis Boxing Blade* (at $4 an article) and Lew was doing some sports reportage for a couple of small-town Manitoba papers. "Why don't you come out and see me?" he had written. An invitation I promptly accepted.

I crossed into the states at Niagara Falls, made my way west through Buffalo, Erie, Cleveland, South Bend, Chicago Heights, Dubuque, Mason City, Fargo, and Winnipeg. My luck was good and I averaged two hundred miles a day. The people who gave me lifts occasionally bought me meals, but mostly offered coffee. As a matter of fact, at the time I still had ring ambitions, and didn't drink coffee. A glass of milk and two doughnuts cost only a dime, and that would be my modest request when a driver would say, "I'm hungry, lad. What say we stop for a bite to eat?"

I stayed with Lew for a couple of weeks, then headed home by way of Winnipeg, Minneapolis, Rockford, Mouth Bend, Toledo, Cleveland, Buffalo, Syracuse, and Watertown.

I worked at several odd jobs that summer. A cheapo subcontractor hired a dozen of us youngsters to work on road construction several miles out of town. We slept in tents and were fed mostly on bread and jam. After ten days the boss announced that he was broke, sorry, we were fired and he couldn't pay us. One of the lads said his father was a friend of a Kingston lawyer. We decided to go to see this lawyer. He listened to our story, said not to worry, began making phone calls. A couple of days later we were paid our wages. We asked what the lawyer's fee would be, and were told he wasn't charging us anything. His name was Nichol, and at one time he was the Attorney-General of Ontario in the Ferguson government. I worked a couple of weeks in the Kingston shipyards, and two days in a quarry on Wolf Island.

Then Ken Robinson and I took off for Toronto to see the Wrigley Marathon Swim, twenty-one miles in the ice-cold waters of Lake Ontario. Canada's hope was George Young, but he was forced to drop out after five miles. The famous Gertrude Ederle, who in 1926 had become the first woman to swim the English Channel, also failed to complete the course. The event was won by a German named Vierkotter.

In September I hiked north to Kirkland Lake, and got a job at the Conroyal Mine, four miles out of town, where my dad was a hoistman. For the first couple of weeks I unloaded coal, dug spuds, painted the cookhouse veranda, helped the blacksmith. Then I got a mucking job at the five-hundred-foot level.

The Conroyal was a small gold mine, with some sixty workers. It operated on a two-shift basis. The day shift drilled and blasted, the night shift mucked and prepared the face for the next day shift. My partner and I were mucking in a drift which extended some hundred yards from the shaft. We handled about twenty tonnes a shift, which meant each of us had to fill ten one-tonne cars, push them to the shaft and send them up top, wait for an empty to come down, and push it back to the face.

My "partner" was a squat, husky Yugoslav who refused to water the muck. Dry muck is lighter but also makes it easier for the fine silica dust to seep into the lungs and condemn you to a painful death from silicosis. Steve didn't give a damn about the future. We started the night shift at 8 p.m. and could leave as soon as we had mucked out the drift. Working like fury, with dry muck, we could be through by midnight. That gave him a chance to wash, walk the four miles to Kirkland Lake, and visit a blind pig.

By the time I had pushed my full car to the shaft and returned with an empty, Steve would be waiting at the switch with a full car, fuming, impatient to get going. But by the time he brought an empty, my car would be only half or two-thirds filled. Although I was in excellent physical shape, no youngster just turned eighteen could compete with a solidly muscled thirty-year-old experienced manual labourer.

"To hell with him," my peers told me. "Steve knows it is dangerous and technically illegal to shovel dry muck. You have eight hours to finish the job. Anybody can do it in six but why bust your ass to try and do it in four?" Nevertheless, I felt uncomfortable. But when the opportunity arose to go above ground and take on the job of night fireman, seven days a week, ten hours a shift, at 45 cents an hour — I jumped at the chance.

In the spring of 1928 the urge to travel hit me again. I quit the Conroyal, hitched my way around southern Ontario for a couple of weeks, came north with Ken Robinson and worked very briefly at the Murphy Mine, then took off again with no definite destination in mind. After crossing the New Peace Bridge and finding myself in the United States,

I flipped a dime to decide whether to head east or west. Go west, young man, the dime commanded.

A few days later I crossed the Mississippi River at Clinton, Ohio. Seeing a rowboat hauled halfway out of the water onto a sandbank, with no owner in sight, I considered stealing it and floating down the river, like Huck Finn. But I lacked the nerve.

My last lift that day left me between towns. It grew dark and I curled up in a dry ditch by the side of the highway to get some sleep, for it is useless to thumb at night. I awoke at midnight, chilled to the bone, and decided to walk a few miles and try to find a barn or a haystack near the road. I had only gone a few hundred yards when a car with a New York licence plate passed me, slowed down, and the driver yelled, "Wanna ride?" I climbed in and away we went, weaving a bit and hitting sixty or seventy, while my drunken benefactor explained in great detail that if I had tried to hail him he'd have stepped on the gas. There was very little traffic, for which I was thankful, and we made Marshalltown, Iowa, some seventy-five miles, without mishap. He put up at a small hotel and I slept in the car, under an old army blanket. It was a lucky break for me.

The following evening I was tramping out of Albert Lea, Minnesota, when it began to rain. I made a beeline for a ballpark and spent the night in the ticket office underneath the grandstand. A cop came around in the morning but was friendly. When the rain stopped I started north for Minneapolis. Just as it began to drizzle again I struck a through lift.

Somewhere along the line a jolly character driving a truck picked me up, offered me a shot of bourbon, which I refused, then handed me a bottle of beer, which I drank. When we stopped at a gas station, he showed me a very big, ugly snake he kept in a glass case in the back of the truck.

"He's my worker," the owner explained. "At hick towns I put up a tent, back the truck into it, and charge the yokels a dime, 10 cents, one-tenth of a dollar, it will neither make you, break you, buy a farm, pay the mortgage, or grow in your hand like your cock, to see this thirty-foot, man-eating python, come one, come all, step right up ..." The snake, actually about twelve feet long, lived on chickens and could eat a dozen at a time, the owner explained. "I paid $500 for him, and he's paid me back over and over, though when the dimes are scarce, I don't feed him at all for weeks on end."

The next lift I got was from a circus couple, and they, too, were by no means sober. Three drunken drivers in one week. Very unusual. The circus lady was fat and on the shady side of fifty. She called me "baby" and kept falling asleep on my shoulder. Her husband was a boaster, and claimed acquaintance with Dempsey and Lindy. "I knew them when they didn't have a dime."

I hitchhiked north to Winnipeg, then west to Saskatchewan, where I stayed a month with various uncles, aunts, and cousins in Innes and Bengough. From the latter village I began the long hike home, taking the Regina-Yellowstone trail. Arriving at Ecobey, Montana, a tough little cow town, I turned my face eastward.

On my birthday, July 27, just outside Fergus Falls, Minnesota, I caught my longest lift ever, nine hundred miles to Toledo, Ohio, in a Chrysler with Tom Brown of Seattle. He proved to be an interesting companion. Young, thirtyish, handsome, travelled, well-to-do (from a wealthy New York family). He had served overseas during the last year of the World War. Played semi-pro baseball at one time. Became a songwriter on the west coast. Worked as an executive for an insurance company in the southern states. And when I met him he was representing a carbon company in Seattle, but was on his holidays, and planning to spend two weeks at a summer camp in the Adirondacks.

I didn't learn all this at once, of course. When I casually asked, "How far are you going?" he answered just as casually, "A few miles." But as we talked of this and that, it turned out that we had many common interests, and when, after covering 250 miles, we rolled into the town of Wing, he said: "Look, Bert, I'm driving all the way to New York, and I like someone to talk to. Now, I've scads of money, so don't argue, I'll pay for your hotel bill and meals, and you'll earn your bed and board by keeping me entertained on the road."

It was a genuine offer and I didn't argue. We took two rooms in an expensive hotel that night, and the next morning ate a marvelous breakfast of bacon and eggs and toast, preceded by something new in my experience — half a grapefruit with a maraschino cherry in the middle, set in a silver bowl filled with crushed ice. We drove four hundred miles that day, ate a late dinner of filet mignon and stayed overnight at the Hotel Clayton in Waukegan, Illinois.

All good things have to end. I told Tom that I would be splitting off when we reached Toledo, as I had arranged to visit a friend who was working in Dayton. "Look, why don't you come along with me to New York, and in a couple of days a group of us will be heading for the Adirondacks. My young brother is just a few years older than you, and about the same build. He can supply you with all the clothes you'll need, and I'm damn sure you will like my friends. Then when our holiday is over I'll be driving back west and can drop you off at Toledo. What do you say?"

It was an offer hard to refuse. But my common sense warned me that his family and friends might not be all that enthusiastic about hosting a road kid whom they knew nothing about, and that it was far from certain that I would fit in with a bunch of sophisticated New Yorkers, most of them ten or more years my senior. So I thanked Tom warmly for the invitation, but when we drove into Toledo I said goodbye and headed south on the Dixie Highway.

Lew McKenzie had left Brandon some months before and was now working in a print shop in Dayton. He put me up for a week, and we saw a professional boxing match at McCabe's Arena (Mike Dundee knocked out Frankie Lloyd in three rounds). I also noted in my diary that "the girls here are much snappier dressed than in the west, and a few follow the new stockingless fad." Lew took me to my first "talking picture" featuring Conrad Nagel and Dolores Costello in *Tenderloin*. If I remember correctly, it was mostly a silent film, but at one point some people gathered around a piano and burst into song.

Back to Work

When I landed back in Kingston I was badly in need of a job. My luck was in: a friend clerking in a haberdashery was quitting and I was taken on to replace him.

"So you're working for Barney the Jew!" some of my friends chortled.

"Yes, I'm working for Barney the Jew," I said. "And you want to know something? He's a damn sight better to work for than Billy Mills."

As the months went by I began to piece together, like bits of a jigsaw puzzle, the picture of Barney Lipman's hard life. From somewhere in pogrom-ravished central Europe (Poland? Russia? Lithuania?) he had emigrated to New York around the turn of the century when the words on a tablet on the Statue of Liberty still, perhaps, had some meaning:

Give me your tired, your poor,
Your huddled masses yearning to breathe free,
The wretched refuse of your teeming shore.
Send these, the homeless, tempest-tost to me,
I lift my lamp beside the golden door!

Maybe a golden door, but no golden streets, Barney soon discovered. Like so many immigrant Jews, he gravitated to the Garment Centre, where he worked fourteen hours a day in a sweatshop, and slept on the cutting table. Still, in three or four years he had saved enough money from his meagre wages to buy a handcart and a few dozen pairs of glasses. Thus equipped, he left New York and pushed his cart around the countryside, stopping at farms and letting farmers try on glasses until they found a pair that suited them. Then would come the hard bargaining over price.

In a small way Barney prospered, and married, and decided to search for the Golden Fleece in Canada. During the World War of 1914–1918 he graduated from selling glasses to peddling clothes, and by the time the war ended had signed a long-term lease for a narrow-fronted store on Princess Street. True, it was on the "wrong" side of the street (every business street has its "right" and "wrong" sides) but Barney had achieved his aim, a store of his own. It was never a money maker, but money wasn't Barney's main concern. Independence was.

Barney must have been in his seventies when I began to work for him. He was a small man; even standing on tiptoe he never reached five feet above the earth's crust. His home life was a mess; he and his wife had become estranged some ten years before, and never spoke to one another. I acted as go-between when, on rare occasions, she entered the store. "Tell Mr. Lipman to be home for dinner at six o'clock."

I repeated her words. "Tell Mrs. Lipman I will be on time."
Sad. I never learned what had caused the rift.

My first day on the job, Barney decided to test my honesty. Ringing up "no sale" on the giant old cash register, he made a great fuss about dropping a few bills on the floor and stooping to pick them up, then told me: "I am going to the bank, you will be in charge of the store. If a customer comes in, don't let it out." From the window I watched him cross the street, turn a corner, then peek back. It was obvious that he had something devious in mind. I walked over to the cash register and saw a $5 bill on the floor. I picked up the money and pocketed it. Barney was still peeking around the corner every minute or so. What if I should miss the bill, and a customer came in and took it? Soon he returned, wandered over to the cash register, scanned the floor, then rang up "no sale" and counted the cash, began to walk up and down, his brow furrowed. I let him sweat a bit, then said casually, "Oh, Mr. Lipman, you must have dropped this money on the floor, I didn't know how to operate the cash register," and handed him the five-spot. His face lit up like a pinball machine.

Customers were few and far between, and when a window shopper would stop for a few moments, either Barney or I would sally forth to try and drag him in. Because we were "a Jew store" many customers tried to "jew us down." But in this game Barney was in his element. Naturally our prices were inflated to cover the situation. A pair of socks marked a dollar had cost us forty cents. The bargaining proceeded from fifty–ninety to sixty–eighty and usually ended at seventy-five, which gave us a nice profit. Notice the "us," for after a couple of months I had begun to feel a strong affection for old Barney and shared his problems.

Problems. There was, for instance, the problem of raising the monthly rent, and of paying my wages ($12 a week and one per cent commission, which was more than Mills had ever paid me). And the problem of stalling off our numerous creditors. A shirt salesman from Toronto would drop in, crack a few jokes, show his samples. Barney would order three dozen shirts. "Ah, Mr. Lipman, I can only take your order for two dozen. You see, you still owe us $35 on your last order, and payment is long overdue." Barney would explain that business was bad, but we were planning to hold a sale, the money would be sent next week, without fail. We would try, but couldn't always make it. So I would compose a letter to the firm. "Enclosed please find $10 on our account." In the course of a month I sent dozens of such letters. And the firms continued to trust Barney up to limited accounts, for they knew he was an honest man, and would pay up in the long run.

When finances became too desperate, Barney would write to his son in New York, who had apparently become prosperous by owning a factory which made buttonholes. I never could quite understand this: it seemed like making holes for doughnuts. In any case, once or twice a year, to avoid us going down the drain, Barney would himself write (in Yiddish) to his son, and would receive a cheque (I guessed for perhaps $200) by return mail.

Barney had health problems, too. Rheumatism. We would go to the rear of the long, narrow store and Barney would peel off his coat and lift his shirt, while I applied a mustard plaster to his aching back.

Then there was the problem of putting on the storm windows. So after work I went home with him, lugged the storm windows out of the cellar, and put them up. Barney was grateful — he had long since begun calling me Bert — and gave me some sweet Passover wine. He had also stopped opening the store at 8:30 a.m. and entrusted me with a key.

Once a week we were supposed to dress the windows, but Barney often forgot and I never reminded him. His idea was to jam all the goods possible into the windows, making our store look like a junk shop, which in a way it was. We sold suits and pants and sweaters and socks and shirts and blankets and jewellery (our jewellery case contained three watches, several leather watchbands, a compass, tie pins, cufflinks).

One day an unusual event occurred. A tall, well-dressed Englishman entered the store and without wasting any time, bought from me six shirts, a couple of ties, half a dozen pairs of socks. The bill totalled about $30. He paid in cash, and departed. I was delighted, but Barney snorted. What kind of a numbskull paid the marked price on everything without even an attempt at bargaining? What kind of buying and selling was that? He was disgusted.

Barney owned a car which had been sitting on blocks in a garage for eight years. It had never been driven. Or rather, the day he bought it he had got behind the wheel (without a driver's licence) and made a trial run of a couple of blocks before mounting the curb. He had promptly put it in storage and tried to sell it, but refused all offers less than what he had paid for it. No buyers, naturally. So it sat on blocks, year after year. Eventually this vintage auto (a Gray-Dort?) would have fetched a fancy price, of course. What became of it, I do not know.

Trying to recall with exactitude more than a half century of episodia is difficult (as A.J. Liebling's friend Colonel Stingo so often remarked, "Memory grows furtive"), but from the cryptic entry in my diary, "Refused to identify McFee," I will try to reconstruct what happened with reasonable accuracy.

One day in late February 1930 a young lad entered the store, bought a pair of socks, and offered a cheque in payment. Barney accepted the cheque, then took it to the bank after the customer left, only to find there was no such account. He phoned the police, who picked up the youngster as he was trying to hitch his way out of town. Barney and I went over to the jail to pick out the bogus cheque artist in a lineup. Barney, whose eyesight wasn't too good, admitted he wasn't sure if the young man, name of McFee, was the party who had cashed the cheque in our store. I was quite sure he was, but when Barney failed to identify him, I had second thoughts about fingering him. Why send a road kid to jail over a lousy couple of dollars? So I said, no, I can't be sure, I think this fellow is taller. One of the cops guessed I was lying, and snarled, "You know damn well this is the same little bastard." "No," I repeated, "I can't be sure. In fact, I remember only the other fellow was a couple of inches shorter than this chap." So they had to release him.

For many months Jim McLaughlin and I had been planning a return to nature. At the end of May 1930, Jim quit his job as a bank teller and I said goodbye to Barney Lipman. The local press duly recorded our departure for the north country:

"J.A. (Bert) Whyte and James R. McLaughlin, two local young men left the city today for Gowganda, Ontario, a small silver mining town about 50 miles north-east of Cobalt, from which point they will strike into the bush to set up a camp near Leta Lake in the Temagami Forest Reserve. The youthful adventurers intend to spend the next six months at this camp site, and are contemplating a canoe trip by way of the Mattagami and Montreal rivers to James Bay early in August ..."

"When they leave the steel at Gowganda, to which place they are travelling by train, both young men will carry pack sacks weighing approximately 65 or 70 pounds each. Stowed away in the pack sacks will be knives, hatchets, a small tent, fishing tackle, cameras and several rolls of film, as well as clothing and other necessities . . ."

In the event, we lived in the bush for two months, not six, and abandoned the idea of a canoe trip to James Bay. We travelled on the Temiskaming & Northern Ontario Railway to Earlton, changed to the slow train to Elk Lake, where we stocked up on grub—flour, rice, oatmeal, bacon, Klim, powdered milk, lard, salt, sugar, prunes, tea, coffee, etc. A truck gave us a rough ride for several miles, then we packed our stuff the rest of the way to Leta Lake, had a dip in ice-cold water, and were bitten by swarms of blackflies. We had forgotten to buy any fly dope. Our first few days in the wilderness were pure misery. The mosquitoes and blackflies made a feast of us, and our attempts at cooking were disastrous — mostly a slumgullion of rice and raisins, or paystreak bacon and half-cooked greasy beans.

In the words of Dollar Bill, a famous janitor-philosopher at Queen's University: "On the apex of the horizon I see perplexity." We fished and caught no fish, a bear swiped our side of bacon one night (we had left it hanging from one branch of a tree) and several rainstorms soaked us to the skin.

We walked to Gowganda one day to buy more food and some fly dope. Back in 1909 the slogan was "Gowganda or Bust " and the silver rush had brought ten thousand miners and prospectors to the straggling shack town. A thousand teams were on the trail, and five hundred canoes would be lined along the lakeshore. The Gowganda "boom" had been short-lived. The town we walked into had a single street and a population under two hundred. It had one Chinese restaurant and one general store. However, at sky-high prices we were able to buy some supplies.

Jim and I decided to move our camp south, and make for bigger timber and better fishing country. This had been the advice given us by Ed Parker, caretaker at a closed-down mine. Ed was pushing seventy, sported a magnificent grey beard, and looked more like an aging youth than a vigorous old man. He chuckled when he saw my chin whiskers, which I was assiduously cultivating. "I have a patent on that."

We packed and lugged our stuff to Longpoint, caught an eight-mile ride to the Beauty Lake trail, and in a couple of hours entered real timber country, pine, tamarack and birch trees, from forty to seventy-five feet in height. Beauty Lake is one lake, but a narrow passage seems to divide it into two, Beauty and Little Beauty. At the head of the main lake New Liskeard's ice cream king, Sam Eplett, had a cottage. He and a few friends would come up for an occasional weekend fishing trip, and at other times he gave us permission to use his canoe and rowboat. We got to know him better in the following month, but more on that later.

Borrowing the skiff, we rowed the two miles to the opposite end of the lake. Passing through the narrows we came close up to three moose swimming across. A moose can be a powerful enemy on land, but in the water he's as helpless as a baby.

At the very end of Little Beauty we found an abandoned one-room cabin, complete with table, bench, and a bed of poles. We had to clean out some mice and a couple of garter snakes and bring in some fresh branches for the bed. We unpacked our library — a dozen books we had brought with us, ranging from the poems of Robert Service to Nietzsche to the Bible. Paradise!

We woke early the next morning, had a wonderful swim, took the canoe out and began trawling, caught a two-pound trout which we fried for breakfast. Jim constructed a stove out of a tin box while I chopped some wood. In the evening Jim tried his hand at verse. Doggerel, but it pleased us:

There's our cabin on the hillside,
With the sunny poplars round it,
Ship your oars and let the boat ride,
Look, my friend, at last we've found it.
There's a pathway leading on it,
Past the wild rose bushes laid,
There's a sunbeam streaming through it
From a hole the mice have made.
There's a rocky hill behind it
And a valley splashed with green,
'Twas an artist that designed it,
And he made it for a Queen.

We made up a "back to nature" menu:

Stewed Rabbit

Take .22, insert shell. Hunt through bush until well done.
Return without rabbit, eat handful of raisins and
go to bed.

Bean Soup

Take pail of water, add one bean. Boil contents
until water is brown on both sides. Remove bean and
serve soup piping hot. If too thick, add more water.
(Bean may be used for bait.)

Mouse Rarebit

Put cheese in trap, catch mouse.
Remove mouse, eat cheese.

As time passed, our food situation improved. We averaged two trout every day, shot a few partridge, and once Jim even bagged a duck. We caught frogs and kept them in a pail of water; when we had a dozen or so we feasted on frogs' legs. We began to bake "rockcakes" in our tin oven, and flapjacks of a sort.

Suddenly there were no more fish. We trawled and trawled, but had no luck. It was Sam Eplett who saved the day. A storm on the lake drove him in to visit us one Sunday. We offered him coffee and rockcakes. He gnawed his way through one rock cake but politely declined a second. When we told him about our fishing problem he laughed and said, "I can see you aren't fishermen. In this hot July weather the fish go deeper. Just add fifty feet to your line and they'll bite again." He was right. That evening we caught a couple of beauties, each weighing well over two pounds.

Sam looked at our ten-volume "library" but professed ignorance of all the authors except Service and the Bible. He patted the latter and said, "As long as you follow the advice in this book you won't go far wrong." When we began to talk about Plato and his idea of a perfect society, Sam confessed he had never found time to worry about such things. He had been working since a kid of thirteen and "didn't know nothing but business." He started to tell us about his ice cream plant in New Liskeard and asked if we'd ever heard of it and was delighted when I said, "Heard of it? I grew up on Eplett's Ice Cream!" and explained that I had lived in Haileybury until the great fire of 1922.

Our good relations with Sam Eplett continued for the remainder of our stay. Once he brought his son Gordon with him. We talked and drank mugs of tea but both our visitors refused rockcakes, saying that they had just had a big lunch. We pretended to believe this excuse.

On July 27 I celebrated my twenty-first birthday. Boiled beans and bannock for breakfast, pancakes for lunch, and fried trout for supper. The next morning we packed our belongings and hiked to Elk Lake, then turned south. A few days later we tried to cross into the United States at Sarnia, but were turned back because we could only produce 50 cents when asked about our financial status.

After we landed flat broke in Kingston, Jim's parents put me up (reluctantly) for a couple of days. Then blamed me, of course, for "luring" Jim away from his safe job in the bank. I scored a few days' work on a dump which was being levelled off to make a Kiwanis children's playground. Then I somehow managed to survive the next couple of months on odd jobs, and on October 18, 1930, was hired at $12 a week by Sam Simmons, owner of the Fifteen Dollar Clothing Store, 79 Princess Street.

Simmons was a go-getter. To survive on a profit of from $3 to $6 a suit required fast turnover. A couple of blocks up the street was the big rival, Tip Top Tailors, one-price suits, $24. In between was Barney Lipman, no threat. But a block south, near the farmers' market, was the Lion Clothing store, a long-established firm, pulling in the country trade.

Life with Barney Lipman had had a certain dreamy quality. On rainy days we never expected any customers. "It's raining cats and rats," Barney would say, and sit down in an armchair to rest, facing the door, but half hidden by a counter piled high with sweaters. In a few minutes his head would begin to nod and he would fall asleep. I would take another chair a few feet behind him, and soon doze off myself. Thus, we spent many an afternoon, disturbed only when some oddball decided to come in and buy a tie or a pair of socks.

With Simmons it was go-go-go. If the weather was bad and business slow, we'd clean out the tiny window and dress it again using our best stock, including the 16-ounce blue serge. These suits cost $12 wholesale, and usually we tried not to sell them, but pushed our regular stock, costing $8 or $9 wholesale. Only if the customer proved tough would we produce the blue serge: "Just feel it, sir ... 18-ounce serge ... the same as Tip Top charges $24 for ..."

Mrs. Simmons spent a lot of time in the store when Sam was away on business trips. She was a pleasant woman but kept a sharp eye on things. When Sam was present she sometimes took me to do her shopping at the market. Unlike Barney Lipman, who was an Orthodox Jew, the Simmons paid little attention to their professed religion, though in the small Jewish community in Kingston it was impossible to ignore all religious taboos. Still, at the farmers' market Mrs. Simmons would nod her head towards a fat chicken she fancied, and I would buy it while she sauntered on. At home they paid no attention to special meat and dairy dishes, and when I was invited up for breakfast one Sunday it turned out to be bacon and eggs. When I had dinner with them on a Saturday, however, she produced the customary Sabbath meal of chicken soup (Jewish penicillin, as they say today), gefilte fish, and chicken. A chicken is a chicken in any language or religion, but this was my introduction to gefilte fish and it turned into a lifelong love. I had yet to meet such culinary rivals as delicatessen chopped liver on rye with fresh dills, blintzes with sour cream, Siberian pelmeni [dumplings] with vinegar, Peking duck, shark's fins, shashlyk [kebabs], Russian cabbage rolls and their cousin dolma ... all delights of the future.

The winter passed quickly and soon spring was bursting out all over. Business had been good and Simmons began talking of opening a branch store in Belleville, with me in charge of a staff of one. Came a day in May when my feet refused to carry me to work. I called up Jim McLaughlin and we set out for Toronto.

Jimmy Black, whom I had known in Kingston, was now working as a chocolate dipper at Eaton's. He put us up in his room on John Street. I spent my days in the reference library, reading and studying. Jim McLaughlin began working at a packing house, in and out of a refrigerator room, tossing hams around and picking up colds. The two Jims each gave me a dollar a week to live on — 25 cents a day for food and an extra two bits "in case I wanted to take a girl out."

In September we said so-long to Blackie and hitched our way to Sudbury. Then Jim received a wire from home, offering him the chance of a job in the army, clerical staff, and he decided to try for it. I stayed another week in Sudbury, then headed for Kirkland Lake, where I luckily met Miles McMillan on a street corner. We spent the afternoon talking over old times, when we had worked together at the Conroyal Mine in 1927–28. We agreed that Kirkland Lake had "declined" and become "effeminate" since the streets had been paved. At 5 p.m. I boarded a train for Rouyn, Miles having sprung for the ticket.

In Rouyn I ran into my dad, in town buying winter supplies. His days as a hoistman were over; one eye had gone blind, and Jack Hammel had given him a job as caretaker of the closed-down Green-Stabell Mine. Dad and I took a bus to Amos, an ordinary little French-Canadian town. Its only distinguishing features were the numerous steamboats and other craft on the Harricana River, the presence of two mail planes, the CNR station, and a beautiful Catholic church. The river flows north into James Bay, but all traffic was to the south, the mining country.

On September 28, 1931, we pulled out from Amos and travelled upstream in the *Tit Willow*, a fifty-three-foot steamboat which Dad had hired to bring in supplies — food for Dad and mother, hay for the horse. As we were towing a scow behind, our progress was slow. We journeyed forty-five miles south through Lake La Motte and Lake Malartic, and tied up in the river overnight. We continued on our way the following morning, passed the Milky River leading into Lake Montigny, locally called by the Indian name of Kenowesick, and shortly after 12 p.m. landed at the Stabell dock, Lake Blouin. The mine is a mile inland from the lake; there is a wooden railway to haul in supplies. I recorded in my diary that it was "quite likely that I will find work and stay in this vicinity all winter."

[At Rouyn, Whyte met memorable characters, among them Penny Ante.] Penny Ante had the worst job in the Noranda copper smelter — bringing cars of red roaster dust to the reverb furnaces. He was an ugly little runt of a man with a monkey face and brown, decayed stumps of teeth. His name — the only one we ever knew — came from his passion for penny ante poker, at which he invariably lost.

His nationality? Oh, some kind of a bohunk from the slums of central Europe. We never thought to ask. For us, in the arrogance and strength of our youth, he was the butt of daily practical jokes, the spluttering target of fluent English tongues. He was the immigrant, we were Canadian. He was old and we were young. He was apparently happy to hold down the filthiest job in the smelter while we felt free at any time to tell the boss to take his job and shove it.

I was a fettler on No. 1 furnace — a feeder, that is — and every shift had to take two or three tons of Penny Ante's dust and mix it with the charge. The dust was poured into hoppers, or bins, above the furnace and was fed in along with the calcine. Too much dust would sweep the calcine into the middle of the furnace, where a nasty crust of half-smelted ore would form and cause trouble for the crew on the next shift. When we needed to get rid of more calcine than the furnace could handle we'd mix dust with the charge in all the hoppers, let it sweep the heavier ore into the centre of the furnaces, and to hell with the guys who inherited the mess. We often were victims of similar action on the part of the preceding shift. Penny Ante's job was to bring the dust to the furnaces and run his dust cars back and forth over the hoppers, while he sat at his motor and was completely hidden from view by billowing red clouds of dust.

After a dozen or more years at the same hopeless, dead-end occupation, Penny himself carried around several pounds of copper dust on his person. When he dies, we joked, he'll be fed into the furnace and smelted down. The dust had eaten into the pores of his skin, ingrained itself in the lines of his face, giving his grizzly hair a tinge of red. His clothes, which he never changed, were stiff with the stuff. Clap him on the back and clouds of dust would choke you.

Penny Ante had a vocabulary of perhaps five hundred English words — half of them rich profanity and half the remainder relating to sex. For he regarded himself as quite a guy with the ladies. Whenever he had the good fortune to find a girl so down and out that she was willing to come and stay in his one-room log shack, he would boast and strut and wish to share his prize. "Goddam son-o-mo-bitch, you come by my place after shift tonight, I got best goddam lay in Rouyn."

When we young bucks were flush and had anywhere else to go we never went near Penny Ante. But when we were broke and finished with the restaurants, poolrooms and whorehouses of Noranda and Rouyn, we might decide to drop in on Penny at three or four o'clock in the morning. We would pound on the door and after a while it would open a crack and when he saw his "friends" he would throw wide the door, a happy grin on his face. "Come in my bes' frans, wait, I get beer and whisky!" he would cry delightedly. Then he would give his current girlfriend, snoring on the bed, a hefty kick on the rump: "Gaddap, goddam you, doan you see my frans here, gaddup and get bottles beer. You treat my frans right, onnerstand?" And the old gal — usually a whore down on her luck who had found Penny an easy mark for room and board — would get up tiredly and prepare herself for whatever might come.

Penny Ante's log cabin had the usual potbellied cast-iron stove, a wide bed covered with a few filthy blankets, one chair, and a kitchen table. Blocks of wood served for other chairs. One corner of the room was piled high with empty beer bottles. A single dim bulb hung from a long cord in the centre of the ceiling.

We often stayed and drank until the sun came up. Penny Ante would talk and sing and drink — it was at such moments, in the company of his fellow workers, that he felt "accepted" as a member of the human race. Sometimes we sensed this and felt ashamed. It even occurred to us that the difference between Penny and ourselves was not so wide as we had always assumed — weren't we also wasting away our lives drinking, gambling, and fornicating? How had we used our advantages of birth and education? Who were we to sneer at this illiterate immigrant and his broken-down whores? Such thoughts, at five o'clock on a drunken morning, often led to maudlin tears. We felt sorry for ourselves, sorry for all mankind.

Then, one day, Penny fell in love. The first indication we had was when he came into the dry after a shift and took a shower. Nothing like this had ever happened before and several of us gathered to watch — with something approaching awe — the streams of rust-coloured dirt that poured down his body and formed little reddish puddles on the floor.

"What the hell are you doing?" we wanted to know.

"I got a girl," said Penny Ante proudly. "Bes' goddam girl in Rouyn. Boy, she nice and goddam fat, she sleep nobody but me. Maybe get goddam married, how you like that, goddam son-o-mo-bitch?"

Everyone laughed and the story was spread around, all over the smelter. As the days passed and Penny failed to invite us to see his girl, curiosity mounted. "How about letting us try your new girlfriend?" someone asked. The reply was a stream of unprintable oaths, the gist of it contained in the final sentence: "My goddam girl no goddam whore for you son-o-mo-bitches, she no give her ass to no-good bastards like you."

Penny had had many girls before; none had been able to put up with him for more than a week. But this affair seemed permanent; one day, three weeks after it began, Penny took a second shower bath and donned a bow tie. The effect was startling, as he continued to wear his dust-encrusted, stinking, stiff old clothes.

Finally, three of us called unexpectedly at Penny Ante's shack one morning just before sunrise. We were half shot and determined to take a look at the female who had wrought such a metamorphosis in Penny's life. He came to the door, suspiciously, but when we entered boisterously his natural hospitality asserted itself and he dragged out a case of lukewarm beer and shook his girlfriend gently until she woke and rolled over, yawning and wanting to know just what the hell was going on. "My best frans," said Penny, "Gaddup, I wantya meet them."

The flabby old girl muttered something under her breath but obeyed. She reached for a proffered bottle of beer and drank it in two gulps, went outside to relieve herself, came back and settled down to some heavy drinking. Soon we were all very friendly and Penny was in heaven. "Scuse me, frans," he said, "I gotta go." And stepped outside.

"Hear you're gonna marry Penny," said one of the boys. "Congrats."

"Marry that guy?" she said. "You think I'm crazy in the head? Lissen, boys, I'm just out-a-luck now, thassall. When I get on my feet I say goodbye to that dirty bastard. For crissake, when we go to town all that comes outta him is a squirt of goddam smelter dust!"

We laughed, but stopped when Penny Ante walked in from the yard, still buttoning his fly. He slipped his arm around his beloved and said: "Hey now, my goddam frans, I got high class girl, you bet, eh?" One day, perhaps a week later, Penny came to work with a long face. He delivered his first load of dust sullenly; when we tried our usual jokes on him he failed to respond. Brutally we continued to bait him, until someone finally managed to touch the open wound.

"When you gonna invite us to your wedding, Penny?"

Penny Ante looked us over, very carefully, as if seeing us clearly for the first time.

"She gone," he said simply. Two tears rolled down his cheeks, making white streaks through the red copper dust. None of us felt like laughing.

CHAPTER TWO

The 1930s

The Great Depression

The pop song "Happy Days Are Here Again" was introduced on October 24, 1929, just five days before prices plummeted on the New York stock exchange, ushering in the Great Depression. The stock market crash on October 29 marked the end of the 1923–29 temporary stabilization of capitalism, "The Decade of Illusions." Stock losses for 1929–31 were estimated at $50 billion.

Canada soon felt the consequences of the New York stock market crash. In 1931 there were some five thousand bankruptcies in our country and more than a million and a quarter people (of a population of ten million) were in urgent need of relief. Western farmers were hard hit as the price of wheat dropped from $1.60 a bushel to 38 cents. Farmers fought back under the slogan "No foreclosures, no evictions." Demonstrations of unemployed took place in Toronto, Montreal, Vancouver, and other cities, demanding relief, work, or full maintenance.

The government reacted by launching savage attacks on the working class. RCMP Commissioner James Mac-Brien declared that if Canada would rid itself of foreigners there would be "no unemployment." In 1932 more than 7,600 "suspected communists" were deported. Tim Buck and seven other Communist Party leaders were sentenced to long terms in Kingston Penitentiary, where an attempt was made to murder Buck in his cell. Despite the repression, CPC membership in the next two years more than doubled.

In 1933 a new left-wing party, the Co-operative Commonwealth Federation (CCF), was born, with J.S. Woodsworth at its head. It was destined to become Canada's third strongest party in the years that followed.

The Communist-organized Workers Unity League (WUL) mushroomed and led militant trade union struggles (in 1934, of 109 strikes in Canada, 93 were led by the WUL, of which 73 were won — the only successful strikes that year). The farmers' resistance to foreclosure was so strong that the Bennett government was forced to introduce the Farm Creditors Arrangements Act. And for the first time in the history of Canada (and contrary to the BNA Act) Ottawa had to step into the relief field. Bennett opened his infamous 20-cent-a-day camps (which in turn gave birth to the Relief Camp Workers' Union).

A great national campaign for the release of Tim Buck and repeal of section 98 of the Criminal Code — under which the Communist Party had been declared illegal and its property confiscated — resulted in 483,000 Canadians signing a petition issued by the Canadian Labor Defense League. When Buck was released from penitentiary seventeen thousand people jammed Maple Leaf Gardens to welcome him. The two front rows were filled with RCMP and Provincial Police. Buck threw down the gauntlet, defied them to arrest him (he had been warned he must abstain from political activities). The fuzz remained silent. When King was elected prime minister in 1935 he kept an election promise and repealed section 98 the following year.

The Depression eased up somewhat in the mid-1930s, but times remained tough until the outbreak of the Second World War in 1939. In 1936 Sir Edward Beatty, President of the CPR, revealed to the *Financial Post* his plan to end the Depression: "It is not a platitude to say that the cure for unemployment is for men and women to go to work."

The following are excerpts from the official notice of a relief cut in the town of Pembroke, Ontario, as published in the press:

(3) All deserted families are to be cut off relief March 1, 1936, and advised to secure sufficient from their fathers or husbands. No 'Grass Widow' will receive relief while her husband remains at liberty.

(13) Single persons who marry and apply for relief will not be granted some until they have been married at least one year and a half.

(14) Single persons will not be granted relief unless they are physically or mentally incapacitated, in such cases arrangements will be made to transfer them to an institution.

(15) The following food allowances are effective after February, 1936:

Number in family	Monthly food allowances
Man and wife (2)	8.67 dollars
Man, wife and 1 child (3)	10.83 dollars
Man, wife and 6 children (8)	18.42 dollars

The maximum monthly food allowance will be 18.42.

(17) All relief recipients who are unable to work for their relief shall receive 10% less than those that work.

(20) Relief recipients who are not satisfied with the relief distribution after publication of this notice and who create any disturbance whatsoever will be cut off relief entirely.

Welfare payments in Newfoundland were 6 cents a day.

During several of the Depression years I worked at Noranda Mines as a smelter-man, earning good wages. Had I not become fed up with the job and quit in the spring of 1934, it is unlikely that I would ever have experienced the Depression first-hand, spending a year on the freights and in Bennett's 20-cents-a-day "slave camps."

While a quarter of all Canadian workers suffered directly from the Depression, those who had steady jobs benefited to some extent. With business in a slump and small businessmen slashing prices in a desperate (and often losing) attempt to avoid bankruptcy, consumers with a few dollars in their pocket could take advantage of the bargains available.

A Loblaws advertisement in the *Globe and Mail* of March 1, 1934, offered peach jam, 32 oz. jar, 27 cents; corned beef, 12 oz. tin, 11 cents; flour, 24 lbs., 57 cents; cheese, ½ kg., 9 cents; iceberg lettuce, 6 cents each; bread, 24 oz. wrapped loaf, 7 cents.

Other bargains: Eaton's Women's Wear: topcoat suits, $16.95; knitted suits, $13.95; shoes, $1.98 pair. Eaton's Annex: men's trousers, $1.45; men's sox (no delivery) 25 cents pair; men's shirts in plain shades, $1.24; men's suits for spring, $16.50. In houses listed for rent there were ads like this one: "Parkdale, 18 dollars per month, 6 bright rooms, decorate to suit tenant."

And for entertainment: "Saturday 8.30 p.m. fastest sport

in the world. Detroit Red Wings at Maple Leaf Gardens. Good seats available, 40 cents to $2.25."

Few jobs were offered in the columns of the papers, but the "Situation Wanted" ads were many. A sample: "Farm hand; respectable Canadian; Protestant; Life experience; single man wants employment on farm by the year; good milker; good stockman; steady and reliable; non-smoker; asking 20 dollars per month."

O Canada!

On the Road

Noranda, Quebec, May 12, 1934. I had been working in the Noranda Smelter since October 25, 1931, and was thoroughly fed up with the place. Not that I wasn't doing well. Starting on gas analysis at 50 cents an hour ($4 a day), I had been promoted to fettling (feeding calcine to the reverberatory furnaces) with a nickel raise, and now was skimming (in charge of a furnace) with a further dime raise. Good money at that time. In Toronto and other cities there were plenty of workers with families glad to be earning 30 cents an hour. And, of course, in those bitter Depression years there were over a million unemployed — a quarter of the workforce.

Well, I knew all that, but I was single and had no family responsibilities, and I was sick of the smelter dust, and wanted to get away from a world of matte, slag, roasters, converters, and reverb furnaces. And I was tired of living in a town which had only one movie theatre and no public library, but where dozens of sleazy whorehouses dotted an area known as Vimy Ridge.

So, after coming off afternoon shift at 11 p.m., I dropped in on a dance at the Polish Hall in Rouyn, and met Leo Katinen, a congenial night owl and fellow elbow bender.

Leo was of Finnish descent, born in the United States but long a resident of Canada. His job as a mine electrician paid well and he had a comfortable one-room flat above the liquor store.

The dance wasn't interesting, so we repaired to Leo's place and settled down to some serious drinking. As always, we got around to bitching about our work and the monotony of our lives. I spoke about my hitchhiking days, glamorized life on the open road. By 6 a.m. we had polished off two quarts of Scotch and decided to quit Noranda. Later that morning I called on shift foreman Harvey Woods for a pink slip, collected my pay from Scotty Coburn in the front office and met Leo at the railway station, where we took a train for Toronto. We continued drinking and for the next few days lived in a kind of blur, pissing away our money on booze and girls. We were kicked out of a room in Toronto by an indignant landlady. Took a bus to Windsor and crossed over to Detroit. Drank in a bar with some college girls. They disappeared, and Leo and I staggered along unfamiliar streets looking for our hotel. But what we actually did was board a Greyhound bus for Chicago. I woke some hours later, feeling an urgent need to urinate. Leo was still sleeping beside me, on the floor at the back of the bus. He had a never-ending thirst but was blessed with a gigantic bladder. I crawled up to the driver and explained my plight. He wasn't very friendly, but pulled over to the side of the road and let me get out and relieve myself.

We had left a couple of suitcases and a camera in our Detroit hotel room, and never saw them again. Leo had a sister living in Chicago, whom he hadn't been in touch with for many years. But he remembered her address on 64th St. East, so we looked her up and booked a room for the night. Counting our money, we were surprised to find how little we had left. Still, Chicago is Chicago and we set out to have a fling. The last time I had been in the Windy City was in 1927, the Capone era. Now it had become Depression City. We came across a "One Cent Cafeteria" and had a meal: one cent for a pat of butter, one cent for a sausage, one cent for a scoop of mashed potatoes, one cent for coffee, one cent for sugar, and one cent for cream.

Having "saved" so much money on food, we next found a noisy bar, sat down at a table and began drinking mugs of beer. Our waitress asked us to place a 50-cent piece on the corner of the table, and she would perform a trick. Wondering what the name of the game was, we complied. Quick as a little red fox, she pulled up her skirt, showing she was wearing nothing underneath, and snatched up the coin, no pun intended. Of course it's an old trick, practised in many countries, but it was new to us at the time, and we donated several more half-dollars just to marvel at her muscular control. Look, ma, no hands.

Later we asked a taxi driver to take us to a house he could recommend. He said he knew a Negro girl who did a little on the side. Fine. He rang the bell and talked a minute or two, then we were allowed in. At a kitchen table half a dozen Negroes were playing stud poker. They paid no attention to us. Dorothy, very pretty, led us upstairs. Leo and I flipped a coin to see who would get a wet deck. Leo lost, curled up on a sofa, and went to sleep. As I was pulling off my red sweater in the bedroom Dorothy saw the "Made in Canada" label. She laughed and said, "Now I'll show you something as red as that sweater, made in the USA."

The next day we took the "L" to Maywood and began walking west. After stopping at several hot dog stands and swilling beer, we flagged down a bus which took us to Minneapolis. The taxi drivers were on strike there, traffic was tied up, and there were clashes between pickets and police.

At St. Cloud we bought swim trunks, drank beer, and slept in a tourist cabin. At Fargo we had a shower and swim at the YMCA, crossed the Red River to Moorhead and headed north for Winnipeg. Thumbing was easy.

Ham and eggs in a Winnipeg greasy spoon. Turned down by the Sally Ann on Logan Avenue. So we checked in at Immigration Hall on Water Street. "From here on it's going to be tougher," I said to Leo, who had never been on the road before (whereas I had logged over fifteen thousand miles by thumb while still in my teens).

"Hurry up, get your clothes off," said a surly attendant. We stripped and waited in a bathroom while he took away our things to be fumigated. Leo tried the door. "The bastard's locked us in!" When our clothes were returned, smelling strongly of disinfectant, we crawled into three-decker bunks (mattress but no blanket) in a barn-like room, and soon fell asleep, or were asphyxiated. At 7 a.m. we were kicked out, and went to ding our breakfast. That's when I discovered that Leo, who had a slight speech impediment, became completely tongue-tied when he tried to hit somebody up for a dime. A skilled electrician, Leo had never been without a job. He had always had money in his pocket, even in the worst of times. He had open fingers, too. During the bush-workers' strike in Rouyn the loggers used to line up near the bank where we cashed our paycheques. Most of us would ask for three or four dollars in 50-cent pieces, and would hand them out to the strikers. Leo, who earned higher wages, would invariably double our donations. But giving and asking are two different things. Leo couldn't bring himself to ask anyone for the price of a coffee and, Hell, if he needed a light he would stutter while asking for the loan of a match. So I had to be our mouth. We made out all right that day — one chap took us into a cafe and bought us meals. When I hit him up on the street, he said, "No cash, boys. But if you're really hungry I'll take you to a meal. I want to see if you have good appetites." This kind of response is not unusual. I've often done the same thing. Not that I question the right of a panhandler to spend one's donation on a glass of beer if he so desires. But I dislike a lying sob story: he hasn't eaten since the Flood, and so on. A guy that's really hungry scoffs everything up, and deserves a hunk of pie to round off his meal. But if he pushes his food around on his plate and finds it hard to get it all down, you know he's a phony; neither a hobo nor a tramp, just a bum. (A hobo is a migratory worker; a tramp is a migratory non-worker; a bum is a non-migratory, non-worker.)

Although we were now on the bum, Leo and I classified ourselves as hoboes, working-class stiffs. Our vague plan at the time was to thumb our way across the prairies and try to get jobs at the smelter in Trail, BC.

We slept at Immigration Hall for two nights, were refused a ticket for a third night, so had to blow town. Found shelter in a country schoolhouse. On the road early the following morning, but got caught in a shower. We hustled to a farmhouse and an active old granny invited us in, gave us fried eggs, bread, and tea. The shower over, we hit the highway and caught a through lift to Regina, some four hundred miles, in a Willys-Overland. A shave in the YMCA washroom, after which we explored the town. Tried to sleep on park benches that night, but after midnight it grew cold, so at 2 a.m. we went to the police station on 11th Ave. and slept in clean cells. The Sally Ann gave us a breakfast of porridge, bread, jam, and tea. Feeling chipper, we walked to the city's new artificial lake, donned our swim trunks, and had a refreshing dip. In the afternoon we hadn't walked more than half a mile before the driver of an ancient Ford picked us up and took us the 150 miles to Swift Current. Called at the police station but were refused a flop. Leo had been hanging onto a sawbuck so we went to the Regal Cafe (the locals pronounced it Gaff) and bartered for a room — 55 cents for a double. We went to bed hungry but in the morning I gave the cafe owner my fountain pen in return for two orders of bacon and eggs. Like everywhere in the West, french fries were included.

We walked for miles with no sign of a lift. The cars were few and far between, and none stopped. Footsore and weary, we came across a little spring and stopped to rest and wash our feet. This part of southern Saskatchewan looked terrible. Flat country, alkali lakes, and few farmhouses. Times hard. Many farmers pulling out in old-style covered wagons or "Bennett Buggies" — old automobiles pulled by a team of horses.

We had talked to one farmer who was heading for BC with his family. "My farm just blew away one day," he said. "There was a strong wind and the topsoil took off and is probably down somewhere in Montana by now. You know, I haven't had a crop in five years. And not a drop of rain this spring. Wells dried up. Grasshoppers. Millions of gophers. Tumbling mustard and sand storms. I've had it."

At one farmhouse where I asked the woman for something to eat we had a chastening experience. The farmer's wife, a pleasant but tired-looking woman in her forties, said, "I'm afraid all I can give you is a couple of slices of homemade bread." That would be fine, I said. She had just cut two thick slices when the door burst open and an angry husband yelled at us: "Get out of here. You tramps ain't going to take the bread out of my children's mouths." Then he calmed down a little. He looked at our hands and said, "I see you guys are workers. But I can't feed you. We have two kids, and all we can give them is bread and jam. We're at the end of our tether. I guess we'll have to abandon the farm, though God knows where we'll go. So you see why I won't let the wife give you any of that bread."

We understood, we said, and wished him better luck in the future. Back on the highway, Leo and I didn't speak to each other for some time, but we were undoubtedly thinking the same thoughts. How we had blithely thrown up good jobs, and spent our money on booze and whoring, and were now begging bread from honest, hard-working folk who were suffering from prolonged hunger.

Finally Leo said, "I guess I'm not made for life on the road. If and when we get to Vancouver, I'm going to head for Seattle and join the US Army. There must be jobs in the army for a qualified electrician."

A couple of short lifts in an Essex and a Ford, and at dusk we reached the village of Tompkins. The first person we saw was the local cop. "We're just passing through and are looking for something to eat and a place to sleep," I told him, not at all sure what his attitude would be. "Say now, you fellows can sleep in the town hall," he said. "It's warm and dry and the door is always open. And you go and see Mr. McAllister, the overseer of the town, for something to eat. He's a pretty good fellow and he'll give you a ticket for a restaurant meal, only don't tell him I sent you, for there's too many hungry people these days."

Mr. McAllister greeted us cheerily, wrote out an order for two 25-cent meals at the Empire Cafe. So we surrounded some cold pork and potato salad, bread, butter, and coffee, and bedded down in the town hall.

We arrived in Medicine Hat the next afternoon, asked a

chap how to get to the Sally Ann, were given directions, four bits, and a handful of Christian tracts. After eating, we called at the town hall and shaved "blind" in the public washroom, then crossed the bridge and had a swim in the cold, swift-flowing South Saskatchewan River. We spent the night in a trailer cabin with a road worker. He gave us supper and a couple of blankets to sleep on the floor. In the morning we hit the pike for Lethbridge. The police there advised us to go to a relief camp two miles out of town. We went, were given a towel and soap, blankets, and a cold meal of bologna, bread, and tea. We slept in clean bunks, had a breakfast of hotcakes, gruel bread, and coffee, and pulled out.

Fort Macleod, Alberta, proved to be a hostile town, so we didn't tarry, but moved right on. It began to rain, at first lightly, then heavily. In the downpour we were soon soaked to the skin. Plodding along the muddy road we spied a railway section house. The section gang were friendly, invited us in to dry a bit, but when we asked if we could stay overnight they hesitated, explained it was CPR property and they'd have to ask the boss at the station house. He gave his okay. We had a good night's rest and in the morning, our bellies filled with hotcakes, bacon and eggs, bread and coffee, we headed west. Two days later we crossed into beautiful British Columbia.

Tramping Through the Rockies
On June 2, 1934, Leo Katainen and I came through Crowsnest Pass in the back seat of an ancient Ford driven by a miner from Coleman, Alberta. He was doing us a big favour. In the Hungry Thirties, BC was In if you could get in. Police tried to turn back the jobless youth from other provinces who flocked to Canada's west coast because of its mild winter

climate. The miner who had picked us up went out of his way to take us several miles past the border patrol before dropping us off and turning back.

We spent the night in Natal, after I had bartered my Sheaffer pencil for a room in a small hotel. The next day we caught a lift to Fernie. At the police station a genial cop gave us a loaf of bread, two cans of sardines, and a can of beans. "The natives are friendly," Leo observed later.

Cars were scarce so we tramped the next dozen miles or so. Superb scenery. Snow-capped peaks surrounded us. At every turn in the road we found something new to exclaim about. Far below on our left the Elk River followed its winding course through the mountains. It began to rain. We holed up for the night in an abandoned shack. Leo made a little fireplace with stones while I gathered wood, and with shavings we started a wigwam fire. During the night some large animal kept prowling around. The shack had no door, so we took turns sleeping and keeping the fire going. At dawn we loaded wood on the fire and slept fitfully for a couple of hours before hitting the road again.

Elko. Carter's Tourist Cabins. Carter's Refreshment Stand, Carter's Gasoline Station. We looked up Mrs. Carter and asked for something to eat. The good woman sighed. "I don't know what's going to happen to this country. The politicians don't seem able to do anything. I often think things are coming to such a pass that God will come down and fix things. We should all get down on our knees and pray." Then she gave us two egg sandwiches each and five glasses of milk. "And there is 50 cents you'll need to cross on the ferry," she said in parting. (A year later, when I was back working at Noranda smelter, I mailed her a $5 bill with a note signed, "One of the many jobless young men you fed in these hard times.")

We reached Cranbrook footsore and hungry and decided to sign up for a relief camp. These 20-cents-a-day camps were set up by the government under the Department of National Defence to reduce the eyesore of thousands of young unemployed on the streets of cities and towns. The camps were tucked away in the mountains or established on the prairies far from urban centres. Out of sight, out of mind. It was a bandaid approach to the problem of unemployment.

We filled out some papers at city hall, received an order for 40 cents worth of groceries and train tickets to Camp 64, Goatfell, some fifty miles southwest of Cranbrook. Our train came through at 4:30 a.m., so we spent most of the night sleeping in the waiting room of the CPR station. At Goatfell camp we were issued sox, underwear, boots, shirts, and pants. There were about sixty young men in the camp, including local boys from nearby villages. We joined the road gang, handling mucksticks. Near us a sign read: SLOW MEN AT WORK. It didn't lie.

We became friends with a rambler named Al. He was twenty-six, had left his home in Vancouver at the tender age of eleven, had passed the intervening years in the United States. He could roll a cigarette with one hand (using Bull Durham tobacco). He was a professional gambler. He wrote doggerel verse in which he related his experiences on the road. "I ain't done nothing since I run away from home, that's why I keep so young," he explained. "Don't you ever intend to work?" "I intend to get mine. Workers are suckers. They make dough for somebody else. I make dough for nobody but me. That's why I became a gambler."

During our first week in camp Leo and I had sent a few dinging letters to friends back in Noranda, and these resulted in a small shower of dollar bills.

The inhabitants of the camp were of two types — the "Home Guards" and the "Ramblers." Every evening the Ramblers would gather around the potbellied bunkhouse stoves and tell tales of the road:

"I had ten thou ($10) and got into a crap game in Butte ..."

"I was holding down a flyer from Fargo to Chicago, and in the Milwaukee yards ..."

"So I nabbed a hot shot and rode her to Frisco ..."

"We held her to the Peg and the Bulls were waiting for us at Transcona ..."

"I goes up to the door and rings and out comes the town clown ..."

"A bunch of stiffs was riding the Big G over the hump last summer ..."

One evening, after we had been in Goatfell camp for about three weeks Al, Leo, and I walked to the village of Kitchener and had a few beers. The bartender was a good fellow and gave us a couple on the house. As we were leaving Al suddenly grabbed a small basket of cherries from the counter and made a dash for the door. We followed him, with the bartender behind us yelling, "Come back, you thieves!" But he couldn't leave his post to chase us. We stopped running about a hundred yards down the road and angrily asked Al: "What in hell did you do that for?" "I just wanted some cherries," he said.

We had walked about a mile when we heard the sound of a siren. We hid in the bushes and the cop car passed. Later it returned and we hid again. There were two Goatfell camps, East and West, and the bartender couldn't have known which camp we came from. We packed our things that night and checked out early the next morning, after drawing our government cheques. We walked to Yahk, bought a gallon of goof, and waited for a west-bound freight. When one finally arrived we climbed on top of a boxcar, as all the cars were sealed. We were feeling no pain and soon threw the empty wine jug away. The sun was shining and the scenery was breathtaking. Two provincial police officers were awaiting us at Creston. They had been combing the country for us all night and were not in a good mood. We were bustled into a car, driven to jail, searched, locked up. Our trial before a JP didn't last long. The Crown brought several witnesses who had seen us snitch the cherries. Their evidence was rambling and conflicting as to who had actually made off with the basket, worth perhaps 50 cents. Except for the bartender, no one seemed to view it as a heinous crime, including the JP, who declared us convicted and discharged.

We were not to escape so easily. The police charged us with violation of the Railway Act. We pleaded guilty and were sentenced to fourteen days in the Provincial Gaol at Nelson. It was a sixty-mile journey and we made it by bus, in charge of a young officer. The highway, which skirted the mountainside, was dangerously narrow in places, but the bus driver drove recklessly and did not deign to blow his horn. At one point we travelled several miles up Kootenay Lake on a ferry. A steady rain and the prospect of our imminent incarceration spoiled the pleasure of the trip.

At 7 p.m. we arrived at Nelson Gaol. All our personal belongings, except combs and cigarettes, were taken from us. We had a shower and changed into prison garb. Then we were hustled to our cells and locked in. "What are you in for?" questioned the other prisoners. "For firing snowballs at passing aeroplanes," said Al. The cell block contained thirteen cells and a corridor ran down the centre. Battleship grey was the predominating colour.

Gaol routine was simple and monotonous. We rose at 7 a.m., cleaned our cells, ate breakfast (a bowl of porridge, one lump of brown sugar in the centre, no milk) and paced the corridor until noon, ate dinner (a plate of beans or a watery stew, with a hunk of bread) and again had the freedom of the corridor until supper (macaroni or rice, mug of tea). Prisoners who worked were allowed to leave the cells again for an evening promenade. This privilege did not extend to us, with the exception of four days when we were to work sweeping the corridor.

The day of our release arrived. We enjoyed a shower and a shave, received good conduct cheques to the value of 40 cents (for our four workdays) and stepped out into the sunshine. We headed for the Standard Cafe, cashed our government cheques, and ordered a substantial 35-cent meal — soup, roast beef, and pie.

To bolster our finances, Al proposed that he sell his packsack and its contents (extra socks and shirt, etc.) which he said he no longer needed, as we'd soon be in Vancouver, where he had relatives. We found a hockshop which offered him 75 cents. Accepted.

We walked out of town, and caught a lift to Trail. We should have stopped at Castlegar and grabbed a freight, but our jailmates had warned us of a hostile bull in Castlegar, who delighted in picking up stiffs just released from Nelson Gaol and sending them back for another fourteen-day stretch. We bought some bread and cheese in Trail, and started the six-mile uphill hike to Rossland. As night fell we crawled into an empty boxcar and slept a few hours. Up at

3 a.m., built a little fire to warm up, then took to the road again. When we reached the town we sat down to rest on the bandstand steps opposite the post office, waiting for the stores to open. A breakfast of baloney and bread perked us up somewhat. We caught a lift up a long snake-back road and walked down the other side. Stayed overnight at an abandoned relief camp at Sheep Creek, after buying some macaroni and potatoes from a covered wagon caravan from Saskatchewan, heading west, destination uncertain — anywhere to escape from the prairie dust bowl.

A Doukhobor couple gave us a lift in their truck all the way to Grand Forks, where we decided to abandon the highway and travel by rail. A westbound freight was not due for twenty-four hours so we settled down in the jungle to wait. It turned cold during the night, and we didn't sleep much, but sat around the fire and talked. The next day was sunny and we grabbed a few hours shut-eye, then ate the last of our grub while our train was making up. "Never hang around the yards or you'll have the switchmen on your back," Al advised us. "You'll have plenty of time to make it when they test the air brakes before giving the highball."

We rode the top of a boxcar eighteen miles upgrade to Eholt. Before entering tunnels we took a deep breath, crooked an arm over our faces and exhaled very slowly. This procedure, which Al taught us, prevented dizziness from smoke and gas. At Eholt the two engines returned to Grand Forks to pick up the remainder of the train. It was horribly cold up in the mountains so we found some old ties and built a fire. When we started again we rode an empty. At Midway we had another stopover and built another fire. We came through the hump at dawn, and saw Okanagan Lake and Penticton in the distance, far below.

The jungle at Penticton was a large one, the home of

more than a hundred stiffs. The Home Guards lived in slab shacks or packing boxes along the riverside, and the Ramblers jungled all over the place. Hunger drove us uptown to the Provincial Relief Centre, where we were given a relief order to the value of $2.10. We blew the works on bread, beans, bacon, coffee, butter, and canned sausages. What you could buy for a few cents in those days! The Depression was the only period in Canadian history when prices actually fell for a time.

Midnight, and our drag made up. We climbed aboard a flatcar. "Toot-toot," highballed the heats engine. "Toot-toot!" answered the hind push. We picked up speed and roared across the bridge leaving the Penticton yards, but soon slowed on the steep grade. After a few miles our comfortable flatcar, which was carrying some bales of hay, was sidetracked, and as no empties were available we rode blind baggage between a boxcar and an oilcar. The boxcar broke the wind for us, but it was cold and extremely uncomfortable. We shivered and clung doggedly to the arm rail. I hooked one arm through it and dropped into snatches of sleep, awakening by instinct when my knees began to buckle and threatened to tumble me beneath the wheels.

At Princeton we stopped a half-hour and warmed up around a feeble fire. At Brookmere we repeated the performance, and at Hope, where we joined the main line, we built a fire and brewed coffee. We had been travelling some sixteen hours without eating and now we hungrily demolished the last of our supplies. When our train pulled out over fifty stiffs were aboard, including one girl. We were all riding the tops of boxcars. At Coquitlam there was a lot of switching around, so Al, Leo, and I took to the highway at 10 p.m. and footed it the fourteen miles to Vancouver, arriving at 3:30 a.m.

"So long," said Al casually, and walked out of our lives.

Leo and I spent our last dime for doughnuts and coffee, and then curled up on benches in a small park opposite the *Daily Province* building. When we awoke the sun was shining brightly and old women were throwing bread crumbs to innumerable pigeons and seagulls.

"How far have you fellows come?" a clerk in relief headquarters asked us.

"From Quebec."

"Well, I might as well send you all the way, to a relief camp on Vancouver Island. If you want to go further west, you'll have to swim the Pacific."

Milligan's Camp was the best I ever struck. Leo left after receiving his first pay and hitchhiked to Seattle, where he joined the US Army. I spent three months in camp, then left the Island in order to meet Jimmy Black in Vancouver. From then on we bounced around together from one relief camp to another.

Hell on Wheels

December 1934. We were up in the mountains, building a road at 20 cents a day, when the news filtered in that all the relief camp boys were on strike in Vancouver. So we called a meeting in the mess hall, and after a hot discussion about half voted to join the strike. Jimmy Black and I, along with a dozen or so other lads, caught a lift to Princeton in a truck and collected our cheques. Mine was for $2, for ten days' work.

The weather was cold. We picked up a passenger train, after successfully evading the local yard bull. As the train gained speed we derisively thumbed our noses at him. Our jubilation was short-lived, however, for at Brookmere the conductor came up to the tender and called out, "Boys, you'll have to get off." We laughed, until he said, "All right, lads, this train stays right here. There are snowslides in the Coquihalla Pass and I won't have you freeze on my train if I'm held up for a few hours, and that's all I have to say."

"I think he's telling the truth," said Jimmy. "Let's wait for a freight."

We pulled off and walked to the small waiting room at the station. A red-hot, pot-bellied stove welcomed us with its warmth and we curled around it, lying on the floor. The wireless operator took a long look at us, shook his head and said, "You stiffs have no right to be in here, that's my orders, but I'm damned if I kick you out. It's a tough world." We slept around the stove all night. In the morning a blustering station agent arrived, chewed out the operator, and told us to vamoose from CPR property. We left the station but gathered in the sand house. A freight train rolled up in the afternoon and we made for the tender as all the boxcar doors were sealed.

The train switched north towards Spences Bridge. This jog meant an extra hundred miles in sub-zero weather. In all we faced 250 miles of cold, bitter travelling. We clapped hands and pounded our knees to keep the blood circulating in our feet. It was mighty cold. At Merritt we stumbled into the tiny station and found it empty, the stove in the waiting room unlit. We took rolls of toilet paper from the lavatory and began to burn them in an attempt to warm our half-frozen hands. "Toot-Toot," highballed the drag, and we dashed out and made her as she began to roll. Two lads with frostbitten feet stayed behind.

Colder and colder. My feet became numb. I took off my boots and socks and Jimmy rubbed my feet until they began to burn. Then I did the same for him. In two hours we reached Spences Bridge and had a stopover until the fast

Seaboard came through. We called at the hotel, washed the grime and grit and coal dust from our hands and faces, ate a hot meal for 35 cents. I spent a nickel for a stogie, and believe me, a Corona-Corona was never smoked with more relish.

At midnight we caught the Seaboard and began to roll down to Vancouver. With food in our bellies we were now able to enjoy the grand scenery, majestic mountain peaks, deep canyons. I had stuffed dry paper in my shoes, and my feet remained warm for half an hour or so. One hour passed. Blackie complained that his feet were freezing. He stood up and began a crazy dance on the tender. The train roared along, swaying from side to side. We pounded on through the night.

North Bend. Into the roundhouse. Off with coats, boots and socks, and we hopped around the boilers, toes tingling. When a friendly yardman warned us that our drag was ready to pull out, several lads refused to budge from the boilers. The rest of us donned our clothes and soon were on our way again. We lost altitude rapidly west of the Bend, but our resistance was lowered and we shivered more than ever. We sat down, spread knees and joined together in human links. Our engine was an oil-burner, so Blackie climbed on the tank and fell asleep. It began to snow. It turned to sleet. I also made for the tank — it was slightly warm — and tried to sleep. Sleet stung my face. Then big gobs of snow fell softly. The snow and the grease and the oil mixed and formed a dirty mess an inch thick on top of the tank. In this we lay, because it was warm. It soaked through our clothes and we swore, but mostly we suffered in silence.

At Mission two more boys gave up. It was now raining, pouring. The engine spent an hour switching. We were too miserable to even leave the tender; just stood up and let the water drip, drip, drip down our legs. A well-dressed voter waiting on a covered station platform for a passenger train glanced at me contemptuously, as though I were a dog, so I bared my fangs and snarled at him, like a dog.

Soon we reached Coquitlam, only a hop, step, and jump from Vancouver. Twelve of us were left, twelve good men and tough. A big coal burner took us the rest of the way. We laughed at the driving rain and sang revolutionary songs. For we had made it, through storm and cold and sleet, snow and wind and rain; we had successfully made our way to join the strike.

A delegate from the relief camp committee met us as we swung off the train in downtown Vancouver. We followed him to the Union Hall on Cordova Street. As we entered, a meeting was in progress, but it stopped for a moment and every man rose and gave us a cheer. We checked our packs and received meal tickets. No doubt we looked like scarecrows, dirty and tired, as we marched across to a restaurant, but inside our breasts was a warm, warm glow.

Under the Boxcar Wheels

There is a saying on the road that you don't beat the freight trains, the freight trains beat you. Four of us sat near a water tank waiting for a freight. Three were old-timers. We had known many foodless days and bedless nights until life taught us the art of panhandling. The fourth was a green kid who had been walking the highway all day and his feet were swollen and blistered. On our advice he was turning his socks inside out — there is a certain freshness derived from this trick.

A train came along and stopped to take water. We searched for an empty boxcar, but all were sealed, so we climbed on top. Soon we were rolling along towards North Bay. As darkness fell it began to rain. We shivered in our damp clothing and the cold raindrops stung our faces. At the Bay we decided to seek lodging for the night.

The jail was old and crummy, but warm. We registered in the accepted manner, declared our religious, political, and moral convictions, the names and ages of our maiden aunts and other information necessary to the police. Having done this to the apparent satisfaction of the uniform on duty we were ushered into the coal hole, where we spent the remainder of the night beside the furnace.

Outside, the rain descended and the wind blew. Inside, the air was heavy with the perfume of unwashed bodies and dirty feet. The kid and I sat beside the furnace, not wishing to lie down on the filthy cement or the crawling sand-pile in the corner. "Have you eaten?" I asked him, knowing that green youngsters often go hungry rather than beg a bit of bread. "Not since yesterday," he answered. So I opened my pack and pulled out a crushed package of sandwiches and we ate.

A Halifax rambler awoke and began brewing tea in a tin can. The water boiled quickly when the can was set on the banked coals inside the furnace door, and the Bluenose added tea and sugar from a paper sack. We passed him a sandwich and drank some of his tea. We talked and discovered that we were all heading west. The local railway bulls were hostile. We'd have to make our train on the fly. The pale-faced kid looked nervous; he had never caught a fast freight.

The hours crawled slowly along. At dawn we and other residents of the coal hole scattered in all directions, some to catch freights east, west, north, or south, others to batter a morning handout in town. The kid and I and two companions of the previous day walked west beyond the yards and waited for a freight. It was a cold, grey dawn and a drizzle of rain was falling; none of us were in a talkative mood and all felt sullen and bitter towards everything.

We heard our drag coming and began to separate, looking for good footing. Before I walked away from the kid I said, "Don't be nervous. Just catch her as though she was standing still." Then the train was on us and I took a short run and nabbed a front ladder. It was slippery but I held my grip, got a foot on a rung, and climbed on top.

When we stopped at the next town I began looking for the kid but could not find him anywhere. I searched the train from end to end but there was no trace of him. The next day I picked up a newspaper from a park bench and read a one-inch item on an inside page: "An unidentified body found on railroad property is thought to be that of a transient, crushed beneath the wheels of a freight train."

The Canadian Jungle

The night is dark, no moon, no stars. The small town is silent, it is midnight, everyone is sleeping. We follow the railroad around a bend, walk a quarter-mile, and come to the giant roundhouse. Clink of hammers, an engine puffing, the fireman shovelling coal. In the darkness beyond the roundhouse flickering lights of small fires can be seen here, there, all about. We enter the Canadian Jungle.

The Jungle is alive, restless. Shadows slink about, congregate at the water hole. Nomads squat on their haunches or sprawl on the grass beside campfires, talk, smoke, eat. Few sleep, for soon it will be time for the night freight. We search for and find some twigs and branches to start a fire while someone goes to the creek for water. In fifteen minutes the water is boiling merrily in an old tin can and soon we are gulping down great, hot swigs of tea. Warm our bellies now, for it will surely be a cold ride tonight.

Six yards away two veteran hoboes are frying bacon and potatoes over their fire. They pay no attention to us but when we ask what time our drag is due to pull out one replies shortly, "In half an hour." And here she comes. Better not miss it — a long wait till the next one comes along. We split, each of us testing the ground for solid footing. We are on a steep grade only a hundred yards from the Jungle, and the freight will have two engines, a head and a hind "push."

She's coming! Fast! The engine flashes past and a young lad makes a grab at the tender but misses and is sent rolling down the embankment. A dozen sealed boxcars go whizzing by me. I wait, knowing that the grade will soon slow down the train. The two engines are snorting and panting angrily now, fighting to conquer the grade. Several of the stiffs are already on board and I hitch my pack and begin to run, grip a front ladder firmly with my hands and let my feet swing clear of the ground. My knees bang against the ladder, and I scramble up the side of the car. Now to locate my partners, and walking back over the tops I see some of them, standing on a narrow ledge at the front end of an oiler, clinging to the arm rail. I join them, the boxcar ahead breaks the wind; we roll cigarettes and talk. "Did the youngster make it?" I ask, referring to the lad who had failed to catch the tender. "Yes," someone replied, "I saw him a few cars behind. His face is all scratched and bleeding from the cinders."

At the top of the divide, "the hump," one engine is no longer needed so it toots goodbye and starts back for the roundhouse. During this brief stop we run the length of the train in search of an empty boxcar and are lucky enough to find one. When the highball is given and our freight begins to roll some of us are installed more or less comfortably in a large and airy "side-door pullman," and spirits soar. Everyone starts to talk except the lad with the scratched face. He is spitting on a dirty handkerchief and dabbing at his cheeks, trying to get the cinders out. "You're lucky you weren't pulled under the wheels," a lanky fellow tells the youngster. The conversation naturally enough turns to accidents on the road. Our new companion says: "I've seen four stiffs killed. One hopped off a drag onto a piece of ice, his feet slipped and he had both legs cut off. He died in the hospital, I heard. Two guys were riding with me last year on the Big G (Great Northern) and they lay down at the end of a pile of steel. The steel shifted and they were mashed to jelly. Then there was a lad — just a mere punk — who stood up to stretch himself while we were holding down a tender last month. The engine lurched and flung him off: he landed on his head and his brains got scrambled."

Rolling stock. That is what we are, rolling stock of bones and blood and brain and muscle, fit for work and "there ain't no work to do."

People
Jimmy Black

I knew Jimmy Black for half his lifetime — from the age of thirteen in Kingston until his untimely but heroic death at twenty-six. Yet to say that I was his close friend would be something of an exaggeration, though we shared many experiences, including girls, jails, and Depression 20-cent-a-day relief camps.

Jimmy came around to the Kingston YMCA gym one day back in 1925, to watch some of us amateur boxers working out. Not that he was interested in boxing particularly — his athletic abilities lay in another direction. We soon found out that he was tumbling most of the girls at the biscuit factory where he worked, but even more exciting, was having a real love affair with a thirty-year-old married woman.

Jimmy didn't look the part of a great lover. Not quite fourteen, just over five foot two, eyes of blue, sandy hair, few faint freckles on a pitted face, and an Irish grin. How did he do it, succeed where we so often failed, we wondered. And most of us were fifteen or sixteen, a couple of years his senior.

We remained fairly close acquaintances, and Jimmy continued his philandering, if it could be called that. Perhaps better to say that he was by temperament a lover. Like Casanova. And while some of his affairs lasted only a few days, all his "exes" continued to adore him.

This became even more evident to me after the Great Depression struck in 1929, and Jimmy lost his job. He moved to Toronto and became a chocolate dipper at Eaton's. And when Jim McLaughlin and I hit the road a couple of years later, we stayed a few weeks with Jimmie in his room on John Street, just behind Grange Park.

Jimmy had landed in a Happy Hunting Ground. That needs a little explaining. The house next door contained, at any given time, a dozen or more young, and beautiful, Finnish maids. When I say maids I don't just mean maidens, I mean maids — the kind that worked for the rich in Forest Hill. Depression or no Depression, the rich couldn't get along without servants. Good maids were hard to find, but in the interests of economy the rich were only prepared to pay $30 a month. The Finnish girls were well aware of their worth and demanded $60. And although they weren't card-carrying members of a Maids' Union they knew the value of solidarity. So they rented a house, these independent Finns, shared the cost among several dozen of them, and lived there while temporarily out of work, waiting patiently for the rich to surrender — which the rich did, for there were no maids as neat and efficient as the Finnish maids.

Jimmy found this situation much to his taste, and wasted no time. He was soon known as "our Jimmy" to Ija and Auli and Riitta and Anja and Seija and Leena and and and ... His score at the time Jim McLaughlin and I arrived was fifty-seven. This period was, I believe, the apex of Jimmy Black's career of amorous dalliance. When next we met it was in Vancouver, a few years later.

People weren't buying so many chocolates and the chocolate dipper had proved redundant. So he had taken to the road and wound up in Vancouver, the Mecca of the jobless youth of the land. We shared a 25-cent-a-night room in a small Japanese-run hotel on Water Street, and when our money ran out signed up for one of Prime Minister R.B. Bennett's 20-cent-a-day slave camps. The drill was to receive the government issue of green sweater, pants, work boots, and underwear, stay a couple of weeks in a camp, then take off for Vancouver and sell the stuff to the longshoremen for a few bucks, remain in town as long as you were solvent, then sign up for another camp and repeat the process.

We were shipped forty miles north to a camp at Half-moon Bay. The foreman was an old-style army type, ram-rod back, hardwood head. All that he lacked was a swagger stick. One rainy day fifteen of us, sopping wet, returned to our bunkhouse from the work site without "awaiting orders" and were kicked out of the camp and put on the Department of National Defence blacklist. In Vancouver we applied for reinstatement and while awaiting a decision lived on city relief — $1.05 a week for a room and a meal ticket. You could get a good meal for 25 cents in those days, and when we ran out of money we stood outside one or another beer parlour in the gut of the town, and hit up patrons as they were leaving. Couples were the best bet, the woman usually urging her escort to loosen up and "give the kids a quarter."

At that time — and for years afterwards — Vancouver beer parlours were divided into two sections — one for men only and the other for "ladies and escorts." Quite a few of the "ladies" in our stamping ground were ladies of the pavement, and they were the ones who invariably made their johns cross our palms with silver.

One evening we counted our loot and found we had over three bucks. Jimmy suggested that we had been chaste for some weeks, that we were not monks and had never taken a vow of celibacy, that the bow should not be too tightly strung, and that we should pay a visit to Union Street, where the girls inside the houses of pleasure sat by the front windows and tapped out invitations on the glass with knitting needles. It seemed like a good idea, and a highly moral one, since we would be returning to the sisterhood some of the bread they had cast upon the waters.

Most of the "Halfmoon Bay 15" were reinstated by the DND; others had to adopt new names, including Jimmy Black, who became Jimmy Kelly. We spent the next three months in various camps — Camp 3459, Saddleback; Camp 330, Spences Bridge; and a real stinker at Annis, BC. It was here that a shit-house rumour aroused our interest. In Halifax, it was said, the DND was issuing blue sailor pants to all relief camp stiffs. This sounded like an opportunity not to be missed. Jimmy and I and three other guys decided we'd cross Canada and get a pair of those blue pants. If you think we were nutty, just remember that soldier in the Second World War who said, "I sure hope I get out of this alive so I can wear one of them zoot suits."

I sold my "front" (civvy coat and pants) for a fin, and Jimmy and I figured this would feed us as far as Winnipeg, which turned out to be good figuring. But in the Peg we had to sign on for another relief camp and were put on board a CNR passenger bound for Hudson, Ontario, almost two divisions east. From there they shipped a bunch of us thirty-five miles or so up north to Lac Seul, via tractors and cabooses.

The camp officials turned out to be a gang of robbers. Instead of receiving our government issue of new underwear, boots, shirt, pants, and sweater, we were given worn, dirty underwear and told to melt snow over our bunkhouse stove and wash them. We were handed patched sweaters, second-hand boots, etc. We threw this junk back at the storekeeper and suggested what he could do with it.

The following day three Ontario Provincial Police flew in to take us out. Sixty lads decided to come with us. But the police were only interested in the five of us from BC. They put us in a caboose and sat with drawn guns. We had one stiff called Sheep, because of a certain sexual proclivity. (Remember the old joke: "What is virgin wool?" "Any sheep that can run faster than Errol Flynn.") Anyway, Sheep had plenty of moxie. He gave some lip to a cop, who prodded his gun into Sheep's belly and said "Another word out of you and I'll pull this trigger." "If you've got the guts to pull it, you bastard, I've got the guts to take it!" Sheep replied. And we all gave the cops a Bronx cheer.

We were handcuffed at Hudson, taken by train to Sioux Lookout and lodged in the local jail. It soon became evident to us that the town cops had little use for the provincials. We were treated as guests, served home-cooked meals and provided with reading material. After spending the weekend in the calaboose we came up before a sympathetic justice of the peace who found us guilty of "intimidating the storekeeper at Camp 10, Lac Seul" and gave us sixty days' suspended sentence.

The trial itself had its ludicrous moments. While on the train we had talked loudly about raising the red flag to signal the start of the revolution, discussed hidden caches of weapons and arms, and sung what words we could remember of "The Internationale." Passengers quickly grasped that we were having a bit of fun at the expense of the cops, but the latter solemnly took notes of everything we said. So at the trial they charged that we were Communists, Wobblies, and Anarchists, who sang the "Third Internationale" (sic!) and had machine guns and other weapons hidden somewhere. The JP could barely repress a smile.

After the trial we had nowhere to sleep that night so our friendly jailer said we would return to our cells and his wife would rustle us up a supper. And what a supper! Pork chops and mashed potatoes! And apple pie! She served us herself and we thanked her profusely. Then the JP visited us and said, "Boys, if you will give me your word not to raise a rumpus I'll get you jobs with the Northern Ontario Development Company at 25 cents an hour. You'll have ten days or two weeks' work before the spring breakup — enough time to earn a little grubstake."

We worked a fortnight and were laid off about the middle of April, returned to Sioux, caught a freight and headed for Toronto, seven divisions away. We slid our boxcar door open to grab some scenery. It was very cold, so someone (our number had grown to fifteen) hauled out a set of new boxing gloves from his pack, and he and I battered each other around to warm up. Once he clipped me a dandy which almost knocked me through the open door. Philo Vance [a fictional character in a dozen crime novels of the 1920s and 1930s written by S.S. Van Dine] mystery: tramp wearing boxing gloves found frozen to death on railroad embankment, miles from nearest town.

At Nakina three of our BC lads decided to turn around and travel west again, but Jimmy and I held her down: Hornepayne (blinding snowstorm), Foleyet, Capreol (we kept a sharp eye open for the infamous yard bull "Capreol Red," who liked to beat up hoboes), Parry Sound, and Toronto. We swung off at Queen Street in the Don Valley, ate at a fish-and-chip joint, washed the grime from our hands and faces, and looked up Jimmy's latest Finnish girl friend, Elmi, at 122 McCall. Jimmy moved in with Elmi and I took a front room at a dollar a week. I did not spend my nights alone — hundreds of cockroaches kept me company.

Not long afterwards we abandoned our dream of sailor pants and our paths diverged for a couple of years. I headed north and was rehired by Noranda Mines on May 13, 1935. Jimmy joined Canada's standing army, was assigned to the medical corps, and became a first aid man.

We met next in Toronto late in 1936. In the meantime I had joined the Communist Party and been fired from Noranda for trying to revive union activities (the union that had called a strike in 1934 had been smashed and many of its leaders jailed). Jimmy had left or been bounced out of the army in circumstances which never became clear to me. He was currently working as a masseur in a hotel known far and wide as the "Bay Street Riding Academy." Some of his clients were stripteasers from the old Casino Theatre on Queen.

I suggested to Jimmy that he join the Communist Party. He said he couldn't sit through so many dull meetings, but "when the crunch comes, I'll be on the right side of the barricades." Meanwhile he was deep in a study of Irish history, and had advanced as far as 1649, when the Scots proclaimed Charles II in Edinburgh and the Irish rose in his favour under Ormond. Jimmy was highly incensed by Cromwell's massacre of the Irish garrisons in Drogheda and Wexford. Jimmy was always a voracious reader, but only on matters relating to Ireland and Finland.

Sometime that summer we went to Montreal and opened a massage parlour in a one-room basement flat on Drummond Street. Most such establishments were simply disguised whorehouses, but we were strictly legit. Our most reliable customer was a retired army officer who had a game leg from an old war wound. Jimmy mixed his oils and potions and did most of the work, though he showed me how to give a good rubdown and massage, and occasionally I handled a customer. There weren't many. The ex-officer's five bucks a week kept our heads above water for a few weeks, then we tired of the whole thing and moved back to Toronto.

I became rather active politically, speaking at street-corner meetings, and working closely with Dewar Ferguson, who was trying to form a seamen's union on the Great Lakes. So I did not see as much of Jimmy Black as formerly. Then one day he came around to my rooming house and said, "I'd like to join the Party."

"Just like that?"

"Well you asked me before."

"And you said no."

I knew quite well, of course, what Jimmy wanted. The Spanish Civil War had broken out on July 18, 1936, when a fascist military junta moved to overthrow the democratically elected Republican government. Nazi Germany and fascist Italy gave military support to the insurgents. The position of the Spanish Republic became desperate. International Brigades were formed, made up of anti-fascist volunteers from many countries. In Canada, which eventually sent twelve hundred men [new studies put the figure at almost seventeen hundred men and women], the Communist Party handled recruiting. Screening was conducted by Paul

Phillips, at that time party organizer in Ward Four, with a tiny office on the third floor of a decrepit building at the corner of Spadina and Queen. I was working as an assistant party organizer (salary, $4 — later $7 — a week) and did a little peripheral work in connection with the recruiting project.

So, of course, I knew what Jimmy wanted, and he knew that I knew that he wanted to volunteer to Spain, and that holding a party card would help pave the way. But there was more to it than that. During the Second World War thousands of Soviet soldiers, before going into battle, asked to join the party. If they were to die in the anti-fascist struggle, they wanted to die as Communists. Jimmy, a member of the working class from the age of twelve, had the same feeling.

He was accepted into the party, and a few weeks later, after receiving his visa (stamped "Not Valid for Spain"), was on his way to Spain with $15 in his pocket. And in company with a group of shipboard tourists, similarly endowed, who were ostensibly on their way to visit the Paris Exposition. I received one letter from Spain, with a photo enclosed, showing Jimmy, wearing his Irish grin, posed with several other volunteers, none of whom I recognized.

After the Battle of Fuentes de Ebro, in October 1937, Jimmy was posted missing, presumed dead. His epitaph could be a paragraph from the book of the XVth International Brigade, p. 293, quoted in Victor Hoar's book, *The Mackenzie-Papineau Battalion* [Toronto: Copp Clark, 1969], p. 146: "One of the most inspiring sights on the battlegrounds was two Mac-Pap first aid men, James Black and James Rose of No. One Company who moved out with the first waves, stopping to attend the wounded, dragging men into shell holes. Again and again, through the day and far into the night, Black and Rose dared the fire to save lives."

Sam Scarlett

"Order! Order!" shouted the courtroom clerk.

"Two beers!" yelled the Wobblies in the dock.

Not since Robin Hood and his Merry Men warred against the rich has the class war been carried on with such élan as displayed by the Industrial Workers of the World in the first quarter of this century.

"The working class and the employing class have nothing in common," read the opening sentence of the IWW Constitution, adopted at the founding convention of the organization in 1905. "We are going down into the gutter to get at the mass of the workers and bring them up to a decent plane of living," said Big Bill Haywood, who chaired the session.

Within a few years tens of thousands of nomadic workers were carrying the little red membership cards, and preaching the gospel of "One Big Union." They organized and won — and lost — strikes in the woods, mines, and mills. They fought the greatest "free speech" battles this continent has ever seen.

Although the US Constitution guarantees freedom of speech, city officials and vigilantes denied this right to Wobblies, who therefore staged some thirty "free speech" fights in the period from 1909 to 1917. The tactic was to call in Wobblies from all over the country to take part in a particular struggle. They were not to avoid arrest, but to welcome it. When all the jails were full the authorities usually had to cave in and allow some soapboxing in that town. In 1909, for example, after an IWW organizer had been arrested for street-corner speaking, the union paper published a call: "Wanted — Men to Fill the Jails of Spokane." Within a month more than six hundred Wobblies were in the cells, and more were confined in a schoolhouse. Finally the authorities were forced to release the prisoners and recognize the organization's right to rent a hall, publish a newspaper, and hold street meetings.

Wobblies opposed the First World War and went to jail for their beliefs. Many received vicious sentences. But for all their courage and energy, they never succeeded in achieving their goal of "One Big Union," which would paralyze capitalism and enable the workers to take control of production and distribution. After flashing like a meteor across the sky, the IWW failed to keep up with changing times, rejected political action as useless, scorned the Russian Revolution as a "haystack revolution," and declared they wanted a "smokestack revolution." By the end of the 1920s they were a spent force.

Yet there was something grand about their failure. For they left behind a precious legacy — poetry, folk music, revolutionary songs, and literature. Yes, and a combination of revolutionary zeal and humour, which is sadly lacking in most contemporary progressive organizations.

Sam Scarlett, a blowed-in-the-glass Wobbly for most of his life, loved to bait his enemies in courtrooms. On one occasion, as Sam was bound for Leavenworth along with fifty-one comrades, the prosecutor was trying to pin him down on his nationality. But Sam, Scottish by birth, always claimed he was a "citizen of industry" and had no other nationality.

"Where is your home?" the prosecutor asked.

"Cook County Jail."

"Before that?"

"County Jail, Cleveland, Ohio."

"And before that?"

"City Jail, Akron, Ohio."

"Are you an American citizen?"

"No."

"That's enough."

While he was in Leavenworth the heating system broke down one day and Sam, a skilled machinist and electrician, offered to fix it. Thereafter he was in charge of the boiler room and managed to get Jack Johnson, the former heavyweight boxing champion, as his assistant. Sam set out to turn the great Negro fighter into a revolutionary, and according to Sam "he was a quick learner."

To go back a bit, Sam Scarlett was a direct descendant of General Scarlett, in command of the Heavy Brigade at the Battle of Balaclava, which rescued what was left of the Light Brigade after their ill-fated charge.

Sam became a footballer and once played on the Scottish national team, I was told. After coming to the United States he coached a soccer team in Salt Lake City. When the famous English revolutionary Tom Mann visited America, Scarlett organized a mass meeting in Salt Lake City which turned out to be the biggest turnout for Mann on his entire speaking tour.

I don't know when Sam, after amassing a total of ninety-nine years in prison sentences in the United States, decided to move to Canada. But a veteran Canadian revolutionary told me that he was for many years the scourge of Communist agitators in the prairie provinces. The One Big Union was long dead but Sam clung to his Wobbly card and philosophy, and whenever a Communist speaker would mount a soapbox, Sam would set up another one nearby and proceed to steal the audience. For Sam was a master spieler; he could charm the birds out of trees. It didn't matter what he talked about, his audience would be spellbound.

I must interject here that most Wobbly street-corner speakers were superb orators and knew how to attract and hold crowds. Joyce Kornbluh, in her fascinating IWW anthology, *Rebel Voices* [Ann Arbor: University of Michigan Press, 1964], relates that one Jack Phelan, called the silver-tongued boy orator, would mount the box and start yelling, "I've been robbed!" When enough of a sympathetic crowd gathered to hear him, he would start, "I've been robbed by the capitalist system!"

There came a day when Sam Scarlett decided to join the Communist Party. I once asked him what had caused him to take that step. "As long as the authorities were directing their main blows against the Wobblies, I felt I was on the right track," said Sam. "But when they began attacking the Communists and ignoring us, I realized I had to switch parties. If capitalism recognized communism as its chief enemy, then I belonged with the communists."

During a miners' strike in Saskatchewan in 1931, the Mounted Police killed three strikers in Estevan as the strikers were assembling for a public meeting. The police then arrested Sam Scarlett and Annie Buller, who had been helping the strikers, and they were sentenced to jail terms. Sam did a year in a western jail. He soon made friends with some of the guards, and began to discuss sports and politics with them. For Sam would not only preach to mass audiences, he would also talk to a crowd of one. When the day of his release came, in dead winter, he was shown out of the prison gates wearing summer clothing and with a $10 bill in his pocket. Heading between huge snowdrifts in the general direction of the station, he suddenly heard "Pssst" from behind a snowbank. One, then two of his former guards appeared. "Come on, Sam," they said, "The missus has supper all ready, you can stay the night at my place and we'll see you off in the morning."

I first met Sam Scarlett in 1936 or 1937, when I was working as an assistant Communist Party organizer in Toronto's Ward Four. We had set up a social club in an old house at 905 Bathurst Street, just north of Bloor, and held regular public meetings. I had to line up speakers, and Sam's name was on the list of possibilities, along with those of Joe Wallace, Harvey Murphy, Bert Kenny, and others. Sam willingly agreed to speak — talking was his meat and drink. But while he had a wealth of background experience and was a graduate of the University of Life, he was not very strong in Marxist theory. So on one occasion he created some confusion when he told the audience that "we must never forget Lenin's advice to take one step forward, two steps back!" I was a beginner in those days and it took me some time to dig up Lenin's book *One Step Forward Two Steps Back (The Crisis in Our Party)* and realize that Lenin was castigating those who in his opinion were pursuing wrong organizational (and hence political) tactics.

A couple of weeks later I had a chance to see Sam at his best, attracting and holding an outdoor audience. It so happened that for several weeks I had been soapboxing at Queen and Spadina with fair success. The unemployed in that area had no money to go to the movies, so the Red and Rationalist "orators" provided free entertainment. At first the Rationalist speakers were fierce competition ("You fought for King and Country and what did you get? A little round service button — and the King kept the Country!") But they were good fellows and we soon agreed on sharing the corner — one hour for each.

After speaking to crowds of fifty or a hundred I became a bit conceited, and suggested to my club members, who always turned out to form an initial nucleus, that we try our hand in "bourgeois" territory up north — on rich Bloor Street. Surrounded by seven comrades, I confidently mounted my box at Bloor and launched into one of my better harangues. The art of street-corner speaking is to hammer away at a simple theme, and because of shifting crowds, to return to your central point every five minutes. Some twenty minutes later, I still had my original audience of seven. Ten minutes more passed, and the situation hadn't changed. I was becoming desperate. Then suddenly I spied Sam Scarlett walking along the street. "Sam!" I called. He came over and I said, "Sam, will you give me a hand? I can't get anybody to stop." Sam mounted the soapbox (actually a broken chair). "A little closer," he told the comrades. And he began to speak, not in a strong voice, but fairly low. In a minute or so a couple stopped, straining to hear what he was saying. A few more people joined. "Come in a little closer," coaxed Sam. The crowd began to grow. Sam began to raise his voice. He now had about forty listeners. Sam talked for half an hour. He had his audience eating out of the palm of his hand. And what was he talking about? Revolution? No, as I remember, he was describing the system of traffic lights in Moscow. Now THAT'S a soapboxer!

Not long before his death from a heart attack in Buffalo in 1941 I ran into Sam by accident in Toronto and we spent three hours together in a downtown beer parlour. The party was illegal at the time and we were both working underground. The beer kept coming and the talk flowed. One anecdote of Sam's I remember well. After the Wobblies were released from Leavenworth a rich New York supporter of the movement invited the boys to come to town and relax.

"A dozen of us accepted," said Sam. "We were given a swank apartment, well stocked with booze and groceries, and we all got a fistful of greenbacks. Well, for three weeks we really hit it up. Then we decided it was time to go back to work, so we told our benefactor that we'd be shoving off for the midwest the next day. 'But why?' he asked. 'You guys have more than done your bit for the movement. You need more money, it's yours. I'm rolling in the stuff.' We said no thanks, we've enjoyed every minute of our stay — but now it was time to grab a handful of boxcars and head for the Mesabi Range, where we had to organize the miners into the One Big Union."

Sam's reminiscences continued, hours passed. When the time came for us to part and go our separate ways, we shook hands warmly and said goodbye, neither of us knowing that it was a final farewell.

Harvey Murphy

Harvey Murphy's brusqueness covered up an innate shyness. The blunt-speaking Communist trade union leader in public was in private a sensitive romantic.

When we walked across Red Square in Moscow some years ago, Harvey's eyes filled with tears as he stood in front of the Lenin Mausoleum. And he was emotionally moved when I arranged to have his picture taken beside the plaque and ashes in a niche in the Kremlin Wall of Big Bill Haywood, the famous IWW leader.

I first met Harvey in 1936, in Toronto. At that time he was organizing the unemployed. With typical acuteness, he had rejected the conventional "Unemployed Organization" title in favour of "Ontario Federation on Unemployment." It added a touch of class, and sounded vaguely official. And indeed, minor bureaucrats in various government offices often accepted it as such. Harvey's secretary, name of Raefield, an upper-class Englishman who had somehow strayed into the Communist orbit, would phone the relevant department and say, with marbles in his mouth: "Mr. Strang? Ah, good. Raefield here — the Ontario Federation, you know. It seems we have a little problem, a Mrs. Saxon on Robert Street has complained to us that she's had her water cut off. A mistake, of course. Could you look into it, old man, and see that things get straightened out?" Sometimes it worked.

Harvey was addressing some sixty jobless in the third-floor meeting hall at 441 Queen St. West when I poked my head in the door. I saw a chunky, bald-headed man on the platform. "We must stick together," he was saying. "Remember what happened to the bananas. As soon as they left the bunch they got skinned."

That was Harvey, the master of the apt phrase. Years later, when he was leader of the Mine-Mill union, the Steelworkers announced to the press that they were going to raid Mine-Mill in Trail and "chase Harvey Murphy right out of town." Newspaper reporters swarmed around Harvey and asked for his reaction. Without a second's hesitation he said, "If you don't run, they can't chase you!" Mine-Mill won that battle, thanks largely to Harvey's leadership, but events later led to a logical combining of the two unions.

Murphy had been involved in labour's struggles since his early youth. In his book *Thirty Years: The Story of the Communist Movement in Canada* [Toronto: Progress Books, 1952], Tim Buck wrote:

> The workers of the National Steel Car plant at Hamilton, Ontario, fought a major strike for six weeks in 1928. That struggle illustrated both the will of the workers to struggle and the fruit of the party's work in developing youthful leadership. Harvey Murphy, then 22 years of age, led that strike like a veteran. The union had no treasury, the families of many of the workers went hungry until a relief committee was organized and set to work by a young comrade (Minnie Davis) then 20 years of age.

In his tape-recorded reminiscences Tim Buck told another story about Harvey Murphy. In those days, he said, we did a lot of travelling via boxcar. We wanted to send Harvey to help a strike in Coalhurst, Alberta, but there was no money. However, a comrade who ran a small restaurant donated $5 and made up a huge food parcel. "I went back to the office with $5 and a seven-quart fruit basket loaded with food, including some canned fruit and an opener," Tim said. "Away went Murphy with a basket of food and $5 in his pocket. He arrived in Coalhurst all right."

Harvey and his wife Isabel landed in Moscow one time when I was away on a journalists' trip. When they called at our flat, as they usually did, Monica, my wife, said, "Oh, Harvey, you should have phoned and let me know you were coming ... I'm afraid I haven't got a drink in the house, and it's after hours." Harvey, naturally, looked disappointed. "Nothing at all?" he said. "Well," Monica admitted, "Bert has a case of Vat 69 stashed away for Christmas, but it's away up in that recess on top of the kitchen, and too heavy to get down."

"Don't worry, I'll manage," said Harvey, and climbing onto a stool balanced on a chair, and standing on tiptoe, he began tugging at the case. His face grew redder and redder and he was puffing like a grampus. "I was afraid he'd have a stroke," Monica told me afterwards. But success finally crowned his efforts, and deep inroads were made into my holiday Scotch.

The Canadian labour movement doesn't produce many colourful figures. Murphy was an exception.

A Murphy quote:

"What a day it was in Blairmore, Alberta, in 1933, after the strike, when the coal miners elected a mayor and a full council of workers! We renamed the main street Tim

Buck Boulevard. When Tim and the others, the Kingston Eight, had all been released and Tim visited Blairmore, we shut down the mine and declared a school holiday and celebrated a great victory." Murphy pushed the miners' council into doing more than that. The mine owners had pedigreed dogs, the miners had mutts. So council passed a law that all owners of pedigreed dogs had to pay a dog licence, while the mutts were given the freedom of the town.

Years later, during the period when Claude Jodoin was head of the Canadian Labour Congress, Murphy acquired a dog which he promptly named Claude. Mine-Mill was outside the Congress at that time and the target of its raiding activities. Murphy would bring his dog to union meetings (so the story goes) and on taking the platform would order, "To heel, Claude!"

After the Mine-Mill and Steel unions merged (to the benefit of Canada's mine workers) Harvey was presented with a car by the union. His son Rae described to me Harvey's method of driving. "He would aim for his objective and step hard on the gas. Anyone standing in his way had better step out of it." One day Murphy came roaring into the driveway alongside the old union office in Toronto. There was a car in his parking spot. At the last moment he swerved to the left, ran the car up a guy wire slanting down from a telephone pole. His car neatly turned over and came to rest, upside down, on top of the parked car. Harvey crawled out, unhurt, and phoned the wreckers. They came, two of them, gawped at the scene, and one said, in a tone of awe, "Now how in hell did you manage THAT, Harvey?"

Harvey was a home-loving man, deeply attached to his wife and children.

Many of his political and union foes were nevertheless personal friends. When Harvey died a few years ago [in

1977] — slipping away quietly while watching television —
thousands of Canadians felt a sense of loss. Among them
were some of the Steelworkers' leaders who had once vowed
to "chase Murphy right out of Trail."

Harvey Murphy's kind don't come down the pike too
often.

Dewar Ferguson

Some wealthy citizens, before they die, arrange to leave
money to build a new hospital wing, or an addition to a library, or a home for stray dogs and cats. But damn few leave
any money to their employees, whose labour created their
wealth. Dewar Ferguson, a well-to-do but far from rich em-
ployer, was one who did.

"Fergie" was the subject of an interview front-paged by
the *Daily Commercial News* of Toronto on May 14, 1973, not
long before he died of cancer. The sixty-three-year-old president of A.N. Shaw & Sons Ltd., a building restoration company, had decided to set up an $80,000-dollar trust fund for
forty-three of his long-term employees.

"In the past few years," wrote *DCN* staff reporter Patricia
Williams, "the firm has done most of the restoration work
on historical buildings in Metro Toronto." She cited a few:
Osgoode Hall, exterior of the legislative assembly at Queen's
Park, complete exterior restoration of Little Trinity Church,
the Coach House at Casa Loma, exterior of the Royal York
Hotel. And further afield: exterior cleaning and restoration
of Kingston City Hall, the Brock Monument at Queenston,
a federal building in Sault Ste. Marie.

"My men have been with me for a long time. They have
worked very hard and have helped me earn my money. I
feel they deserve a portion of it," Fergie told his interviewer.
"Most of the men are as conscientious about their work as

I am. I've been blessed with a good staff, both in the office and in the field. Setting up the trust fund was the very least I could do for them."

I met Claude Dewar Ferguson ("Fergie" to everyone) in 1936, when he was a beached seaman trying to organize a union on the Great Lakes. We were as poor as church mice, as lean and hungry as a couple of wolves in a Russian fairy tale. I was working in Toronto's Ward Four as an assistant Communist Party organizer, paid $7a week when money was available. Fergie's income came in pennies; he owned three one-cent peanut vending machines, located in cafes in the Dundas-Bay area. After cleaning out the machines, we would sit at a cafe counter and pay for our hamburger dinners with handfuls of coppers.

We shared a $3-a-week room in a gloomy Finnish rooming house on Spadina near Queen. Later we rented an attic room on Augusta Street, which was fine after we managed to get rid of the bedbugs. Every day Fergie would make a tour of the waterfront, and I would often accompany him. Captains and mates had strict orders not to let Fergie on their vessels, but most of them turned a blind eye while Fergie would slip aboard and talk union. He had sailed the Great Lakes for seven years and was known to hundreds of sailors. Many would sign union cards, while at the same time stating they didn't think a union could be built in the middle of the Depression.

The men's grievances were many. Since 1932 many companies had been following the rotten practice of carrying "skeleton crews." Ships going up the Lakes would lay off their deckhands at Port Colborne and operate on the upper lakes with a "skeleton crew," the remainder of the men having to do the deckhands' work without extra pay. One day down the Lakes the crew would be picked up again in preparation for the arduous canal grind between Cardinal and Montreal. Thus seamen were robbed of part of their wages each month.

How Fergie obtained the money to open a union office at 8 Bay Street and purchase a typewriter is a story known to only a handful of people. A well-known gambler owed Fergie a favour. Gamblers like to pay their debts, and apparently this was a rather important one (though just what it was, I was never told). So one day this gambler turned up and told Fergie that in the next few days, at obscure race tracks in the United States, three "fixed" races would be run. "I will let you know a few hours in advance," he said. "Put every cent you can raise on each race. Nothing can go wrong."

The first tip came, but we could only bet five bucks with a bookie, for that was all we had. The horse came in and paid something like twenty to one, but bookies, of course, never paid off at higher than sixteen to one. Nevertheless, we had over $75 in the kitty, and Fergie promptly paid a month's rent and acquired a union office.

On the second tip, we bet $15, and the payoff was six to one. We collected, and Fergie bought an office typewriter.

We put the bundle, something like $25, on the third tip. Fergie's small-time bookie wouldn't handle it all, splitting it with some cronies. The result came over the wire: our horse had finished second. But wait! An objection had been lodged! The revised result: objection sustained, our horse placed first! Our affluence was temporary, as Fergie socked most of the gains into office furniture, printing of new membership books, etc.

About this time the *Sand Merchant* foundered in Lake Erie, sending nineteen people to a watery grave. It was the third major marine disaster on the Great Lakes that year, and the question of safety regulations stirred wide interest.

Seamen began joining the union in ever-increasing numbers. In Montreal an office had been opened at 658 Common St. under the leadership of Pat Sullivan, who became secretary of the Canadian Seamen's Union (CSU). (A decade later Pat, by that time a big wheel in the Trades and Labour Congress, sold out the seamen and disappeared from view. That does not alter the fact that in the early days of the union he played a progressive role.)

The main aims of the union, as outlined by Fergie at that time, were higher wages, full crews and clean quarters; wireless on all ships irrespective of tonnage; compulsory lifeboat drill at regular intervals; and transportation to and from ships on fitting out and laying up.

But I am not writing a history, or even a sketch, of the birth of the CSU. Nor am I trying to present a shorthand version of Fergie's life. My aim is more modest; to pay tribute to a friend of more than thirty-five years. I have known many trade unionists who were better public speakers than Fergie, many who were better strategists, better negotiators. None more honest, though; and none with his ability to recruit members, not en masse but on a personal basis. Fergie was the kind of a union leader that everyone trusted.

Many of the early members and builders of the CSU were communists. And we received considerable help and advice from leaders of the Communist Party — particularly from J.B. Salsberg, at that time head of the party's trade union bureau. Yet I remember one occasion when Fergie saved all our trade union "wise men" from making a mistake that might have spelled the end of the union.

The spectacular success of "sit-down" strikes in France during the early years of Popular Front, and the successful application of this strike technique to US plants, led certain

Canadian trade union leaders to reach the conclusion that it was high time to introduce "sit-downs" in our country.

A seamen's strike was in the cards, so it was not entirely unexpected when Pat Sullivan arrived to take part in an emergency meeting of communist trade union leaders and announced that the Lakes seamen would stage a "sit-down" when the 1938 navigation season opened a few days later. He had arranged a simultaneous telephone tie-in with CSU organizers in all the ports to give last-minute instructions.

Present at the meeting were J.B. Salsberg, several prominent Toronto unionists, Pat, Fergie, and myself. It had become customary that I should take time off from my job on the *Clarion* whenever the CSU called a strike, in order to handle union public relations. Pat's idea was enthusiastically welcomed. Typical arguments in favour of the sit-down were:

"The strike is being called on four days' notice. Something spectacular must be done to get nation-wide publicity. A sit-down will achieve this."

"It might be the lever to start a wave of sit-downs in Canada and introduce the French and US techniques here."

"Sit-downs could be the spark needed to revitalize our unions and lead to organization of the unorganized."

"It is the ideal place to start the sit-down movement. Seamen can lock themselves in the galleys and have enough food to last for weeks."

I voiced my full support and predicted that the sit-down "would make headlines from coast to coast."

Just when we seemed to have reached unanimous agreement, Fergie, who had remained silent up to this point, took the floor. He said: "All the arguments so far have been one-sided and don't take into account the actual situation. The actual situation is that our members will fight like tigers on the picket line, but they will not go for a sit-down, or if they do, they won't stick it out. And I'll tell you why. It all hinges on the background of the men, on traditions of the sea, and other factors. Most of our members come from small towns along the Lakes — I do myself. There's a Bible in every home and they're brought up with strict ideas of 'right' and 'wrong'. The first law of the sea is that the captain is master of his ship. A revolt aboard ship is mutiny and our lads have ideas way back in their minds that they can be hanged for mutiny, or imprisoned for life. Even if they go on a sit-down they'll feel they are doing something illegal. There'll be squabbling in the galley about penalties and so on. Then the captain will bring the cops aboard and threaten them, read the law to them — and the strike will be lost from that moment. On the other hand, the seamen know that all workers have a right to strike and picket. The purpose of picketing is to keep scabs off the ships. Our guys will fight to do that — they'll feel that they are in the right and that any cops who try to break the picket line will be acting illegally — and they'll fight like tigers on the picket lines — and we can win such a battle."

Fergie also reviewed the short history of the union, the relative inexperience of the men in strike action, the need to teach them strike tactics, to educate them in the process of the strike — all things that couldn't be done if they were "holed up" aboard the strike-bound ships.

Another round of discussion followed. Some of us were reluctant to abandon the sit-down "dream" but eventually a unanimous decision was reached to conduct a conventional strike. The strike was called. The men did, as Fergie predicted, "fight like tigers," stopped the scabs, kept the vessels tied up, and won the strike.

An interesting point is that at Fort Williams, where only one ship was berthed, the CSU representative misunderstood orders and pulled a sit-down. The men locked themselves in the galley. The captain called police aboard, read the riot act, the law on mutiny, or whatever. The men walked ashore and meekly watched a scab crew go aboard. They offered no resistance when the vessel sailed away — to them the strike was "lost" when the sit-in failed.

The tiny CSU office at the bottom of Bay Street could only accommodate half a dozen people at one time, so Fergie rented a large-one-room shack, called Sailors' Rest or something similar, on the waterfront. In summer the Christian group which owned the building held Sunday services for seamen and distributed religious tracts. When the shipping season ended the place was locked up until spring. Fergie's offer of $7 a month rent in winter was gladly accepted.

It was in this shack that the nucleus of the union was built. In the nearby freight marshalling yard, where steam locomotives shunted boxcars around all day, Fergie and I would pick up chunks of coal and feed the pot-bellied stove which heated the drafty shack on days when recruiting meetings were held. Communist trade unionists like Fred Collins and Sam Scarlett would come down and give a rousing speech to an audience of twenty or thirty seamen. Then Fergie would try to sign up those who weren't already CSU members.

I remember one cold day when we ran out of coal and had to resort to burning piles of religious tracts and pamphlets. I also remember that a couple of young sailors demurred, saying that we were committing sacrilege. "Nonsense, these tracts have never been put to better use," said a veteran seaman named Hughie, a Wobbly, almost the last of a vanishing breed. He signed up and paid a year's union dues in advance.

The sinking of the sand sucker *Sand Merchant* in Lake Erie on October 17, 1936, carrying eighteen of her crew and the wife of the first mate to a watery grave, enraged seamen and resulted in an influx of new union members. A judicial inquiry into the disaster revealed that the vessel had only eighteen inches of freeboard when she left port. She carried no wireless. As an open-hatch ship she was a veritable death trap. There were no means of preventing the ship from filling with water in a storm.

Had the *Sand Merchant* carried wireless, help could have arrived from Cleveland, barely more than sixteen miles from the scene of the disaster, in time to save many of the nineteen who perished. There were only seven survivors.

A month later, on November 21, the motorship *Hibou* suddenly listed forty-five degrees in calm waters off Square Point in Georgian Bay. The captain gave the order to abandon ship before she sank. Seven crew members were drowned and ten survived. A coroner's jury at the inquest of one victim reached a verdict that "we cannot determine the exact cause of the disaster, but from the evidence we believe that the boat was not properly stabilized, and we recommend that a thorough and searching inquiry be held forthwith to try to determine the cause."

The *Hibou* had lurched and rolled over just a hundred yards from shore. This suggested she was either top-heavy or unseaworthy. No stability test had been made of the motorship after her conversion from steam engines some years earlier. Stowage of cargo and such things as lifeboat drill were left entirely up to the ship's officers. Giving evidence, the mate said there had been no lifeboat drill since the boats were lowered for inspection in the spring.

The CSU won the support of all Great Lakes seamen by pressing for much-needed safety measures. "It is absolutely imperative," Dewar Ferguson told the press, "that in future all ships, regardless of tonnage or the length of their runs, should be compelled by law to carry wireless. Let the Marine department get to work and draft some up-to-date legislation for the protection of those thousands of young men who risk their lives each year sailing on the Lakes. Volume of shipping has increased this year; profits have likewise gone up. Higher wages and more protection for seamen should be next on the program."

The war came along and our paths diverged. While I was overseas we kept up a desultory correspondence. Back in Canada I became Toronto organizer of the Labor-Progressive Party. In civic elections Dewar Ferguson had won an aldermanic seat in Ward Six. He was a good alderman, but the Cold War was just getting underway and the right-wing crowd united to defeat him for a second term.

I moved to Vancouver in 1948 and lived there until 1960. During this period I saw Fergie infrequently. The Liberal government, with the aid of imported gangsters from the United States, had succeeded in smashing the Canadian Seamen's Union. In 1955 Fergie went to work for Shaw & Son Ltd. Within a year he was sales manager. Later he acquired a controlling interest in the company. Under his presidency business boomed, growing at a rate of more than 20 per cent annually.

From 1960 to the beginning of 1964 I was stationed in Peking as correspondent for the *Canadian Tribune*. When Monica and I returned to Toronto for a two-year period we saw a lot of the Fergusons, Dewar and Marge. Then I was assigned to Moscow. On my rare visits to Canada I stayed at Fergie's. In 1973 I was shocked at my old friend's appearance. Cancer had him in its grip. He had sold controlling interest in the building restoration firm and was busy setting up the trust fund for his long-time employees.

The night before I was to fly back to Moscow we sat watching television for a few minutes, then talked a little about the early days of the CSU. But Fergie was very pale and tired, and at 9 p.m. said, "I think I'll go to bed." Those were the last words my old chum spoke to me.

From Pool Table to "Politician"

As mentioned elsewhere in these rambling reminiscences, after spending a year in 20-cent-a-day relief camps, I decided to return to Noranda and try to get my old job back. I arrived in town broke and slept that night on a pool table — the same table on which I had so often played money pool in the past. Next morning I turned up at the smelter office and applied for work. I knew skilled hands were needed. There had been a strike at Noranda the previous year; nineteen strikers were serving jail terms and hundreds of foreign-born workers had been fired. Many illiterate French-Canadian farmers had been used as strikebreakers; some had stayed on while others had returned to their farms or villages.

I was given a cool welcome and told that the only job available was on the slag pile, at 50 cents an hour, working under an Italian foreman who had an all-Italian crew. Everyone knew that this foreman demanded a kickback from his gang on paydays. Pasty-faced Jack Anderson, the assistant superintendent, made me this offer and half-sneered as he waited my reply. "Fine," I said. Actually, the job wasn't all that bad.

There was some heavy lifting at times, laying new rails or shifting them. But we worked in the fresh air, free from the gas and dust of the smelter.

I knew that I was being punished for the manner in which I had thrown up my job the year before. It was inevitable that sooner or later I would be again put in charge of a reverb furnace. The call came in less than two weeks. One of the smelter foremen whom I had worked under, Ben Anderson, came out to the dump, said, "Okay, Bert, you can go back to skimming No. 2 furnace." I grinned and said, "I don't think so, Ben. I like it here." "When it hits 30 below zero next winter?" Ben asked. "Come off it, lad, you know why you were put out here, to do penance. Now you're wanted inside, and you have no choice in the matter. So cut the comedy."

Only one or two of my old furnace crew were left. The matte tapper had joined the unsuccessful strike and been fired, and so had the slag tapper and fettler. When tapping matte the new man often failed to shut off the stream and I had to be ready with another doby in a matter of seconds. Some of the crew moaned over the bad working conditions, and recalled the "good old days" of the strike, when they had been paid double wages and given free work gloves for helping to break the strike. I pointed out that they were now complaining about the very conditions that had led to the strike.

In the year I had spent on the road and in the camps my political opinions had changed considerably. I had always taken an offbeat and somewhat anarchistic attitude to society. On the west coast I had come in contact with IWW, CCF, and Communist Party members, had joined the Relief Camp Workers' Union, and participated in strikes. With other RCWU members we had responded to a call to beef up the picket lines during a strike of lumber workers, and had waged a battle with the police. I had become a reader of *The Worker.*

One day, while I was working the 3:00-to-11:00 shift, a Ukrainian came up to me and said someone from Toronto wanted to meet me at midnight and would be waiting in Louis Smith's cafe, which operated round the clock.

I arrived at the cafe on time, ordered ham and eggs, and looked around to try and guess who wanted to speak to me. There were a few drunks at one table, a prostitute whom I knew quite well at another. I had often spent an hour or so with her in this cafe. She would show me pictures of her younger sister, a convent girl in Montreal, and read me letters from her mother, who was not aware of the profession her elder daughter had chosen.

The door opened and a small man sidled in, glanced swiftly about the room, slid into a chair next to me, leaned close and said into my ear softly, "You wanna join Party?"

"Which party?" I asked.

"Communist Party!"

"Sure," I said. "I've been waiting for someone to ask me that for some time."

In Vancouver I had been attracted to the IWW, but suddenly realized that at their meetings, for all the fiery speeches, everyone was either grey-headed or bald. I listened to CCF orators and all they seemed to want was my vote, with a promise that by 1955 they would be elected to power federally. I couldn't see that outfit doing anything very revolutionary. I knew that many of the leaders of the Relief Camp Workers' Union were Reds, but I was never sure which ones, and nobody had ever approached me to join the Communist Party.

We got down to business the following night. I was given

a membership card and paid six months' dues in advance. I also gave a dollar to something called the National Party Fund. I paid for a subscription to *The Worker,* which I would pick up at a Finnish comrade's store. The paper would be addressed to "Valkonen" — a name I suggested because it means "white" in Finnish. I bought some "literature" which I was to study. I was asked for a donation to help finance some local project.

By this time I was becoming a little suspicious. What if I was being conned by this chap from Toronto? Perhaps he was pocketing all the money himself. No, that couldn't be. His clothes were threadbare and he looked as if he needed a good meal. In any case, his face was honest. His English was poor (he was some kind of a Slav, I suppose), but every word was sincere and expressed deep convictions. I was to try, he told me, to form a party club of native-born Canadians, and send articles to our English and French press about conditions in the mine and smelter. A comrade in Timmins would ship us bundles of leaflets urging the need of a new union at Noranda, and we should find ways to distribute them among the workers.

Surprisingly, it was not difficult to recruit members. I brought in two friends, they asked other friends, and within a month we had a party club of nine members, four of them smelter workers and five miners. Three were French-Canadians. As we were never all on the same shift, only four or five of us were able to get together at any one time. Our meetings, if you could call them that, took place in a Chinese cafe. Not having the faintest notion of how to prepare an agenda, we spent most of our time discussing how to get another union started. Leaflets had arrived from Timmins and we passed them around though many workers refused to take them. The shadow of the lost strike still hung over Noranda.

I wrote an article on the bad working conditions in the smelter and sent it to Tom McEwen, editor of *Unity*, published by the Workers Unity League. It was printed and this encouraged me to continue writing. I described Dave Galt's death in a story which *The Worker* printed:

> On a night in March, Dave Galt walked to work and never walked home again. At this time he was swamping in the converter aisle and also working on the anode or copper furnace. It was a part of his duties to operate the tilting ladle, which poured its tons of molten metal into the anode furnace. No one knows just what happened on this night, but for some reason Dave stopped beneath the ladle while the motor which operated it was still running. *There was no safety catch.* The ladle tilted beyond a certain point, the motor continued to run, there was a crash and the eight-ton pot fell back upon its platform, pinning the helpless worker beneath it. Death was instantaneous.

I had met Dave Galt in 1931 when I first began working at Noranda. Indeed, for a period of six months I had rented a room in his flat. On many an evening we sat at home planning our respective futures. I spoke of my desire to write. Dave's mind was filled with the idea of becoming a first-class radio technician. He had been a "sparkie" on the Great Lakes boats in his youth, and when he spoke of this period his voice often revealed a vague regret that such days were gone. "Here I am tied down to this damn stink-hole of a smelter, when I should be following my trade," he would say. "I took a Marconi course in radio, and now look at me. The trouble is I need the money and cannot afford to quit just now. As soon as I can save a few dollars ahead I'm going to open a small radio shop of my own. My health is all shot, and if I don't get out soon I'll die in this smelter."

The *Toronto Star* carried a small item datelined Noranda: "Crushed beneath a tilting ladle here today, David Galt, 29, was instantly killed. He had been employed at the Noranda mines for three and a half years.... He is survived by his widow and one child."

It didn't take very long for the security man at Noranda to find out who the leaflet distributors were. So one fine day half a dozen of our club members were fired. Most of them sought jobs at other smelters or mines in the district. I decided to move to Toronto.

I had about $50 in my pocket, enough to keep me afloat for several weeks if I lived frugally. I rented a room in a Finnish house on Beverly St. for two bucks a week, ate two 20-cent meals a day in a Finnish restaurant on Spadina near Queen (long since demolished). The menu gave you a choice of meatballs and mash or sausages and mash, plus soup, dessert, coffee, and all the bread you could eat.

I began doing some voluntary work for the party, then was taken on staff as an assistant to Paul Phillips, the Ward Four organizer. When Paul, a talented young man who spoke six or seven languages fluently, was moved to the party's national office, he was replaced by Muni Erlich (who was killed in the Second World War). The club I belonged to decided that we should hold street-corner meetings twice a week. I was chosen to be the speaker. My first attempt was rather ghastly. I mounted a box at one corner, while the Salvation Army was holding a meeting on the opposite corner. Determined to draw away part of their audience, which in this district was composed mainly of unemployed workers, I took a deep breath and roared: "COMRADES AND FELLOW WORKERS!" The sound of my own voice paralyzed me. I couldn't think what to say next. I had no experience in public speaking, my mind was a blank, and though I managed to utter a few sentences, at the end of a minute I was a spent force. Just then who did I see in my dwindling audience but Jim Davis, one of the party stalwarts and a noted street-corner speaker, almost as good as Sam Scarlett. "I will now call on our main speaker," I said, and beckoned to Jim. He responded brilliantly, and soon had a crowd of fifty or sixty people. Later, over a coffee, he gave me some tips on how to win and interest the crowd. "Remember that you are not giving a lecture to a captive audience in a hall," he said. "People will drift away, others will join your listeners. So stick to a simple theme, and don't be afraid to repeat yourself every few minutes. Hammer home your main points — the fight for jobs, or the need to stop evictions, or whatever. You are an agitator — that means getting across a few ideas that will stick in people's minds."

Jim Davis talked on in this vein, and as the weeks passed I became more adept at soapboxing, though never a spellbinder. And I learned how to handle hecklers. There was one old chap, however, who gave me a bit of trouble one night. I was doing fine until he suddenly shouted, "What about Daniel De Leon?" I had never heard the name before. So I ignored the interruption and tried to continue my speech. But a minute later it came again, loud and clear: "What about Daniel De Leon?" I faced the heckler and pointed a finger at him. "My friend," I said, "you may be interested in De Leon, and I may be interested in De Leon, but these other good people are interested right now in work or wages. So please do not disrupt our meeting, and this time tomorrow night I promise you I'll deal with your question about Daniel De Leon. Fair enough?" The crowd was with me and the heckler subsided. The next morning I cornered Paul Phillips in our party office and said, "Look, Paul, I'm in trouble. Who in hell is Daniel De Leon? I have to know all about him by tonight." Paul laughed and gave a rundown on the famous American leftist [who died in 1914]. But at the street-corner meeting that evening my heckler didn't show up.

Dewar Ferguson was a member of my party club. We became friends, roomed together for a time, and I played a small role in helping him to organize a union of Great Lakes seaman, described above.

It was decided that *The Worker* should become a daily. I had been contributing articles, mainly on mining, relief camps, and seafaring. When the *Daily Clarion* was born I became a staff writer, thus beginning my long association with the left-wing press.

Bert Whyte, age four, with his brother, Clinton, age seven, at Pembroke, Ontario, in 1913

Whyte in about 1928, outside a pool hall, holding a cue

Whyte at the age of about seventeen, an avid boxer and boxing writer

Riding the rails in the 1930s: Whyte (second row, third from left)

A rare photo, taken by Whyte in 1935, of the inside of "one of Prime Minister R.B. Bennett's 20-cent-a-day slave camps," probably in British Columbia

Jimmy Black, left, and comrades in 1937, during the Spanish Civil War

Opposite: Whyte in army uniform during World War II

Above: Whyte in Germany, February 1945, wearing Canadian Army uniform and "looking 1,000 years old," he writes on the reverse

CHAPTER THREE

The War

Underground

When, on August 23, 1939, a Soviet-German non-aggression treaty was signed, it caused, said Tim Buck, "a state of confusion" in Canadian communist ranks. The confusion grew worse when Germany attacked Poland on September 1 and Britain and France declared war on Germany September 3. What stand should the Communist Party take? Neutrality? Critical support to the British government? Opposition to Canada's participating in the war? After a period of indecision, the CPC declared that it was an imperialist war, between imperialist powers, for imperialist aims on both sides.

As the RCMP had already arrested a number of communists, raided our offices, and seized copies of the *Clarion*, it became necessary to work underground. Shortly after this, wrote Tim Buck, "the Defense of the Realm Act was enacted in Ottawa; our Party was banned and declared illegal."

I was sent to Ottawa to replace district organizer Harry Binder, who had been arrested. My "parish" included the capital city and also Pembroke, Cornwall, Brockville, and Kingston. I was ostensibly a salesman, and arrived in

Ottawa carrying a dozen samples of picture frames, supplied by a sympathizer who ran a picture-frame factory in Toronto. Of course, this flimsy cover wouldn't have stood scrutiny for five minutes if the RCMP ever became suspicious of me.

My first task was to set up a new district committee. Binder had been fingered by a youthful member of his committee who, under pressure, had turned informer. My committee, assembled with care, consisted of a newspaper reporter, an artist, one male and two female government employees, and the manager of a shoe store — part of a national chain. I also made contact with a Ukrainian farm woman, who handled distribution of our "literature" in the countryside.

There are two basic ways of working underground. One is to sit tight in your room all day, and only venture for walks at night. This method has the disadvantage of almost inevitably arousing the curiosity of your landlady, with possible drastic consequences. The other method, which I have always opted for, is to work absolutely in the open, but to change your lifestyle completely. I joined the YMCA and became a member of the bridge club. When I needed a haircut I went to the expensive barber shop in the Chateau Laurier. I avoided eating in cheap cafes and often conferred with the chain store manager over a good dinner at a respectable hotel dining room — letting him settle the tab. I dressed conservatively and wore a blue homburg. In the course of time I became a great "friend" of the editor of a Catholic newspaper, known for its anti-communist views. Members of the bridge club regarded us as complete reactionaries. The puritans among them condemned us for our habit of reciting off-colour limericks:

There was a young fellow named Hyde
Who fell down a privy and died.
His unfortunate brother
Then fell down another
And now they're interred side by side.

And:

An Argentine gaucho named Bruno
Once said: "There is one thing I do know:
A woman is fine,
And a sheep is divine
But a llama is Numero Uno!"

Hanging around with Fay — that was his name, if I remember correctly — eventually paid off. A young red-hot from the Maritimes joined the YMCA staff and set about organizing a discussion club, to deal with such subjects as "What Should Be Our Wartime Aims?" "Is Our Army Fully Democratic?" and "What Changes Do We Envisage in a Progressive Post-War World?" Dangerous topics. Someone suggested that I be invited to join the discussion group. But the red-hot blackballed me, labelled me a jingoist, a chauvinist, a Neanderthal type that a progressive Canada could well do without. Naturally, this delighted me, as it strengthened my cover.

I had brought two gelatin duplicating machines to Ottawa, and began publishing twice-a-month editions of the *Clarion* (organ of the Ottawa District of the Communist Party of Canada). It usually ran to six pages, came out in two hundred copies, and contained material sent from the party centre in Toronto as well as local stories. Distribution had to be selective. One method was to use the public library, inserting copies into books which progressive readers would be most likely to take from the shelves (political biographies, John Steinbeck, Clifford Odets, etc.). The authorities set a silly trap. Near the librarian's desk, in a sector headed "Recommended Reading," they prominently displayed Lenin's *Selected Works*. Only a cretin could have fallen for the invitation to plant our illegal paper there. But they also had a stoolie who wandered up and down between the stacks, trying to look like a person who could read. No sweat.

We sent copies of the *Clarion* to the *Toronto Globe and Mail*. This aroused the editor's ire and on January 18, 1941 an editorial entitled "The Ubiquitous *Clarion*" appeared, which said, in part:

> When publication of the Toronto Communist newspaper, *The Clarion*, was prohibited, the public thought that was the end of it. Perhaps it was of this particular *Clarion*. But a Winnipeg *Clarion* continued with the same kind of stuff. And now there is published in Ottawa, right under the Government's nose, *The Clarion*, boldly announced as "organ of the Ottawa District of the Communist Party of Canada." There is a defiant ignoring of the fact that the Communist Party is declared an unlawful organization in this country.... True to form, *The Clarion* is bent on discouraging the war effort.... Because of its un-Canadian and generally destructive aims, the Communist Party is declared an unlawful organization, but in the Canadian capital *The Clarion*, avowed organ of the Ottawa District of the Communist Party of Canada, carries on its work.

Thus goaded by its Toronto contemporary, the *Ottawa Citizen* called up local RCMP officials to get a story. The

Mounties had little to report. So the *Citizen*, under the heading, "Seek Printing Place of Communist Paper," ran the following story:

> RCMP officials indicated today there is no suspicion that any Communist paper is being published in Ottawa at the present time. While the Communist Party was banned as illegal, after the outbreak of war, under the Defense of Canada regulations, a Communist paper, still called *The Clarion* makes an occasional appearance. The police authorities are actively looking to find where such printing and publication is being carried on, but, as indicated, there is no suspicion that such printing is taking place in Ottawa.

I couldn't resist commenting in the next issue of the *Clarion:*

> In other words, no paper is printed here but the police are actively searching for the printing shop where it isn't being printed. Simple, isn't it? Perhaps the RCMP sleuths lack only a starting clue — a whiff of perfume, a broken comb, a soiled handkerchief, or something. The editor of *The Clarion*, anxious to be of help, is herewith enclosing a lock of his hair with this issue of *The Clarion* going to the *Globe and Mail*. But seriously, boys, do you really imagine that you can outlaw the class struggle?

In my long years in the party I have been accused on more than one occasion of adopting a frivolous attitude to serious matters. Even during the war, while I was facing death every day, one homebody complained that my letters from the front were too "light-hearted." What can be done about such people? Nothing. They were born without a sense of humour and will remain that way until the Grim Reaper (they like that name) carries them off.

I found playing hide-and-seek with the cops stimulating. I was the young fox, bright-eyed and bushy-tailed, and the cops were the eager hounds, sniffing around, trying to pick up my scent. Capture meant internment, of course, not a pleasant prospect; but the game had its piquant aspect.

In my files I have several copies of the *Clarion* published in 1940–41, and I must say that some of the leading articles sent to us from the party centre in Toronto make weird reading today. What our Ottawa committee did not know at the time was that Stewart Smith, in Toronto, was making a bid to take over the party leadership from Tim Buck, who was working from New York and was somewhat isolated. Smith returned to his long-held (and erroneous) thesis that Canada was a captive British colony and that in the event of a Hitler victory the people of Europe would revolt, and Canada would also liberate itself from the British yoke. In pursuance of this line, we received for publication articles containing such nonsense as the following:

> The world awaits the outcome of the Battle of Britain.... The military defeat of British imperialism would be of the greatest benefit to mankind as a whole.... It would not mean what many fear it would, the substitution of German imperialist domination for British, for the defeat of Britain in this war would unleash far greater revolutionary possibilities than the defeat of German imperialism, and German imperialism emerging the military victor would face immediate revolts among the sprawling peoples of Europe.

Every few months I took a swing around my constituency. In Pembroke there was no party group, only one individual contact, a teamster. And he turned out to be a nut, a "joiner." His one-room shack was plastered with Communist leaflets, Seventh-day Adventist papers, material from the Flat Earth Society, the American Association for the Advancement of Atheism, the Rosicrucians — you name it, he had it. Stacks of papers and magazines filled a quarter of the room. It was easy to see why the police never bothered him. He was a harmless eccentric.

He had welcomed me with open arms, fried up half a dozen eggs, told me he liked the *Clarion* but couldn't distribute any because the police ordered him not to bother people with any of his propaganda materials. "But I save them all up," he said proudly.

I wanted to get away, but felt obliged to make a little friendly conversation, so casually asked him how he made a living with his team of horses. His reply electrified me. "I haul in the supplies to that internment camp at Petawawa, where they keep the fascists and our communists," he said. "Do they search you at the gate?" I inquired. "No, everybody knows me, nobody bothers me. They send some of the prisoners to help me unload, but I don't know any of our communists by sight, so I don't talk to anybody." "And do you ever use a helper?" Yes, sometimes, when I have a big load." "Do the guards check on him?" "No, I told you, everybody knows me, they just let my load go through without stopping me at all."

Perfect, I thought. I'd act as his helper and brazenly ride into the concentration camp. When some of our boys came to help unload I'd wink once and then gaze right through them. But I could visualize their jaws dropping and their incredulous looks, though they would have enough presence of mind to pretend they did not know me. Somehow I'd manage to slip someone a stack of party material, including some copies of the *Clarion*.

But first, of course, I must get permission from the centre before I could carry out this little caper. On returning to Ottawa I sent a coded message to Toronto, stressing that the risk would be minimal. Back came orders a few days later: a categorical NO.

My swing around the circuit took me next to Cornwall, where there was an active party club and a staunch and experienced leader. No problems. I stayed overnight and then took a bus to Kingston. I had lived in the Limestone City during the Twenties, so was bound to run into many people who had known me, but it was unlikely that they would be aware of my communist connections. As a test run I dropped into Cotter and Cliff's poolroom, shot a few games of snooker with The Duke and other old cronies. They commented that I'd lost my touch, but showed little interest in me otherwise. "What are you doing for a living, Bert?" "Oh, I'm just another travelling salesman." And that was that. My contact at Queen's University met me for lunch, we discussed the work of his group, and he gave me some money to pass on to the centre.

We had a small industrial club headed by Jim Pople, who had a job at the Kingston Locomotive Works. I had a bit of trouble convincing Jim that I was who I said I was — the District Organizer of the Communist Party. He remembered me as a YMCA boy — a type he held in contempt. To keep in shape, Jim used to work out at the Y gym, and sometimes he would don boxing gloves and go a couple of rounds with me. I had height and reach and skill on my side, but was always careful to keep out of range of Jim's murderous punches. Even when he landed on my arms it hurt.

Jim was a prole through and through. A small man, no more than five feet, he had tremendously developed shoulders and muscles like iron. Fearless as a lion, it was said that once during a strike he had confronted a two-hundred-pound scab, leaped in the air and knocked him cold with a right to the jaw. "You've become a Communist?" he said suspiciously. "But you was one of those store clerks or something!" It took some doing, but finally he accepted me. Years later, when I was Toronto CP organizer, I met Jim Pople again, at an industrial conference called by Leslie Morris and myself. Jim gave me a handshake that left my fingers paralyzed for ten minutes.

Back in my room on Slater Street in Ottawa, I began to publish more anti-war materials. With the help of the committee members a bulletin dealing with civil service grievances came out irregularly; an occasional open letter signed "Jack Canuck;" a news bulletin entitled "Behind the Headlines." In one leaflet we quoted what the *New Republic* (February 10, 1941) had to say about the Defence of Canada Regulations:

Under the Defense of Canada Regulations about 1,500 have been interned. Habeas Corpus does not appear to be applicable in their cases. Only two committees for the whole of Canada, consisting of one man each, can hear appeals. The burden of disproving a case rests on the interned person and proceedings resemble a police investigation, not a trial. As always under such procedure labour leaders find themselves in jail. In Ontario alone 70 trade union leaders are reported to be in custody.

Our underground work proceeded smoothly for a year or more, then one day a couple of RCMP walked into the shoe store and arrested Max, the manager, on the grounds that he was a fascist. The Irony of Fate, in capital letters! For when Max had been managing a shoe store in Toronto some years previously the party had asked him to infiltrate Arcand's fascist group and supply us with information. At a public meeting where Arcand was the main speaker Max could not avoid sitting on the platform, and police had taken a photograph. In their roundup of fascists and communists the RCMP had now got around to the fascist "small fry." To their bewilderment, their search of Max's trunk in a room at the back of the shoe store uncovered a duplicating machine and a score of communist propaganda leaflets, as well as a few copies of the *Clarion*.

All this I learned later, of course. But a girl clerk in the store, on friendly terms with Max, gave me the news of his arrest almost immediately, and said that when they opened the trunk one of the cops had asked Max who was the man in the blue homburg that he had had dinner with the previous Monday. "Let's see, Monday," Max replied, "ah, Monday, that would be my supervisor from Montreal, he visits all the chain stores once a month."

I took a train for Toronto that same day, leaving a member of our executive to carry on the work. Max was interned. When he was released after the character of the war had changed and communists were supporting the war effort, he returned to England, the land of his birth, and ran a shoe store there until his death some years later. I was assigned to work in western Ontario, and lived for the next few months in Hamilton, where a printing press was being installed in the basement of a comrade's home.

On June 22, 1941, however, I happened to be in Windsor when the radio announced that Hitler had attacked the Soviet Union. Working throughout the night with some of the

Windsor comrades, we produced a document which began: "Entrance of the Soviet Union into the war changes the basic character of the conflict. . . . We must demand that the Canadian government send aid to the Soviet Union, which is carrying on a genuine struggle against fascism."

Overseas

We marched along a highway, which had originally been a road to Londinium, built by Roman legions in Nero's time. We were Canadian soldiers, and this twenty-mile route march, in freezing weather, was supposed to "toughen us up" for the upcoming Second Front. As we marched we sang:

> Blow, blow, ye breezes blow
> The kilts fly high and the cocks hang low,
> The biggest balls I ever saw
> Were on our sergeant-major!

And we sang:

> This is number two, and I'm not nearly through
> Roll me over, lay me down and do it again,
> Roll me over, in the clover,
> Roll me over, lay me down and do it again.

And we sang:

> Bless 'em all, bless 'em all,
> As back to the barracks we crawl,
> There'll be no promotion
> This side of the ocean
> So cheer up my lads, bless 'em all.

This song was out of date for us, I reflected. We had crossed the Atlantic and were on the right side of the ocean. Canada lay far behind and Germany lay ahead. My life had certainly taken a 180-degree turn since the day I had volunteered for active service.

I had joined the Canadian Army on January 26, 1942, in Toronto. When I walked into the recruiting office I wasn't sure whether I'd be accepted or arrested. The Communist Party was illegal, a couple of hundred Communists were being held in concentration camps, and the RCMP was still trying to track down Communist organizers who had so far evaded their clutches. People like me.

Not to worry, Ottawa wanted our support. The character of the war had changed since Hitler invaded the Soviet Union on June 22, 1941, and Canadian Communists had become fervent advocates of an anti-Hitler coalition. The government was actually seeking ways to abandon its previous policy and accept us as "allies" for the duration of the war.

So there I was, bedded down that same night in a stall at the Horse Palace in the Exhibition Grounds in Toronto. At some ghastly hour in the morning — it was still black as pitch — we were awoken by the barbaric yowl of bagpipes and the shout of a sadistic sergeant: "Let go your cocks and grab your socks!"

There was a visit to the quartermaster's store to receive clothing and equipment: Anklets, web; Blouses, battle-dress; Bonnet, tam o'shanter; Boots, ankle; Drawers, woollen; Shirts, angola, drab; Trousers, battle-dress; Bag, kit, universal; Brass, cleaning; Brush, button brass; Brush, clothes; Brush, hair; Brush, shaving; Brush, shoe, blacking; Brush, shoe, polishing; Brush, tooth; Comb, hair; Fork, table; Knife, table; Razor, safety, with blade; Spoon N.S., dessert; Bottle, water; Frog, bayonet; Helmet, steel; Tins, mess rect.; Pull-through, single; and much, much more. Including Dog Tags, two, with cord — to be removed from around your neck when you had copped it.

Then came a bad moment when an orderly sergeant looked up from my papers with a gleam in his eye, and said, "Occupation, reporter, eh? So you can type!" I saw the trap right away. The prospect loomed of spending the war years pecking away at a typewriter in this cold, bare office, taking down details of a steady stream of recruits. "No," I said, "unfortunately, I can't type." "But you put down your occupation as reporter." "Yes," I said firmly, "but I never learned to type, I always dictated my stuff." The sarge didn't believe me, but what could he do? I moved along the belt line, away from his little empire.

During the next few days there was some square bashing and attempts to teach us to march. One farm lad couldn't hack it — he was probably good with a gun and might have made a fine sharpshooter. But it was no go — if he couldn't march in step the Canadian Army didn't want him. After three or four days he was given an honourable discharge.

Our Toronto Scottish mob was shipped to North Bay for basic training. Here we soon learned the obligations and privileges of being a soldier (all obligations, no privileges). We were taught how to salute, how to blanco our web and polish our buttons. Once we were taken to a rifle range and allowed to shoot at a target with five real live bullets. But pride of place was given to bayonet drill. An Ol' Bill sergeant, a relic of the Great War, had us charging and plunging our bayonets into a straw dummy, while yelling "Bloody bastards" or "Hitler swine!" If we didn't yell loud enough to satisfy him, he kept us at it till we did. And while teaching us to "fix bayonets" without looking down at our rifles, he blasted our fumbling attempts with the age-old army saw: "You'd soon find the hole if there was hair round it!"

After a month or so, having learned to march, salute, shine our buttons, blanco our web, and make a bayonet charge, we moved on to Trois-Rivières, Quebec, to become "trained soldiers" ready to cross the ocean and tackle the *herrenvolk.*

I was thirty-three years old (most of the lads were in their early twenties) and not too enthusiastic about the various obstacle courses devised by a gung-ho type of college lad who was our lieutenant. The barracks were the local race-track buildings. One variant of training was to gallop around a six-furlong track twice, carrying a section of a machine gun, and at each quarter-pole crawl through a twenty-foot-long piece of concrete pipe lying on the ground. My gambit, which worked quite well initially, was to crawl into the pipe last, lie doggo and wait till the lads came round the track the second time, when I would emerge at the head of the pack and canter to the finishing post in comparatively good shape. Eventually, of course, I was caught and sentenced to kitchen duty.

This sprig of a lieutenant came up with another bright idea. As part of one obstacle course we climbed a wall and dropped into a sandpit some fifteen feet below. Ergo, why not a drop of twenty-five feet? No sooner said than done — and no sooner done than one soldier broke an ankle and several others suffered various injuries. Luckily, the company doctor put an end to this caper.

The Toronto Scottish, in this period, was strictly a machine-gun regiment (later it incorporated 4.2-inch mortars). I'm a slow learner when it comes to anything mechanical, and we had to learn not only how to take apart and reassemble the seemingly innumerable parts of a machine-gun lock, but also how to do it blindfolded.

Just about the time I had become a "trained soldier" and was due to join an overseas draft, I suffered a recurrence of an old back trouble. It had started when I slipped and wrenched my back while firing a boiler with logs at the Conroyal Mine in Kirkland Lake in 1928. In the intervening years it had bothered me off and on. Now I was shipped to a military hospital at Ste. Anne de Beaupré (if memory serves me right) and one doctor advised an operation to remove a disc, another suggested yanking my tonsils out. The latter view prevailed, and when I returned to camp minus tonsils, my draft had gone.

I began to benefit from going-away leaves. On the first one my friends in Toronto treated me handsomely, arranged farewell parties, plied me with liquor and food. On my second leave they were still warm and friendly, arranged a party, gave me food and drink. On my third goodbye tour I was received skeptically, and asked, "When the hell are you going overseas?"

During the period of my back trouble my medical category had fluctuated from A1 to D to A to C. Before I could cross the Atlantic it had to be upgraded. I appeared before a French-Canadian doctor. He looked at me quizzically and said, "One grade lower and you can get your discharge. Do you really want to go overseas?" "Yes," I said. Without examining me, he changed my category to A.

At the time there was quite a discussion among Communists about the role we should play in the army. Some of us were strong advocates of getting to the front and killing as many Nazis as possible. Others thought we should strive to become officers or senior NCO's, remain in Canada and concentrate on educational work in preparing for an anticipated upsurge in left-wing activities in the postwar period. The vast majority of the hundreds of Communists who joined the army went overseas. Many of them were experienced soldiers who had fought fascism in Spain during the civil war. One such was Mike Olynyk, a Ukrainian-Canadian who had been promoted to the rank of captain in a Mackenzie-Papineau Battalion machine-gun group. But if you think that the Canadian Army appreciated acquiring this battle-tested, competent officer, you're wrong. The Toronto Scottish Regiment made him a batman, and Mike spent the war shining his officer's boots and buttons.

Our replacement group crossed the North Atlantic at the beginning of 1943 aboard the former luxury liner *Empress of Japan*, which, however, had been renamed. It was a rough trip; we had no convoy, the ship travelled at top speed and zigzagged every ten minutes or so, the idea being — we were told — that enemy subs wouldn't have time to line us up as a sitting duck. One night, during a violent storm, half a dozen of us were nabbed for "ack-ack" duty topside. We sat in a round gun emplacement booth awash with a foot of water. The ack-ack gun had its barrel wrapped in canvas. There were no shells, and in any case none of us had the faintest idea how to operate the weapon. A typical army SNAFU (Situation Normal, All Fucked Up).

We sailed up the Clyde and disembarked at Greenock (or was it Gourock?), where a young English officer took us in tow. He looked us over and said, "I've never handled any of you Canadians but I'm told you're a rough bunch. Now, I can put you under guard in barracks until we leave for Aldershot by train tomorrow morning. That seems to me the most sensible thing to do. On the other hand, if you blokes will give me your word of honour that you'll all be back in barracks by 6 a.m. I could let you have a free night on the town."

An hour later we were seated among the local pubs, and an old Scot, spotting my Glengarry cap, was asking me about my Scottish background. Suddenly he said, "How do you like the English?" This was a tricky question. In any case, I hadn't met any English as yet, with the exception of the officer who had been sent to convoy us south. I decided that a diplomatic answer was called for. "Very much," I replied. The Scotsman's face did not register joy. After a moment's silence, he spoke again: "And how do you like the Scots?" I had already been clued in. "The Scots?" I said, "why the Scots are my people!" "Aye, laddie, have another drink!" More natives joined us, we drank tankards of wartime beer, everyone got a bit fou [drunk], a man and his wife took me home with them: "Don't worry, laddie, ye'll no have to sleep in those cold barracks, and we'll get ye up in plenty of time."

Every one of our group of Tor-Scots turned up before 6 a.m., as promised.

Aldershot. Wellington Barracks, unchanged since the Battle of Waterloo. A drafty barn of a place, double-decker bunks, a tiny fireplace at each end, with an allowance of one scuttleful of coal a night. Our initial turnout on the parade grounds. It was raining indecisively. We were a miserable-looking bunch. Up comes a sergeant. "Can any of you men handle a motorcycle?" Six volunteers step forward. "Good. Can any of you drive a lorry?" Four more eager beavers advance. "Good. Corporal, march these men to the mess hall for kitchen duty." So we learned the first rule in the army — Never volunteer for ANYthing.

Rule Number Two: If it moves salute it — if it doesn't move, paint it.

There were several thousand replacements in Aldershot, waiting to be sent up to their regiments. Meanwhile we had to be kept occupied. That meant square bashing, route marches, lectures, and other chickenshit activities.

Some mornings we'd have a standard lecture on "The Rifle" by a junior officer from another outfit, and in the afternoon a repeat of the same lecture by a second officer.

The mess served the usual army garbage and the tea shops in town were crammed to the doors with hungry soldiers trying to latch onto a bun and cuppa. I found one spot where it was possible to have a bath for thruppence. Trouble was, the two inches of water allowed in the tub had to be heated in the treacherous-looking contraption called a geyser, whose various knobs and operating instructions would have baffled an engineer. There were sinister bubblings and groans and gurglings while the beast performed its duties. It seemed to me to be always on the point of exploding, and I was much more afraid of it than I ever became of the Nazis.

One day I was caught and put on kitchen duty, faced with a mountain of greasy pots and pans. I had been toiling away for a couple of hours, making no visible progress against the incoming stream of pots, when I heard someone laughing and turned to see Johnny Nevin, in the uniform of an RCAF officer, standing in the doorway. "Ho, ho, ho, *mein* commissar!" said Johnny.

"Listen, you bastard," I said, "If you have any influence get me out of here." "I have already," he replied. "I saw the Colonel and told him we were cousins, and wangled a weekend pass to London for you. So go put on a clean uniform, you filthy pig, and let us away to the Big Smoke."

Johnny had been a member of the Young Communist League in Ottawa when I took over the job of Communist Party area organizer (the CPC was then illegal) following the arrest, trial, and sentencing of Harry Binder to Kingston Penitentiary in the spring of 1940. Johnny was a civil servant, and worked in a filing department, which brought him into daily contact with John Leopold, alias Jack Esselwein, the RCMP agent and stool pigeon who had testified against Tim Buck and other Communist leaders in the 1931 section 98 trial designed to "wipe out communism in Canada." Leopold was now an inspector in the anti-Red section, and would call on Johnny when he wanted a dossier on some Communist or left-winger. Johnny would pass on the information to me and I would put it in the pipeline to Toronto, where presumably it might be of some use, though I never knew, as there was no feedback.

So here was Johnny, RCAF officer, and Private Whyte, B77406, off for a weekend in London. It wasn't the drill for officers and men to mix, but we avoided the haunts of the former, put up in a civilian house, drank draft beer in obscure pubs, and rehashed old times.

"You know," Johnny reminisced, "there was one occasion when I thought Leopold had me nailed. He came into the office, drunk as usual, leaned over my desk and said, 'Johnny, you know I can SMELL a Communist.' My heart was in my mouth for a minute, but all he wanted was a file on someone from Montreal who was supposed to be planning a trip to New York."

Back in Aldershot, not long after that pleasant weekend, I got word that Johnny had been killed on his first mission. I can't even remember if he was a pilot, or a navigator, or gunner, or what.

And I might as well mention here that Harry Binder, on his release from Kingston Penitentiary, joined the army (Regina Rifles), was wounded twice in France, returned to the fighting lines, and survived the war. Some years later he had a sharp political disagreement with the Communist Party and resigned from its ranks.

The day finally came when we were shipped out to join our regiment, which was stationed in a forest on the estate of an English lord. The trees were alive with squirrels, so tame they would climb up your clothes and eat out of your hand. No doubt they had us pegged as harmless nuts.

From our first night we had a lot of trouble with field mice who preferred our Nissen hut to their natural habitat. They had a craving for Buckingham cigarettes, and Tiny Welsh, a 250-pounder who smoked this brand, was the chief sufferer. As soon as lights were out the busy little mice would burrow into his kitbag and chew up two or three decks of smokes. We devised a trap—a tin can with a hole in the top and some cheese and a couple of Buckingham cigarettes for bait — but it didn't work. Finally we had to borrow the quartermaster's cat, who cleaned up the joint in no time.

As we were a Toronto regiment, it was inevitable that the two streets in our forest camp were named Yonge and Bloor. Excitement consisted in a two-mile trek to the nearest village for tea and a muffin, or a visit to the Iron Lung, a forlorn little dance hall with a corrugated iron roof. Most nights we stayed in camp and watched old movies. One night I was going to a show in the mess hall with Ken Skarlett. I'd seen the picture before — *Orchestra Wives* with Glenn Miller and band. "Hurry up or we'll miss the beginning," said Skarlett, prodding me along. "I've seen it before," I said, "So have I," Skarlett admitted. "When?" I asked. "Last night."

Another night we were sitting on our bunks in the hut, some lads reading comic books, others writing letters.

"Jack the Ripper" broke wind loudly. The usual army comments followed:

"Shot himself."

"If he's not careful, he'll shit himself."

"It's a poor arse that never rejoices."

"I'd sure hate to do his laundry."

"It's the beer speaking."

To keep up morale on the home front, we were encouraged to write to wives and sweethearts at least once a week. On the theory that this task might overtax our brains, the army gave us specific advice on what to say in each missive:

A. — The cheerful start. Thanks for gifts.

B. — News. A word about your pals (no gossip). Wise-cracks and jokes (sterilized). Remarks on news from home.

C. — Requests. Information wanted of family. What the next parcel might contain.

D. — Plans, hopes and ambitions. Concerning your duties and rank.

E. — The ending, some praise for someone. A reference to a lovely memory. Never end without a "God bless you."

Give Cheer — Tell the Truth — Keep It Clean
Watch Security!

Even if one followed these instructions, the censor was liable to chop out anything even remotely interesting. The ideal soldier's letter, we discovered, went something like this: "Left where we were and arrived where we are after a trip which was just about as anticipated. The weather here is quite a bit different from where we were, but just about what we expected it would be here. Now I must close before I give away any military secrets."

I spent my leaves in London. Many times I vowed I'd try other cities highly recommended by my mates, but I never did. One chap who went to Manchester came back all aglow: "I made a date with a volunteer YMCA worker the first night," he said. "She took me home to meet her parents and they invited me to stay the night. 'Helen will knock you up in the morning before she goes to work,' her mother told me. I wasn't quite sure what this meant, but it sounded interesting. Well, at 7 a.m. Helen popped into my room and said, 'I'm off now but mother will bring your tea soon.' I protested feebly but gave in, and sure enough, in a few minutes mother came in with bacon and one egg, toast, tea and four cigarettes and a box of matches on a tray. 'Now soldier,' she said, 'I want you to consider this your home while you're in Manchester, so after breakfast go and pick up your things at the Y and move over here.' So I did, and had a real good go for the next few days, and you don't have to guess where I'm intending to spend my next leave."

Nevertheless, I continued to spend all my leaves in London, staying with a Scottish lass who had a room in a house just off Baker Street. Only Sherlock Holmes could have found it in the blackout. "Eat carrots to develop your night sight" advised the food ads. I ate plenty of carrots and any other veg I could get (except the ubiquitous Brussels sprouts) but still walked into the corner of a building one Cimmerian night and gashed my forehead.

Just when we were all becoming a bit squirrelly, regimental orders came through to move to Brighton, on the south coast. This famous old watering hole received us with open arms. Never had we had it so good. Pubs, girls, entertainment. Billeted in an evacuated house; no furniture, of course, but cozy and warm. Demi-Paradise.

It couldn't last. Army regulations don't allow for happiness. In the fall of 1943 Lt.-Col. Ernest George Johnson took over command of the Tor-Scots. "Black Mac" had been playing soldier for many years. Born and educated in Toronto, he was associated with the Canadian Machine Gun Corps as a young man. The Corps later amalgamated with the Toronto Scottish Regiment, in which Johnson held the rank of lieutenant. Mobilized at the beginning of the war, he went overseas with the Tor-Scots as a captain, arriving in England December 17, 1939. In the fall of 1943 he was promoted to command the regiment.

Black Mac went by the manual. He firmly believed in spit and polish, square bashing, long route marches, unarmed combat, arduous training schemes — in short, in all the idiotic system of army life which strives to exclude every comfort and turn human beings into robots. So we polished our brass, blancoed our web, rose at ungodly hours for inspections by lantern-light, marched like the Duke of Marlborough's unhappy sods, dug slit trenches and filled them up again, and slept many a night on the cold moors.

To get ahead of my story a bit, it came as something of a relief when we went to France under Black Mac's command in July 1944. We continued under his leadership until VE Day, when he was appointed in command of the Cameron Highlanders of Ottawa, as part of the occupation force in Germany. But soon he suffered two serious injuries and was invalided home in November 1945. The complications led to his death in Christie Street Hospital, Toronto, at the early age of thirty-seven.

It is impossible to write about the many months we were stationed in Brighton without mentioning two English families, the Greens and Tracys. Just how I first met them has long slipped my memory. The Green family consisted of Harry, a man of around sixty, a fitter in a war plant; Clare ("Mom"), his wife; Clare's sister Alice, a nurse, and Muriel, the daughter, a war bride whose husband was a prisoner of war in Germany. The Greens' house became a home away from home for many Canadians: Dick Steele and Reuben Gorodetsky (killed in France), Joe Levitt, Louis Binder, Wally

Dent, Mike Olynyk, and many others — including a couple of Yanks and a stray Aussie.

"If no one is home, you'll find the door key under the porch mat," said Mom Green the first time I met her. "And you can light the fireplace and make yourself a nice cup of tea — I mean coffee, I know you Canadians like coffee." Tea, of course, was rationed. A typical evening at the Greens, Harry isn't there, he's on night shift. Mom is making tea, coffee, and toast. Alice is playing solitaire. Muriel has just washed her blonde hair and is sitting on a cushion on the floor, while Wally Dent, sprawled in an easy chair, is combing it for her. Rosa Burson, a friend of the family who drives a milk route, is on the couch beside me, telling me about her milk-wagon horse, which during the recent cold spell insisted on descending a steep street by sitting on its rump and sliding down. Rosa's husband, Frank, on a leave from the RAF, is busily modelling a head out of plasticine. Dick Steele and Joe Levitt, near the fireplace, are arguing politics. After our snack we put on some dance music and clear back the chairs — but before that Rosa has managed once again to perform her famous trick, squirm out of her corset ("roll-on") without any of us noticing the intricate operation. The evening ends rather early — all of us except Frank have to scurry back to barracks.

In the false perspective of memory, I've probably run several nights together. Sometimes a few of us would sally forth to the nearest pub and drink gin or Scotch or beer till closing time. One afternoon "Ruby" Gorodetsky and I took Muriel and Rosa to a matinee, an oldie, *The Garden of Allah*, with Charles Boyer and Marlene Dietrich. (A decade later, making another film, Dietrich asked her cameraman why he couldn't make her look as lovely as he had in *The Garden of Allah*. The cameraman diplomatically replied, "Ah, well, you see, I was ten years younger then.") After the film we had tea in a little waterfront cafe, then a few drinks in a pub, and back to the Greens and shared Muriel's dinner with her at 11 p.m. (roast potatoes, mutton bones, cabbage, bread and butter, tea).

Or take the Tracys, Eddie and Gwen, and their little son, Ian. Ed and I had much in common, for at one time he was a taxi driver in New York, and had worked in Cleveland, Calgary, Vancouver, and other cities that I was familiar with. Ed and Gwen opened their door to many Canadians. I well remember a dinner at their place on Boxing Day, 1943. On Christmas Day I was on guard duty. At 2 p.m. a relief took over and our detail was driven to the Brighton dog-racing track, where we had dinner in the grandstand restaurant. For this one day of the year our officers waited on us, served us soup bowls filled with turkey, ham, dressing, peas, and roast potatoes. They also kept the beer flowing. But as soon as we had eaten our fill we had to return to guard duty.

The Tracys had invited Dick Steele, Wally Dent, and me to dinner the following day. By some miracle they had obtained a small turkey (rationing was strict in England). We polished off the turkey and finished with a tart — the kind you eat. But it wasn't the food that was the main attraction, it was the genuine friendliness of these English people to us "colonials" far from home.

After the feast we visited some friends of the Tracys who lived on the same street, and Dick played a disc his wife had recorded with their two-year-old twins back in Toronto. Esther was trying to get them to say "hello" to daddy. Finally one whispers, "Hello, Daddy." And Esther tells him: "Oh, you've got to speak louder than that so daddy can hear you. He's a long way off." The twins also attempted, with indifferent success, to sing, "I've Got Sixpence."

Aside from the Greens and Tracys, I met other English folks in Brighton, and vaguely remember going to a couple of parties and learning several quaint parlour games, one called "Murder," which is too complicated to explain, but requires the run of a house, and is played in the dark most of the time. A sort of adult version of Post Office. (Question: Do infants have more fun in infancy than adults do in adultery?)

Brighton was on the Jerries' milk run and they came over two or three times a week to drop an egg or two on the way to London. Occasionally we'd see a dogfight, but they were mainly nuisance raids. One of my weekend leaves in London I was belting back a few in a Baker Street pub when the air warning sounded. There was an Anderson shelter across the road but none of the civilians made a move from the bar, so how could I, a brave fighting man? One old gal took a deep swallow of her Guinness and remarked, "Old Nasty's at it again!" Soon the all clear sounded.

About this time the British 4.2-inch mortar made its appearance, and the Toronto Scottish decided to form a mortar company. The heavy mortar was manned by a crew of four, could throw a 20-pound bomb a distance of 4,000 yards, had a peak trajectory of 4,000 feet, a flight time of 30 seconds, and a sustained rate of fire of 10 bombs a minute. The 4.2 mortar had done good work in Sicily, and I had a hunch that it would play as important a role in our war as the machine gun played in the First World War. So I signed up for a mortar course and was shipped off somewhere — I can't remember just where — for a few weeks of intensive training.

As usual, I was a slow learner, but eventually got the hang of things, and finished the course at the top, or near the top, of the class. This earned me my second hook when I got back to the regiment, and a suggestion from my major that

I might consider returning to Canada and taking a whack at an officers' training course. "No thanks," I said, "I don't want to miss the big show, and in any case you are forgetting that I'm a dyed-in-the-wool Red." "I don't give a damn if you're red, green, or purple," said the major.

But my captain cared. He definitely didn't want me as one of his corporals, and in a short off-the-record "man-to-man" talk he told me so. "Thanks for being so frank," I said, "and if I had my way I wouldn't choose you to be my captain." Later in France, we both changed our opinions and for the rest of the war got along just fine.

As the months passed and we drew nearer and nearer to the Second Front our training schemes became longer and tougher. On one exercise we went north almost to the Scottish border. The weather was hellish, rain and sometimes snow. We usually slept in slit trenches, shivering in our blankets, but at Doncaster we bedded down in horse stalls at the race track. It was pouring rain and we were dog-tired, but a few of us sneaked out and headed for the nearest pub. As we entered the barmaid shouted at me, "Put wood-in-th'ole, laddie!" I had no idea what she meant, even when she repeated it a couple of times, until someone translated: she was telling me to put the wood in the hole, that is, to close the door behind me.

I chatted up a coal miner's daughter and she turned out to be Redder than Red. "You blokes should go Bolshie when the war is over," she said, "and get rid of Churchill and all that lot." I didn't express my political convictions, so she spent the next half-hour convincing me that revolution was definitely on the postwar agenda. Her father had been injured in the mines and was on pension; grandfather, aged seventy-one, was still working. Her hatred of capitalism was not based on theory, but on the life of the miners of Doncaster.

Back in Brighton, we continued our training on the South Downs, and inspections became more frequent (first a brigadier, then a general, then Colonel James Ralston, Canada's Minister of National Defence). Ralston had been in Sicily and Italy to see the Canadian First Division in action. He began his speech to us in the usual manner . . . people at home proud of you . . . you stood on guard at a difficult period . . . the time is not far distant when . . . know you will accomplish great things . . . Canada looks to you . . .

We were all familiar with this bullshit and barely listened, but our ears pricked up when Ralston finally came to the meat in the sandwich. He spoke of the fluid type of warfare today, and hinted that because of this we Canucks might not be able to fight together as an army but in any case he knew we would do our best whether fighting together or in brigades or divisions attached to other armies. The penny dropped. Ralston was obviously quite willing to hand us over to General Montgomery to be used as shock troops . . . with inevitable heavy casualties.

In barracks that night, thinking over the speech of this jargon-wallah, with its ominous implications, I decided I was definitely underwhelmed. In the event, we did fight together as an army.

Finally General Bernard Montgomery turned up one day to look us over. At the beginning of the war he had been an obscure regular army officer. After Dunkirk he took over command of South-Eastern Command in England, responsible for the defence of the invasion coast. His Spartan regime, with its innumerable forced route marches and passion for dawn physical training, did not endear him to the Canadians under him.

When Monty landed in Africa to take over command of the Eighth Army, the famous British "Desert Rats," he made a chameleon-like change within a matter of days in his methods and manner, even in his dress. The meticulous, fastidious little martinet, the eastern disciplinarian, began wearing corduroy slacks and sweater, suede desert boots and a handkerchief around his neck. The troops had taken quite a beating at the hands of Rommel and the Chief of Staff explained to the new commander that they were planning a withdrawal. "Throw away your plans, there will be no withdrawal", said Monty. "From now on we are going to win victories. We'll let Rommel attack, we'll hold our ground, then we'll begin chasing him." And so it happened. El Alamein, the turning point of the war in Africa, and the beginning of the Monty legend.

We were drawn up in squares, regiment after regiment of the Canadian Second Division. Monty arrived in a jeep, stopped in the centre of the square, waved his arms in a "gather around me" motion, and the moment we broke ranks he had won us. Cocky, tough-looking bastard, we thought.

His speech to us was one that he used over and over again, I learned later. It was simple to the point of absurdity — but it worked. "I came to have a good look at you," he began. "And I want you to have a good look at me. Soon we'll be winning victories together, we'll be chasing the enemy until we put him into the sea. Yes, we'll have a grand time. You must have full confidence in me, just as I have in you. Just remember that we will never lose a battle. It is quite certain that we will win ..." A bit more, along the same line, but somehow his confidence carried us all along with him. We knew that we would win. How could Monty lose?

With so little to do on nights when I was in charge of the guard detail, I found plenty of time to write letters home — to my wife Rita, to numerous friends and to several people who had begun corresponding with me as a result of stories

I had published in the *Tribune*. Rita sent food parcels regularly, the contents of which I shared with my mortar crew and the Greens and Tracys.

Hearing that Joe Turnbull, one of the founders of the Canadian Seamen's Union and a Mackenzie-Papineau Battalion veteran, was somewhere in Italy, a corporal in tanks, I fired off a letter to him on the off-chance that it might reach him. Eventually I received a reply.

"Your letter had a bit of a job finding me," Joe wrote. "It was a surprise, though I fully expected you to be in the army. We have two other guys in my regiment who fought in Spain. One is a New Yorker, who is against everyone and everything in the world. Can find no excuse for existence, except that he likes to eat. The other chap, strange to say, is a Canadian who did his little bit for Franco. He didn't know what it was all about and didn't care. I used to kid him about it, but he readily confesses the error of his ways and says all he wants to do is go home, that he has had enough.

"Well, Bert, this makes six years of army life for me, with what you might call an extended leave in Canada between wars. My 30th year is just around the corner, and I'm a married man now. So far I've remained in good health. I did have a little stay in hospital when my tank hit a high tension wire. Had third degree burns on the right hand which resulted in a skin grafting job. It turned out fairly good.

"The scrap here has not been as tough as it was in Spain. Probably because we have the stuff with which to fight. It is no longer a case of just lie there and take it and hope to hell for a miracle, while you counted your remaining five rounds of ammunition. The same people who gave it to us are getting it back — and with all the accumulated interest. I find a personal satisfaction in it, and I guess the rest of the old International Brigade do as well.

"So Fergie (Dewar Ferguson) is still plugging away for the seamen. He has come a long way since that day we walked off the *Chippewa* together. I'm not surprised to find that Pat (Pat Sullivan) is in the Trades and Labor Congress leadership. Pat always did make out well for himself.

"Give my regards to our mutual friends when you write home. Don't forget to keep the old head down in the days to come: it is always hard to get a new one. Good luck Bert and all the best."

I also had a note from Lieut. Jimmy Garfinkle in Italy. "Haven't done much but have had to duck a bit," he wrote. "If you come this way I could use an English-Italian dictionary. Also a portable slit trench.... If you want any news of what Occupied Italy thinks — well, some are for the King and others paint hammer and sickles all over the place. All mixed up, except naturally, all the fascists 'vanished' overnight."

Came the day when all leaves were cancelled and our regiment shifted from Brighton to Elvington, a small coal-mining village near Dover. We lived in tents in a big field, began waterproofing our carriers, went on route marches. The first evening I was free I headed for the Miners' Club in the village. Where there are miners, I reasoned, there must be some communists. It turned out there were thirty-two. That was how I came to meet the Ashtons and Cranes.

Bernard Ashton was the club treasurer. His wife Alice was a lovely person. While on a twenty-four-hour pass (good only for the local area), I stayed there overnight. It was wonderful to lie between sheets again and remain in bed until noon. Had fish and mashed potatoes and custard for dinner, then went to the club with Bernard for a pint and a game of billiards. The Ashtons had two sons, the elder in the merchant navy, the young lad (sixteen) still at home. When

Mike Olynyk's wife, Olive, would slip down from London for a weekend she would stay with the Ashtons or Cranes.

The Cranes were nice people, if slightly on the eccentric side. Jack was a coal miner. Their home was a madhouse. They had eighteen children, not all at home, of course. And also a collection of animals — a monkey from the Gold Coast, brought home by a sailor son; a racing greyhound, trained by a teenage son; and a large cat. The monkey loved chewing gum; he would skillfully unwrap it, chew it until the taste was gone, then spit it out. Sometimes he would jump on the greyhound's back and there would be a real rumpus until they were separated.

I wrote in my diary at the time:

"Took another chap around to the Cranes last night. Had a whale of a time. Old Mrs. Crane, bare-footed, puffed away on her clay pipe and played a wheezy organ: The Old Rugged Cross, Onward Christian Soldiers, Home on the Range, The Red Flag, Washed in the Blood of the Lamb, etc. Jack sawed away on his violin. We all sang, the monkey and the greyhound and the cat kept running around the room, and a couple of the smallest children crawled about. Mrs. Crane offered to do my washing . . . I gave her some pipe tobacco and promised to get her a new clay pipe."

All the miners were a grand bunch of chaps. For thruppence I was made a "temporary" member of the club and had the use of its facilities.

One day we started out on a scheme, which we knew was the real thing. Buzz-bombs were landing in London as we passed through in the dark of night. Sometime before dawn we boarded a ship (at Tilbury?) and set off for France.

ℓℓℓℓℓℓ

June 6, 1944. Invasion of Normandy. The greatest amphibious operation in history: 1,000 planes and gliders dropped paratroops; 1,000 RAF and 1,400 US bombers attacked installations. Assault troops landed on beaches along the Carentan–Bayeux–Caen line, the US on the west, British-Canadian on the east. Total Allied strength available, 2,875,000, including 14 British divisions, 3 Canadian, 20 US, 1 French, 1 Polish. Also available 5,000 fighter planes, 3,450 heavy bombers, 1,600 light and medium bombers, 2,300 transport aircraft, 2,500 gliders, 835 L.C.T. (Landing Craft Tanks), etc., etc. General Eisenhower was Supreme Commander of Allied Expeditionary Forces; General Montgomery was Commander of Allied Assault Troops. Within a week a beachhead 60 miles long and 10 miles deep was established. Germans had available 65 divisions, including reserves extending back to Germany. Field Marshal Günther von Kluge was the German Commander in France.

Our Second Canadian Division didn't go in with the first wave. That honour went to the Third Division. The Second landed on the narrow beachhead early in July.

This isn't a story of the Canadian Army. It's just my story. And as any soldier knows, as far as he's concerned the war centres around the spot he's in. For a couple of weeks in July my war took place in a quarry, where we had set up our mortars. Unfortunately a German observation post in a village less than a mile away could look right into our position and shell us whenever we moved out of our holes burrowed into the sides of the quarry. Our planes dominated the skies all day, but went home to England at night. Then slow German observation aircraft would take over, drop flares and anti-personnel bombs. It was nerve-wracking.

We quickly became acquainted with the German 88 mm. guns, deadly weapons which gave you only half a second to duck, and his Nebelwerfer mortars, which we called "Moaning Minnies" because the bombs screamed like banshees on the way down (but they gave you plenty of time to hit your hole). There was daily action, and we suffered several casualties. Lieutenant Lea was killed by shrapnel during a shoot. A shell destroyed my mortar and two of the lads were wounded and had to be evacuated. Along with a new mortar I acquired a couple of replacements, fresh from Canada. This didn't make me very happy, but how wrong I was! We remained together as a crew almost up to VE Day.

General Montgomery's strategy was to mount a series of heavy and costly British and Canadian attacks to draw to our front all the German reserves, including most of their Panzer divisions, in order to open the way for the Americans under General Patton to make an end run when all the Jerry reserves had been brought into action against us. Colonel Dick Malone, in *Missing from the Record* [Toronto: Collins, 1946], wrote:

> The road junctions to the south of Caen passing through Falaise and Argentan were the keys to the entire German communications system for Normandy. To shield these arteries the Germans had strengthened their defenses in the Caen area to an unbelievable degree.
>
> Some idea of the German strength may be gained from the fact that during this period the Germans threw in against the Canadians and British four Panzer Divisions, five S.S. Divisions, the 1st (Adolph Hitler), 12th, 21st, 9th and 10th, also the 16th German Air Force Division, the 89th Division rushed from Norway, and the 711th, 346th and 272nd Infantry Divisions ...
>
> The casualties were staggering for such units as

the Calgarys, Maisonneuves and H.L.I.s. Except for a bare handful of men the Black Watch Highlanders were completely wiped out by the concentrated German fire.

Once the break out began to take shape from the American sector, the Germans tried desperately to disengage their armour from the Caen-Falaise sector.... The air force was waiting for just such an attempt at moving the German panzers.... The armour was anni-hilated by the R.A.F.

We knew nothing of all these strategic moves at the time. We only knew that after we'd been plastered for days on end, the way was now open for an attack on Falaise. We crashed through the German defence lines and were on our way. Not all was clear sailing, however; one day we were bombed by British planes, and the next day by the Americans. This SNAFU was caused by drifting smoke lines, which had been laid down to guide the bombers to German positions.

Our Second Canadian Division took Falaise. The Trun Gap was closed. Marshal von Kluge's Army of more than 100,000 was completely wiped out. The remnants that tried to escape through a bottleneck we had left open fell prey to our air force, which had a field day.

When the fighting was over, except for the occasional brave Jerry sniper hiding in a building, I went poking around Falaise with one of my crew. Looking into a cellar I saw a German sitting with his back to the wall and pointing a rifle at me. I gave him a burst from a Sten gun—and then discov-ered I had been pumping bullets into a corpse. He had died from shrapnel wounds, still clinging to his weapon.

After the destruction of the German Seventh Army the remaining Jerry forces were in full retreat. We took off in pursuit, meeting little resistance. Several small groups of the enemy surrendered, some perhaps influenced by the "Safe Conduct" leaflets which our planes dropped on them. "The German soldier who carries this safe-conduct is using it as a sign of his genuine wish to give himself up," the leaflet said. "He is to be disarmed, to be well looked after, to receive food and medical attention as required, and is to be removed from the danger zone as soon as possible."

One morning, during the advance, we passed through a couple of villages where the people gave us a particularly enthusiastic welcome, rushing up with bottles of wine, pitchers of milk, and platters of food. "Les Canadiens sont ici! Le Boche — KAPUT!" they cried. We smiled modestly, like carbon copies of Errol Flynn after cleaning up the mess in Burma single-handed, and showered the grateful peasants with boiled English sweets, guaranteed to give their children caries. Our lieutenant got out his map, studied it a moment, and beckoned an ancient, bearded villager to his side. The ensuing conversation went something like this:

"The village of So-and-So, oui?"

"Non, monsieur."

"You must be mistaken, dans l'erreur. My map, mon carte, says this is village So-and-So."

"Non, monsieur, this village Such-and-Such. I have live here all my life!"

The lieutenant paled, looked at his map again, found the village of Such-and-Such, murmured hoarsely, "My God, we're two miles behind the German lines!"

The French civvies had taken us for the advance guard of our army. We had paid no attention to a few Jerries we had passed on our triumphal joyride, thinking they were waiting to surrender. The Germans presumably had figured we were too strong for their reduced forces to tackle.

We wheeled our carriers around and began a hasty

retreat. The French peasants continued to cheer and wave, though they began to look a little puzzled as we roared past in the direction from which we had originally come. Our luck was in. We made it back to our lines without mishap. By the following day the disorganized Germans had somehow organized themselves, had dug in and begun shelling us. We were going into action under fire, setting up our mortars behind a high, two-foot-thick cement wall in the courtyard of a school area. Moaning Minnies and 88 shells were coming over, often landing uncomfortably close. Suddenly an 88 was on top of us, and I dived for a flowerbed next to the wall. There was a hell of a bang and the wall heaved up and came down on top of me. My tin hat was knocked over my face and a flat section of wall slowly pushed me deeper and deeper into the soft earth. Tons of stuff pressed me down, down — and then I knew I was still alive in the blackness, breathing the air in my helmet.

Far away I heard someone shout, "Whitey's got it! A direct hit! Come and help dig him out!" So I tried to yell for help, then realized I was wasting air I might need, and began to do a Houdini bit, breathing quietly and holding each breath as long as possible. The boys were frantically clawing away at the hunks of wall and yelling to each other, "Get under this corner, all together now, heave! Do you think he's alive? Christ, it was a direct hit. Hey, Whitey, can you hear us? Which end is your head?"

"Yes! My head! Here!" I shouted.

Well, not to bore you, in about ten minutes they had me out. Then another shell landed in the back of the yard, and several of the boys got plinked lightly with bits of shrapnel. Harry Hirschfeld, one of my mortar crew, was injured a little more severely and had to spend a month in hospital before rejoining us. As for myself, I didn't even have a scratch.

"Looks as though I'm indestructible," I wrote to my wife. "If Jerry couldn't get me yesterday he never will. You can expect me home after the war is won."

The man most responsible for saving my life was Dave Nichol, one of the green replacements who came up around Caen, after two members of our original crew were wounded. Nick certainly didn't look much like a Hollywood-type hero, square-jawed, stiff upper lip, clipped sentences. He had not much chin at all, and an inclination to giggle. But from his first day in action he showed himself quick, resourceful, cool under fire. He was the one who shouted, "Whitey's got it — come and dig him out!" which the boys did, while under fire. Dave was married, had worked in a munitions plant in Toronto, but when he was shipped overseas his wife and three-year-old son went to live with her parents in High River, Alberta.

The other replacement, Harry Hirschfeld, twenty-two, also turned out to A-OK. His father, a miner in Timmins, had died of silicosis. The family, a large one, moved to Orillia and was having a hard time getting on. Harry, a good son, was sending most of his meagre army pay home.

To call a soldier courageous doesn't mean that he never shivers with fear. Courage is a sometime thing. All across France and Belgium and Holland I had been expecting a shell or bullet with my number on it. That boastful note to my wife after surviving an 88 hit was simply camouflage.

"Your job is not to die for your country, but to make the enemy die for his," we had been told time and again. But I never believed I was indestructible. *Dulce bellum inexpertis*, commented Erasmus. War is sweet to those who do not fight. I believe, like the philosophers of Central Asia, that death strikes its blows as a blind she-camel kicks — one man is struck, and he breathes no more; another dodges, and lives till old age.

Piles of dead, friends and foes, lay behind us as we fought our way from Normandy to Germany. All these months we mentally accepted the fact that the odds were against living. But when the Nazis were forced back into their homeland, when the war was almost won, when our Soviet allies were hammering at the gates of Berlin — then, for the first time, we began to believe that, having beaten the odds thus far, we might reasonably hope to come out of the war alive.

It was during those last few weeks of World War II that I began to feel fear, in my bowels — the fear that with Germany's inevitable surrender only a matter of days or hours, somewhere a Jerry gunner would fire a last shell blindly and I would be the unlucky target. To be killed by the last shot in the war — my mortar crew often talked about it. For in any war, someone has to be the last soldier to die. The combat soldier who says he never felt fear is a monster or a liar. We all felt fear, but managed to grow a callus over it and do our jobs as fighters against fascism, as killers of Nazis.

Back to Normandy. We kept advancing on the left flank, and by the end of August had crossed the Seine, taken Rouen, and were within a few miles of Dieppe, where two years before more than 3,350 Canadians had been killed, wounded, or taken prisoner during an abortive raid across the Channel. This time the Jerries, after blowing up ammunition dumps and harbour installations, fled before we arrived.

The town was overrun with Canadians, so our mortar company spent the night in the village of Arques-la-Bataille. In the town square the Maquis were administering summary justice to local female collaborators: shaving their hair off and nailing it to the town hall doors. A beautiful young girl approached us and said, "Come wiz me!" Nick, Harry, Skeeze

Simons (our carrier driver), and I followed meekly, wondering what the score was. The score was 4–4: Renée took us home to meet mama and papa and grandmère, and we sat down to a meal of soup, a huge omelet, green beans, cold roast pork, coffee, and calvados. Leaving, we first kissed grandmère, then mama, then papa, and finally our real target, Renée. Incidentally, Renee kept up a correspondence with us for the remainder of the war. Deciphering her letters taxed Nick's high school French to the utmost.

After the Second Division held a victory parade in Dieppe, we continued to chase the Jerries north into Belgium. Five great ports — la Havre, Ostend, Dieppe, Boulogne, and Calais — fell to the First Canadian Army in September. The British Second Army, turned loose by Monty, swept through northern France and Belgium in the fastest drive in military history (225 miles in less than five days). The US armies sped along the German border and began probing at the Siegfried Line. The big job facing the Canadians and British was to clear the Scheldt Estuary surrounding the port of Antwerp. It meant fighting across water-soaked fields and flooded marshland.

Meanwhile we were comfortably enjoying a lull in the fighting. Our mortars were set up at the entrance to a railway station in Antwerp, just across the street from a little pub, or corner café. The Jerries were on the other side of the Albert Canal. They shelled us once or twice a day and we replied with mortar fire, but for some reason we could not fathom, our big drive seemed to have lost its momentum.

What actually had happened was this. Until September 2 Montgomery had been in charge of all the Allied land forces in Europe. At a time when complete victory seemed imminent, the principle of a central command was discarded. Eisenhower, probably to please American sentiment back home, announced that in the future the US armies would be employed to "attack the enemy equally on all fronts." This led to a winter stalemate. Monty's imaginative Arnhem air drop failed because he was refused the use of a few American divisions to secure a corridor across the Rhine and into the Ruhr.

The couple of weeks we spent in Antwerp were for us the best part of the war up to that time. Streetcars were running, cinemas were open, the pubs were doing a roaring business, shops were filled with expensive goods. As I wrote my wife:

> The Belgian people are even more hospitable than the French. Beer is very good and very cheap in our pub or corner café. We are allowed unofficial leaves — for two of us at a time — to go downtown to a movie. Saw Bing Crosby in *Going My Way.* After the show Nick and I strolled round, bought two pounds of green and blue grapes for 20 francs, then went into an ice cream parlour (there are hundreds of them here) and had a fresh fruit sundae for 19 francs. It was our first ice cream since leaving Canada, and we thought it marvellous, though the base is corn starch or something. We skipped supper to save money (a good meal is about 200 francs) and hit back for our mortar site, where the beer in "our" café is only four francs a glass, half the downtown price. The native drill seems to be to enter a café, hang up hat and coat, sit down and order a beer, pinch the café girl's bum, put an arm around her and give her a hug and a kiss, drink your beer, take a turn around the floor if the gramophone is playing dance music, don your hat and coat, bow politely and leave — presumably heading for the next café.

Our pub has three pretty girls, very young. All the action takes place in the café. As one 17-year-old carefully explained to Nick when he wanted to take her for a promenade: "I live in the café, I work in the café, I play in the café, I love in the café, I sleep in the café — all in the café."

Since these little outings we have been selling soap (20 francs) and sox (30 francs) and army shirts (60 francs) in order to accumulate a little capital again. (Primitive accumulation, in Marxist terminology.)

The failure of the Arnhem operation encouraged the Jerries to drop tons of leaflets on us. These "paper bullets" were addressed to "Boys of the 2nd Canadian Division" and reminded us of the heavy losses suffered in the Dieppe raid of August 19, 1942.

"Now your Division is in it for the second time," said the Nazi leaflet. "First your pals — and now you. It was a lousy trick they played on you that time, wasn't it? Why exactly were you forced to do it?

"Every child knows now that the whole Dieppe affair was nothing but a big bluff.

"Firstly the Bolshies had to have their Second Front for which they so urgently clamoured.

"Secondly the Brass Hats needed 'Invasion Experience' and quite naturally they wouldn't think of sacrificing any Limeys on a job like that ...

"We haven't the slightest intention of poking our nose in your affairs. But we Germans honestly despise the idea of having to fight against decent fellows like you, in as much as we know that you're not fighting for yours truly or for Canada. You know that only a few old mouldy scraps of paper bind you to England, an England that in its entire history has never done a damn thing for Canada that would help its future.

"Canada's sole purpose has always been to fight and bleed for England.

"In the next few days this God damn slaughter will start again. WE can't help it, since we are, after all is said and done, fighting for our very existence.

"BUT WE WARN YOU, Hitler didn't give up France for the fun of it!"

The Battle of the Dykes begins. Water, water everywhere, but nary a drink of schnapps. Pity the Poor Bloody Infantry in this godforsaken land. Try to dig a slit trench and you strike water two feet down. Then Jerry lobs over some mortar bombs and you have to hit the mud.

At night all hell breaks loose. Both armies throw across everything but the kitchen sink. Attack and counterattack. Flares light up the scene of carnage and destruction. Stretcher bearers in jeeps pick up the wounded.

Dawn at last ... soldiers sprawled in muddy dugouts and slit trenches, sleeping like the dead ... and some are dead. The rains come again, sleepers wake and shiver and draw their greatcoats closer, curl up in the mud ... the overpowering desire to sleep, sleep, sleep.

Breakfast: mush sans sugar or milk, canned bacon, bread and jam and coffee. Numerous little fires spring up and we heat water in old tin cans. After washing and shaving things look a little brighter. Those fortunate enough to have scored "homes" in Nazi-built concrete dugouts dry their clothes and begin living again, cleaning weapons, washing sox, writing home ("Dear Mom — I'm still okay ...").

Dinner is S.O.S. (Same Old Stew). Then orders come through and we're on the move again, forward a few thousand yards. New positions, set up our mortars, dig slit trenches, prepare ammunition for the next attack. RCAF planes appear and pound the enemy, sweet music to our ears. Tonight we break through again.

Field Marshal Montgomery called the Scheldt campaign "the finest operation of the Western Front." It cost some forty thousand Canadian and British casualties, but by the end of October the winding fifty-mile Scheldt had been cleared to open the way to Antwerp, and by the end of November the great harbour was in use.

I remember an evening when we rolled into Goes, the main city on South Beveland Island, and were billeted in a barroom for the night. We could scarcely credit our good fortune. The bar was dry, true, but trust Canadians to scrounge drinks somewhere.

My crew decided to take a gander at the town. We visited the jail, where members of the Dutch underground forces, wearing bright orange armbands, had rounded up some one hundred male and fifty female collaborators. Next day, we were told, trials would be held in the public square.

An English-speaking civilian invited us to his home for a drink. Over tumblers of gin he told us how, when the Brits and Canucks entered Antwerp, the Jerries in the Scheldt thought the end had come. They threw their tin hats and rifles in the canal and took off in the general direction of Berlin. People finished off the stragglers and celebrated all night, expecting us to arrive the next day. Only we didn't come — our lines were too extended and we were also sorely in need of replacements. Three days later some Jerry officers showed up again, meekly going from door to door and asking politely, "Are there any German soldiers hiding here?" A bunch of soldiers from Breslau crossed the water and reinforced the few officers, other men straggled out from hiding, the platoons and companies were reformed, more support came from Vaterland — and by the time we began our offensive they were ready for us. This same thing happened, said our host, not only in the Scheldt, but in the big cities — Amsterdam, Rotterdam, The Hague.

"I am half-English and half-Dutch," our host continued, pouring us another slug of Bols. "You may find it hard to believe, but one becomes so quickly accustomed to slavery. Only since you entered our town today have we begun to fully realize what we have gradually lost these last few years. It is tragic but true that one soon learns to accept eight o'clock curfews, loss of freedom of speech, freedom of the press, the right to say what one thinks. . . . And the way you Canadian soldiers mix with the people! And officers and men mixing together — it is hard for us to tell what rank you are. One can tell a German officer blocks away, and hear him, too!" But the resistance movement, one felt compelled to remind him, never accepted slavery. In France, Belgium, and Holland thousands of patriots fought for freedom from the day of the Nazi invasion, hiding radios, publishing illegal resistance papers, carrying out acts of sabotage.

For the next couple of months we played a relatively static role. We were shifted here and there, took part in a few skirmishes, suffered only light casualties, and caught up on our mail.

Whenever mail came up from the rear, I was the envy of our mortar platoon. Not only did I receive letters from many people who read my articles in the *Tribune*, but Rita, my wife, had come up with a brilliant idea, namely that at every party, meeting, or conference she passed around airmail forms to the people who knew me, asking them to scribble a note. Sometimes I'd received a dozen of these letters at once, containing notes from forty to fifty people.

"Wonderful party, I'm drinking up your beer ration and being weepy and nostalgic. I feel like the Scot who just had to do something, so when he found a truss in the street he went home and kicked his son in the balls."

"Enjoy your articles — they have a dash of pepper as well as a serious strain."

And so on. Today, nearly four decades later, I still have bundles of those airmail notes from people who took time out to scribble a line to me. A belated thank you, all. Of course, some of the above are long dead, others have strayed into different political pastures, many are still soldiering on in the class struggle.

About that time the *Maple Leaf*, the Canadian Army newspaper, sponsored a writing contest, offering nominal prizes for winners in three essay subjects, to wit:

(A) What should we do with Germany after the war to prevent another world conflict?

(B) What changes would you like to see made in Canada after the war? (politics, industry, world affairs, health, education, sports, entertainment, our laws, or our customs).

(C) What different ideas, habits or methods have you seen abroad that might be well for Canada to adopt after the war? (e.g., should we change our beer parlours into pubs, etc.)

I dashed off a couple of articles on "A" and "B" and was pleased to receive a letter from *Maple Leaf* editor Captain Seth Halton congratulating me on submitting two prize-winning essays and enclosing twelve Dutch *gulden* — thus assuring myself of at least twenty beers when I scored a leave in Europe. What really intrigued me was "C" and I wrote a letter to *Trib* columnist Mel Colby on the subject. (If Colby's humorous column had appeared in a newspaper with a bigger circulation he undoubtedly would have won wider recognition; perhaps, with the current interest in Canadiana, some astute publisher will compile a selection of his vintage columns written over a span of twenty-five years.) Let's dismiss the obvious at once, I wrote Mel. Of course after the war we should change our beer parlours into pubs; and import some buxom, foghorn-voiced barmaids from England to add a homely atmosphere to the joints by booming out, "What'll you 'ave, ducks?" and "Your two bitters, love." And we should establish corner cafés, à la Belgique, with the inevitable blonde café girls, whose duties include dancing with the customers and acting as friends to the lonely and the homeless. Ex-soldiers used to eating garbage out of mess tins would find it mentally confusing to be handed a two-page menu in Canadian restaurants. The solution would be to dish out, unfailingly, the Blue Plate special. Sleeping would present another problem for war vets. Every bedroom should be equipped with a spade or shovel, so that after tossing and turning on a Simmons mattress for a few hours, our battle-scared, bottle-scarred heroes could retire to the backyard and dig themselves a nice, cozy, safe slit trench.

ℓℓℓℓℓℓ

Holland, Nov 12/44: Seventh Heaven is the name of my present residence. It's a one-room shack we constructed yesterday — four poles at the corners, a few braces, and a tarpaulin stretched across the top. The heavenly roof leaks quite a bit, and the weather is cold. Our writing desk is made of broken boxes; our chairs, a few old bomb cases. Bedtime is around 7 p.m., when it grows dark. But in the middle of the night we get up to do two hours' guard duty.

Holland, Nov 23/44: Still a static war, as far as we're concerned. Rains every night, my slit trench is a puddle, so I sit up in our recreation hut, Seventh Heaven, and write letters. We added a real stove yesterday, hauled it from an abandoned house a mile behind the lines. If I ever publish these war jottings I'll call the book "Half Time." At the moment I can think of nothing nicer than finishing off the rest of my three-score-and-ten.

Holland, Dec 18/44: Looks like we're never going to move from here. Aside from a few night shoots, nothing to do. Just a week to Christmas. We've been getting 48-hour leaves, one man a week, and I'm about due, so will revisit either Brussels or Antwerp, probably the former, for there are too many V-2's descending on Antwerp. It is raining as usual, but I'm writing this in Nick and Harry's new shanty, quite warm and comfortable. Seventh Heaven was getting a bit crowded after a new replacement named Bruner joined us, so they set to work and built an elaborate joint, a port of hillbilly Royal York. It has solid walls and a roof, a swinging door, a large range cookstove, a table, chairs, full-length mirror, tapestries hung from the walls (all the result of scrounging in wrecked and abandoned villages) a washbowl and even a jerry under the bed. Oh, yes, there is a bed, an elaborate double bed with spring mattress, white sheets too. Harry even has a lady's blue nightdress with ruffled sleeves, and a pair of Dutch wooden clogs. Quite a sight, he is. . . . This guy Bruner is a bit of a character. He is responsible for an additional word in the army vocabulary — a "Brunerism." On December 3 we were all running around saying "Roosevelt's elected!" Says Bruner, seriously: "What happens to Churchill now?" Then our newspaper, the *Maple Leaf*, reported that the British Second Army had advanced two miles, Bruner shrugs and says, "Probably gone up for coal." (We scrounge our coal from a nearby abandoned village). On another occasion there was a debate on whether it was a V-2 that passed overhead. Commented Bruner: "You couldn't see it today, anyway, because of the low hemisphere."

Had a letter from Rosa Burson recently. She was very cut up over Dick Steele's death and asked about Little Ruby (Reuben Gorodetsky), who stayed several days at her place in London on his last leave. Now I'll have to tell her that he was killed way back in France. Frank (Rosa's husband in RAF bomber command) is finished flying for a year. His plane was shot up badly on his last raid and they only just managed to reach the coast. None of the crew were hurt but their nerves were shattered. Now Frank has to go to Scotland "among the Haggis bashers," as he puts it, and he insists that it should be counted as foreign service.

Holland, Dec 22/44: My back has been behaving nicely; the army pumps so much anti-this and anti-that into your veins that it seems impossible to even catch a cold, despite rain, mud, and slit trenches.

A rare bit of luck for Xmas. Moved into an abandoned village a few days ago, and my crew has a whole house. We use two rooms and have completely furnished same. Two double beds, springs and mattresses, and a dining room–kitchen, stove, table, washstand, and indoor pump, a Christmas tree in one corner decorated with junk we picked up on the scrounge. No civvies in the village as it is under fire daily, but not bad yet, most of the houses fairly intact. Jerry is just across the river; there are no infantry ahead of us, they are several miles in our rear, regrouping. If Jerry attacks right now we've had it. We carry on night shoots, moving to different positions to give the impression we're here in strength.

The news is that down below Jerry has broken through the American lines, in a big counteroffensive south of Aachen. A last effort, I guess.

In his Christmas message General Harry Crerar summed up the work of the First Canadian Army as follows:

> It has fought forward some 450 miles throughout France, Belgium and Holland. It has met and defeated either in the whole or in part 59 enemy divisions, of which 11 were SS (Elite Corps) and Panzer Type and 48 were infantry and other types. It had captured from the enemy nearly 120,000 prisoners. It has a right to be proud of its record.

Yeah, but what have we done lately? Here I am reading books, smoking cigars, and enjoying a long lull in the fighting, except for guards and night shoots. Our crew chew the fat and discuss the meals we'd like best when we get back to Canada. My choice is a Sunday breakfast of six pork sausages, four fried eggs, eight slices of thin toast with marmalade and jelly, and three cups of coffee.

We have acquired pets. I have a big black cat, named — guess what — Blackie. He was a hungry refugee so I adopted him. He is now sleek and well trained. Loves sardines. Right now he's sitting on an easy chair, watching me write this, and purring contentedly. We also have two doves: the lads were poking around and came across them in a cold, dark cellar of a shelled church, half-frozen and half-starved. They found a little bird seed and some grain, and the doves are beginning to perk up a bit — let out their first coos today. We keep them in a big cage in our living room. Once in a while Blackie casts a hungry look their way, but hasn't tried to bother them. They take a bath every morning in a pan of lukewarm water, then ruffle their feathers to dry them. Both grey, and rather nice-looking.

The Battle of the Bulge (as it later came to be called) was a wild gamble on the part of the Germans to break through the American lines, advance to Brussels and Antwerp and recapture the port, while at the same time cutting the Allied forces in two. The counterattack by fifteen German divisions under Field Marshal Model (Field Marshal von Rundstedt Commander-in-Chief) was launched December 16. The breakthrough was successful and the Americans were driven out of Germany in three days. The situation was so serious that Churchill appealed to Stalin to speed up preparations for a planned Soviet push. At the same time, at midnight on December 20, Montgomery was placed in command of the whole northern front (though Eisenhower's headquarters allowed no mention of this at the time). Monty shifted some British forces to support the Americans and stabilized the front in the first two days of his command. After a penetration of sixty miles the Germans were stopped, and then in the following weeks driven back into Germany with losses of 220,000 in dead and wounded.

On February 8, 1945, the First Canadian Army launched a major offensive towards the north German plain to kick off the Allies' spring drive into the Reich. Conditions were appalling; torrents of rain turned the countryside into a huge swamp. But in three weeks we had taken 14,500 prisoners and held 44 miles along the Rhine.

From my letters home, and scrawled notes sent to the *Tribune*:

The Rhine is ahead, and the industrial Ruhr. Let me give you a bit of the picture. We helped start the present push at Bergen Dal, near Nijmegen, Holland, just at the German border, on February 8. It was quite a do. Behind us a thousand artillery guns fired a million shells. Ack-ack also played an artillery role. Our 4.2 mortars threw over two thousand bombs; machine guns rattled off half a million rounds; planes played their part, sending down rockets on enemy strong points; and many other weapons were employed. But despite all this, General Mud prevented any rapid advance. The mud was unbelievable, it simply rolled down the hillsides like lava from a volcano. Tanks bogged down, carriers were stuck all along the roads. Nevertheless we took some prisoners and pushed Jerry back a bit.

After a short respite in Nijmegen we struck south for the Reichswald Forest. On the road another convoy passed us and I had time to shout "hello" to Johnny Miller. We breezed through the Reichswald, then faced tough opposition at the next line of defence. Casualties weren't light, but we managed to advance slowly and take many prisoners.

Cleves was the first big German town we conquered. The RAF had wiped out half the place but we secured billets for the night in a comparatively undamaged sector. I took over a house and made room for my crew in an upstairs room by throwing the owner's possessions out of the window. All the civvies were locked up in the local calaboose. Later I suppose they will be released.

Jerry is a tough fighter and skilled in defence. It is hard to describe what an advance is like — the muddy roads strewn with destroyed enemy guns, tanks, etc., as well as numerous English and Canadian vehicles blown up by German mines; dead bodies of Germans and Canadians, streams of civilian refugees carrying all they now own on their backs, tanks lumbering across fields, infantry plodding doggedly forward, thousands of our vehicles advancing at a snail's pace through the oceans of mud.

So, finally, here we are. Well inside Germany, with the main battles still ahead but conscious that the final result is no longer in doubt. I often find myself wishing that Dick Steele and Muni Erlich and Reuben Gorodetsky and all my other friends who died in France could be with us now. I'd like them to see what we've done. For we are in the enemy's country — these cities and towns we reduced to shambles are German, not French or Belgian or Dutch.

Do I sound particularly bloodthirsty? It isn't that. I'm still a civilian in uniform, and anxious to shed the obnoxious khaki at the earliest possible moment. But one of the peculiarities of this war has been that in order to liberate people, for a period of time we were forced to smash and destroy the very places we liberated. And now, at last, it is the Germans' turn to suffer directly. We are making them pay for their crimes.

Yes, for many years the Germans profited by this war. Their farms have scores of horses and sheep and pigs, hundreds of chickens and ducks and geese — in glaring contrast to the farms in Holland and Belgium and much of France. These cows, horses, pigs, geese were stolen — and it does not matter that the meticulous Hun did it "legally" and paid off in worthless marks for all that he seized.

Now we are having a field day. Army humour is rather broad: "Yesterday 12 chickens, one cow and two pigs counter-attacked at dawn, but were wiped out. The cook has agreed to dispose of the carcasses."

Hitler's "fight to the death" command has made little impression in the countryside. The German farmers bow and scrape (the Russians report similar experiences) and smirk at us.

Well, the war goes on. And the fact remains that the professional German soldier and the fanatical Hitler Youth are tough opponents, determined to fight to the last. Casualties are heavy and reinforcements constantly in demand. Big battles are still ahead and we must not relax. Neither must our people on the home front. But victory is certain.

Germany, February 1945: At long last the rain has stopped and the sun is shining again. Between shellings we come out of our slit trenches to enjoy it. The village behind us is in ruins; our barn nearby has suffered many direct hits and has hardly any roof left; dead cows, bloated, are lying about in the fields, and a live but wounded bull limps painfully around the yard; to our left the air force is dive-bombing an enemy-held section of forest; infantry stream past on our right flank, bound for the front line a few hundred yards away; a few burning buildings are straight ahead of us; now and then a hidden Nazi sniper zings a bullet over; our tanks and carriers and jeeps move up and down the road.

A couple of fellows are shaving; several are writing letters (for we've been too busy to clean up or write the past few days); some of the boys are watching the Typhoons put in their attack; others are playing it safe and sticking to the cellar of the barn or their slit trenches.

I'm sitting at the edge of my trench writing this. About every ten seconds, a Jerry shell whistles, and I stop writing to gauge the sound — ready to dive for cover if it is heading too close. But so far they've been landing 200 yards behind, or to my right in an adjoining field.

An interruption. One of our flyers just bailed out — his plane must have been hit by ack-ack — and is drifting down into the tiny village behind us ...

There's a bit of everything here. A dud V-1 landed about 300 yards away in an open field, Jerry is trying to set it off by shelling it, so we haven't investigated too closely.

Germany, Feb 27/45: At the moment I'm very tired; it is 6 p.m. and we've been on the move since 1 a.m., 16 hours, but have high hopes of a good sleep tonight. We've put the civvies in this house into the cellar, under guard, thrown the furniture out the door and made our beds on the floor. Took a batch of prisoners yesterday.... I'm too tired to write more, so good night, all.

In April we moved back into Holland to clean up a pocket of German troops in Groningen. In Germany, and now in Holland, we liberated a number of Soviet citizens who had been used as slave labour by the enemy. Some were attached to the German army and used to dig trenches, latrines, and so forth; others had been "bought" by German farmers.

I remember coming across two Russians in a building the Germans had used as a barracks before they surrendered. "Russe! Russe!" they shouted, and a glance at their German-stamped documents confirmed the fact. I pulled out a copy of the *Maple Leaf* showing a map of the front lines. "Hitler kaput!" I said. "Russe soldat fifty kilometres from Berlin!" Whereupon they began to sing the "Internationale"! I joined in, then pulled a bottle of schnapps from my pocket and we toasted the Soviet Union, Canada, and victory over Hitlerism. The schnapps proved to be a good international language.

There was a touching scene in a little Dutch town one morning. The Jerries put up a token resistance but our armoured thrust overran them and those who weren't killed or wounded fled in disorder, while a few hundred who couldn't get out surrendered. A number of civilians from the Dutch underground resistance movement, who had been locked up in a schoolhouse, were freed. One of these men, who (I learned later) had been taken from his home by storm troopers a week previously, headed up the street at a run towards some women and children who had come out into the square. His wife let out a shriek when she saw him. They embraced and laughed and cried together. His daughter, overcome by the event, fainted and had to be carried into a house and revived. All the neighbours were hysterical with joy and crowded around the released man, pounding his back and shaking his hand as though they couldn't convince themselves that he was really alive.

About this time I received a letter from Rosa Burson in England, telling me about the dramatic circumstances in which she became a mother: "A rocket (V-2) dropped fairly adjacent the day before the baby was born, and very badly damaged the house. I was in all by myself, sitting reading about half past four in the afternoon when without any warning at all a door hit me in the back of the head and knocked me down. A good thing it did really, because being down and under the door saved me from the glass that was flying about. I picked myself up and climbed over the debris into the street, only to find the place looked like a battlefield — people wandering about smothered in blood and lying around unconscious. All very grim and nightmarish. The baby was born the next morning; everything was perfectly normal and straightforward. I went into the nursing home looking like Tweedledum, and came out a veritable slither. I rode my bike all the time, every day up to twelve hours before he was born — to the absolute horror of all the old women around. The only thing was — if I'd gone on much longer I'd have had to have the saddle moved back a bit."

We shifted back into Germany and our last position before VE Day was outside the city of Oldenburg. Our mortars were set up in a farmyard and we were sleeping in slit trenches.

On April 29 my long-delayed United Kingdom leave came through. I jumped on the back of the dispatch rider's motorcycle and "retreated" a few miles to regimental headquarters; travelled by truck to Nijmegen, Holland; then by train in an unheated, windowless coach to Calais; an overnight stop in a transit camp and then by ship to Folkstone; by train to London, and on to Brighton. How good it was to be in dear old England again! I stayed with the Tracys and visited the Greens.

I celebrated VE Day in a Brighton pub, where a buxom barmaid slipped me extra shots of scotch from under the counter. But I was not feeling boisterous; my thoughts were back with my mortar crew. What if someone had "bought it" during those last few days of fighting I had missed? Not to worry, Corporal Whyte. When I returned from leave I found that Oldenburg had surrendered without our mortars having fired a shot.

After VE Day our Toronto Scottish regiment was billeted in Holland for a time, near the town of Apeldoorn. We slept in pup tents in a huge field. Our officers and senior NCOs fared better, living in houses. But we didn't mind, for we were given permission to reopen a small country pub which had been forced to close for lack of beer. We staffed the place with corporals and privates, and sent trucks to Brussels to pick up a hundred barrels of beer. The pub owner paid for the beer and sold it at reasonable prices, pocketing the modest profit. One of our lads, a talented painter, decorated the outside wall of the pub facing the crossroads with a huge Scottish lion, red against a yellow background. When, after a few weeks, orders came for the regiment to move, the grateful pub owner invited those of us who had acted as his "staff" to a splendid dinner cooked by his wife.

One day I asked for an afternoon pass and caught a lift into town in order to interview the editor of the Apeldoorn (Veluose District) Communist Party paper, *De Waarheid*. Editor P. Clerkx, a slim, quiet-voiced man in his fifties, accepted a Canadian cigarette and smilingly told me that his English was probably inadequate to cope with an interview. "In school many years ago I learned English, French and German. I speak excellent German, but my English and French..." Churchill's election defeat was a key topic of conversation at the time, and Clerkx asked me to write a leading article on the subject. It was splashed over half the front page of *De Waarheid* on July 30, 1945.

Our regiment was moved around from place to place in the weeks that followed, and eventually we landed back in England, where we waited impatiently in a repat depot for news of when and how we were going to be shipped to Canada. On October 13 the *Maple Leaf*, our army newspaper, carried a banner headline: *Queen Elizabeth* On Canada Run. "The *Queen Elizabeth*, world's largest liner and troopship, will sail for Canada within ten days carrying Canadian service personnel," said the lead story. "The *Queen*," wrote John Smaller in a second-front-page story "has covered some 450,000 miles, all on war service, and carried 685,000 passengers to all parts of the world.... She has been known to carry more than 20,000 troops at one time."

Sam Koffman, another staff writer, noted that "the news came like a bolt from the blue" to Canadians in repat depots. "Xmas in Canada had become a mirage. But now, with the Lizzie on their side 'we might make it yet' many said. There was one cluster of that doughty tribe 'The Unbelievers.' They shrugged off the announcement as if it were a rowboat instead of the biggest, fastest liner afloat. 'I suppose they'll fill it with their wives,' said one."

The pessimists weren't entirely wrong. When the *Queen* docked at Halifax on October 26 it included among its civilian passengers Romanian Prince and Princess Matila Ghyka, the Duke and Duchess of Sutherland, the Bishop of Derby, Danish and British newsmen bound to Washington, and other passengers heading for Brazil, Peru, Trinidad, and Bermuda. Still, it brought home 9,022 army veterans, 1,254 air force, 440 Canadian navy, and 16 nursing sisters returning from South Africa.

I'll let a *Toronto Star* reporter (denied a deserved byline) describe our welcome home. Excerpts:

Toronto roared and wept its welcome to some of its most famous fighting sons yesterday afternoon, as the Toronto Scottish, Canada's first unit to go overseas, came home.

The Scottish left just a few weeks under six years ago, landing in England in December, 1939. The Scottish came home, after chalking up one of the most extended campaign records of any Canadian unit, to the biggest crowd that has ever turned out in this city to meet any returning group of men.

More than 75,000 choked downtown streets and all but swamped the marching men as they moved up Front, Bay and Queen Sts. and over to University Ave. for the final 'Break-off,' the last one in a long campaign.

The Scottish, whose heavy machine guns and 4.2-inch mortars tore holes in enemy infantry all the way from the Normandy beachhead last summer to the final march up the shell-broken Unter den Linden in Berlin, ended this war with a string of campaign honours in many ways unique in the entire Canadian Army.

The Scottish were the only Canadian unit to go to the Continent three times: In 1940, just before France fell; at Dieppe on that historic dawn of Aug. 19, 1942; and again, back for keeps this time, in July 1944.... The Scots won three DSO's, three MBE's, four MC's, 10 MM's, 22 Mentioned in Despatches, four French war crosses, and a large handful of other miscellaneous decorations. They were also the first Canadian outfit to bring down an enemy plane. To mention but a few firsts ...

On the main reviewing stand across from the Armories were the dignitaries of the city and of the military district....

The unit's commanding officer, Lt.-Col. Ellis, said farewell to the last parade of his regiment. Remember, he told his men, the others who could not be here at this time. The others who lie in Africa, in France and in Germany.

In the background a band struck up the National Anthem. The regiment stood at stiff attention and the Scottish colours slapped lightly in the evening breeze. There was a pause and the final order snapped out. Dismiss.

The Scottish were home again.

CHAPTER FOUR

Postwar Years

Home Again

On my second day at home, still in uniform, I took part in a mass picket line outside the Imperial Optical Co., whose workers were on strike. A couple of nights later, at a meeting in Massey Hall to celebrate the twenty-eighth anniversary of the Russian Revolution, I found myself on the platform along with Tim Buck, the main speaker. It was the first time I had addressed an audience of three thousand. I spoke in support of the Ford strikers in Windsor. The *Toronto Star* gave me a paragraph: "'A few days ago,' said Cpl. Bert Whyte, 'the Toronto Scottish marched up the avenue to the cheers of thousands of people. Today, there are men of the Toronto Scottish marching in the picket lines at Windsor, facing the guns, clubs and tear gas of the provincial police and the R.C.M.P.'"

I was slated to join the *Canadian Tribune* staff as city editor, and a welcome home party was held for me at the editor's home on November 10. Fate intervened. I woke up the next morning in great pain, my wrists and ankles swollen to twice their size by an extreme attack of arthritis. An ambulance took me to Chorley Park Military Hospital, where I was destined to spend the next few months.

Army doctors are a special breed. The first one who examined me decided to put casts on my legs. After I had passed out a couple of times another medic took off the casts and prescribed heat treatments. A third came along and said cheerily, "You the fellow with the gall stones?" "No, I'm the fellow with arthritis." It took a few days before things got straightened out.

I enjoyed my stay in hospital. After all the shots pumped into me overseas had lost their effectiveness I felt terribly tired, and kept drifting off to sleep between meals. The nurses marvelled at my ability to sleep despite the bustle of daytime activities and the noisy shenanigans of a bunch of Hong Kong vets in the ward. I lay in my warm bed, sweating a bit from the artificial heat, but not uncomfortable. Most days I had afternoon visitors, and every evening my wife Rita brought me a huge milkshake, which I downed, never realizing that I was quietly putting on pound after pound.

After a couple of weeks I slept less and began to read voraciously. I read everything, newspapers, paperbacks, and even *War and Peace*, which I had tackled many times previously but never managed to finish.

At Christmas I was allowed to go home for a day, and sat in an easy chair with my feet up on a stool, and drank Johnny Walker Black Label. The next day, back to Chorley Park. After another month or so my wrists and ankles had returned to normal and I could walk again. On the day of my release a doctor I had never seen before stopped at my bedside and said, "Just remember to take care of that ulcer!"

A Toronto convention of the Labor-Progressive Party elected me as city organizer in 1946. At that time we had a staff of fourteen, a membership approaching two thousand, and played a considerable role in civic politics — we had one communist member on the Board of Control, Stewart Smith, and three communist aldermen, Norman Freed, Charles Sims, and Dewar Ferguson. In provincial politics we had two communist members of the provincial parliament, J.B. Salsberg and A.A. McLeod. During the course of the next several months party membership increased to twenty-two hundred in Toronto, and plans were underway to launch a daily tabloid in 1947.

Given hindsight, it seems to me that all of us failed to sense in time the swift approach of the Cold War, which was to force us to fight a holding action over the next decade. There were signs, though, that a tremendous effort would be made to defeat all communist candidates in the upcoming civic elections. An editorial in the reactionary *Toronto Telegram* (since deceased) said: "There is room for difference of opinion on the merits of the many candidates. There is none where Communists are concerned. Every last one of them seeks office for the single purpose of furthering communism, a religion which is in open conflict with democracy. Every last one of them obeys but one master, Soviet Russia, regardless of the will or the wellbeing of those they were elected to serve."

The *Toronto Star*, however, urged the re-election of the four members of the Board of Control, including Stewart Smith. It editorialized:

> Stewart Smith, the youngest member of the board and the one particularly interested in the masses of the people, was four times elected alderman in Ward Five, and has been a controller for the past two years. He has an excellent record.
>
> In some quarters a dead set is being made upon Controller Smith, who last year came second in the poll with nearly 42,000 votes. He is the hardest working

controller Toronto has. He is closer to the people than any other controller. He has a definite four-plank platform for 1947: The construction of an additional 1,000 homes for veterans; assessment reform with some relief for the home-owner in view; sale of milk at the lowest possible price; traffic reform. He is against the hastily conceived plan of abolition of downtown parking. He has worked out a comprehensive plan for expediting traffic into and out of the downtown district, in part by means of one-way streets. Whether or not this plan is the one which should be followed — and it is certainly one which should be studied — it illustrates the thoroughness of the man, and the pains to which he goes in working and planning for Toronto's future.

Smith polled 42,104 votes but lost his seat, running fifth. Dewar Ferguson lost his aldermanic seat in Ward Six.

At the next civic elections the Cold War was getting well in stride and the *Toronto Star* shied away from recommending a vote for Stewart Smith. Nevertheless, he polled 47,791 votes, again running fifth. The big news in the papers on the day following the election was that Alderman Freed had been defeated in Ward Four. But Freed adamantly refused to concede, claiming that figures given to him by his scrutineers showed he had won by 66 votes. And sure enough, official returns proved that he obtained a majority of 61 votes over Frank Chambers, who was believed on election night to have captured the seat.

Red-baiting attacks hit a new ferocity in civic elections that year. But worse was yet to come. South of the border the voice of McCarthy was fouling the air, and spilling over into Canada.

We began publication of the *Daily Tribune* at the worst possible time. Our primary error lay in a false estimation of objective conditions. Canada was entering a period of political reaction, and despite the obvious increase in Red baiting, we still retained certain illusions — a hangover from the years of wartime advance. Three leading communists even argued, "We are a growing movement — not going backwards. Red-Baiting is not weakening our movement!"

There were subjective reasons also which led to the closing of the daily after some six months. Seeking a broader audience, the strong statements of policy contained in editorials were subordinated to news. Management, circulation, and advertising committed serious errors. Outside pressure against the paper was strong. Our street salesmen were often beaten up, their papers thrown in the gutter. Finally, we had to organize three-man squads of communists or party supporters to protect every paper seller.

We waged and won a political battle to have *Daily Tribune* corner boxes, and these soon proved one of our best means of sales. By early fall circulation was around seven thousand. The decision was made to revert to a weekly. But what was heartbreaking to the staff was that in the final six weeks of its existence, sales were increasing at the rate of two hundred copies a week.

We began with a staff of fourteen, putting out three editions daily. Leslie Morris was editor-in-chief, and Jack Stewart, John Boyd, and I were members of the editorial board. The youngest worker, in the business office, was teenager Marie Barko. More than thirty-five years later Marie was still the *Canadian Tribune* bookkeeper. A fine record of devoted service.

When Leslie approached me to join the staff, I gladly shifted from my post as party organizer in Toronto. Journalism has an attraction that "organizing" lacks — for me at least. The innumerable meetings I had to attend as an organizer bored me — as A.A. McLeod so often remarked, "The mind can absorb only what the seat can endure." When the paper's staff was assembled, we were told that the general practice of equal wages prevailing in the party would not be followed: for various reasons (several children in a family, etc.) some reporters would require higher wages than others. Money was scarce, and each staff member was asked to review his financial circumstances and set his own salary as low as possible. I decided that I could live on $30 a week, $5 less than I had been drawing as an organizer. Nearly all of us took voluntary wage cuts, although two or three comrades decided they needed more money than they had previously been paid. Incidentally, most — but not all — staff members were communists. There was one chap named Walker, an Englishman, who during the few months he was with us — as a reviewer of plays and movies — seemed completely unaware of the politics of the paper he was working for.

Our sports editor, Sam Maltin, had left a job on the *Montreal Herald* to join our staff. Another journalist from one of the big capitalist dailies threw in his lot with us for a couple of months, but then resigned, explaining to me that he found it hard to write for such a small audience. "My ego, I guess," he said. I felt some sympathy for him, knowing his background.

A horse-racing expert phoned in his selections (gratis) every day there was flat racing at Toronto tracks. He was rather good at picking long shots — something like Cayton, the *Daily Worker*'s famous selector. It is said that for years the British Royal Family has taken the *Worker* and its successor the *Morning Star* in order to follow Cayton, whose greatest moment was when he picked Russian Hero at 75 to 1 to win the Grand National. Incidentally, there's a story about how Cayton began his career on *The Worker.* He had selected the name "Nilats" for his column. Just before the presses began to roll an alert deskman noticed that Nilats was simply Stalin spelled backwards. Stop the presses!

The small Dufferin racetrack, long since demolished, was not far from our print shop and office, and on my way to work (I was on the afternoon shift, responsible for putting out the second and third editions) I would sometimes drop in and bet the first or the second race. An honest little plug named Moldy, tilted slightly to port from years of work in this bullring, was usually a good bet at 6 to 1. I had collected on him at least five times, and this day I was at the rail clutching my ticket and they're off to a good start Moldy running an easy fourth and around the bend looking confident as always and at the far turn third and into the stretch and around the bend and down the far side and second time past and Moldy beginning to make his move oh you Moldy you sweet little bastard I knew you could do it and into the stretch and something flashed past on the outside and nipped him at the wire.

A few months after the *Tribune* reverted to a weekly, my arthritis began to bother me again and I decided that a change of scenery would do me good. Ever since the Depression days I had had a hankering to revisit Vancouver. Let's pull up stakes, I said to my wife Rita, and move out to the west coast.

West Coast

In the fall of 1948 I moved from Toronto to Vancouver. My first job was that of publicity director for Effie Jones in her bid for Mayor of Vancouver. The previous year Effie had polled over nineteen thousand votes, the highest progressive vote ever recorded in Vancouver up to that time. The Non-Partisan Association controlling city hall allowed the B.C. Electric Railway to jack up fares and abolish weekly car and bus passes. Their candidate that year was Charles Jones. Inevitably he was dubbed "High Fare Jones" and Effie became "Low Fare" Jones.

We opened an election headquarters on West Pender Street. Elgin Ruddell was campaign manager, Vi Bianco was canvassing director and May Leniszek was secretary. The political lineup was very different from the previous year's, however. In a two-way contest Effie had benefited from the anti-NPA vote, which included most of the CCF supporters. This time the Co-operative Commonwealth Federation (CCF), which would later become the New Democratic Party, nominated Tom Alsbury, thus killing any chance of Effie being elected. Elgin Ruddell, well versed in civic politics, had suggested that Effie should abandon the mayoralty race and instead run for an aldermanic position. However, a majority of the Labor-Progressive Party leadership rejected this proposal.

Effie Jones had a long and honourable record in the progressive movement. Back in the Hungry Thirties, when she went down to volunteer her services during the post office sit-down strike, the first job the strike committee gave her was to peel onions. "I peeled onions for hours straight, and nearly went crazy," Effie told me. The next day she found herself secretary of the emergency committee of women, charged with the task of feeding five hundred boys. Later, after the infamous arrests of the post office occupiers, she was an active member of the Citizens' Defense Committee. But Effie Jones's career of public service went back beyond that period. All her adult life she had been connected with the struggle of the common people for a better life. Born in the Old Country, of Welsh parentage, Effie grew up in a small coal-mining town, getting a first-hand experience of what the struggle for existence meant. The daughter of two school principals, Effie herself became a teacher and taught in schools in Hereford, Ewindon, and Swansea before coming to Canada in 1919.

A talented artist as well as a teacher, Effie won the second prize for still life in watercolours for the Midland Counties, just before she emigrated to Canada. A year later, in Vancouver, she placed first in the still life in oils class.

Since the early 1930s Effie had been associated with a number of progressive undertakings. She was one of the founders of the South Hill CCF club. She gave freely of her time and energy to help the unemployed during the grim Depression years. She was the organizer of the Housewives' League of British Columbia. She played a leading role in the work of the Tenants and Homeowners' League and helped to prevent many evictions. In 1946 she toured Vancouver Island and helped organize mass protests against increases in the price of milk and other foods. At the time of her mayoralty bid she was president of the South Hill Community Association.

If we couldn't elect Effie, the next best thing was to get the maximum publicity during the campaign. Elgin and I put our heads together and came up with some ideas. Streetcar fares were still a hot item, so we placed small ads in the dailies offering free car tickets to the first hundred people who would write to Effie to ask for them. And a book of car tickets to the writer of the best jingle about high fares.

The response was good. I'd never have believed there were so many would-be poets in Vancouver. In follow-up ads we printed some of them, along with our continuing offer of free tickets.

Vote for Effie
Call their bluff
Seven cents
Is fare enough.

And:

Street car fares hit the sky,
Effie Jones tells us why.
I'm not much at writing poems
But I'll vote for Effie Jones.

And:

B.C.E.R. cars are a wreck,
Soon they'll break my bones:
That's why on Dec. 8th
I'll vote for Effie Jones.

Along with a couple of genuine car tickets, we enclosed strips of "Effie Jones' tickets," which soon found their way into fare boxes. And this made news which the dailies picked up. A sample, under the heading "Effie's 'Street Car Tickets' in BCE Fare Box": "Effie 'Low Fare' Jones has issued her own 'street car tickets' and to everyone's embarrass-ment they're turning up in B.C. Electric fare boxes. Company officials said there was no suggestion the depositors hadn't also used an old-fashioned B.C. Electric ticket.

"The advertising tickets are the same shape and size as BCER tickets. Though in strips of four, the 'tickets' are not perforated. But just in case anyone gets the wrong idea, it is illegal to ride on anything but a B.C. Electric ticket."

Charles Thompson, Non-Partisan candidate, and Tom Alsbury, CCF, weakly declared that "nothing could be done about high fares."

Shortly before election day the Non-Partisan Association had their annual dinner meeting in Hotel Vancouver. Half an hour before the affair was scheduled to begin I walked into the hotel dining room, called the head waiter, handed him a bunch of sealed envelopes and instructed him to place them under each plate at the head table. Waiters are accustomed to obeying orders. The next day one of the papers (the *News-Herald*, now defunct) reported, under the heading 'NPA Dinner Gets Food For Thought":

An "enemy" agent apparently got into the Non-Partisan camp when the advocates of "no politics in the city hall" held their annual dinner meeting in Hotel Vancouver.

At each place on the head table and the press table there were square white envelopes marked "Head Table Guests. Open after 7 p.m."

President R.A. Sanderson could not restrain his curiosity and opened his at 6.30. Inside the white envelope was a brown one and in it was a printed card.

In large red capital letters it said, EFFIE WAS HERE.

These publicity stunts were fun, but we also had to get Effie's ideas on civic reform across to the public. So we put Effie on the air, Monday to Friday every week on CKMO, with a five-minute program called "Politics with a Punch."

Voting results, in round figures, resulted in Thompson sweeping in with thirty-two thousand votes, Alsbury second with twenty-three thousand, and Jones with six thousand. Effie had been a delight to work with, a superb campaigner. Her defeat left her undaunted. As she told a rally of her supporters on election night: "We need to go forward from this election and increase the tempo of our fight for civic reforms. We have made thousands of friends during this campaign. We must now unite them under our banner and fight back against reaction on every front until final victory is ours."

I began working for the *Pacific Tribune* in 1949 and remained on staff until the spring of 1960. Tom McEwen, a veteran communist, was editor, but much of the editorial burden was carried by Hal Griffin, an experienced professional journalist, like myself. We worked as a team for many years without any friction. Later Hal became editor of a trade union paper, the *Fisherman*; under his guidance it soon ranked as one of the best publications in its field.

Aside from my work on the *Pacific Tribune* I was active in party circles, a member of provincial and city committees and executives, a teacher in party schools, a public speaker, a candidate in one provincial election, etc.

The early 1950s saw McCarthyism running rampant in the United States, and inevitably this anti-communist witch hunt affected us in Canada. Part of the fight-back campaign was the holding of a Paul Robeson concert in Peace Arch Park near Blaine, Washington, forty kilometres south of Vancouver. The great Negro singer was not allowed to leave the United States, so he sang from the back of a truck parked exactly at the border. Some forty thousand people, most of them Canadians, turned up to hear him. It was a mighty demonstration. The Mine Mill Union played a major role in organization of the concert.

After the Roaring Twenties, the Depression Thirties, and the Wartime Forties came the Dull Fifties. It was a period when left-wing forces had to conduct a holding operation, while waiting for the advent of the Turbulent Sixties.

It was in the Fifties, however, that I met Monica, and lightning struck. This led to the breakup of our respective marriages. Eventually divorces came through and we were free to marry, and did so, though there were dire predictions that our union would not work because of a twenty-five-year age gap. Several decades have passed and we are as much in love as ever.

In March 1960 I was sent to China as correspondent for the *Canadian Tribune*, the Communist Party's main national newspaper. That assignment opened up a new and exciting chapter in my life. When I was settled down Monica joined me and we lived in Peking for almost four years. On our return to Canada I worked a couple of years on the *Tribune* in Toronto; then in the spring of 1966 I was assigned to Moscow as the paper's correspondent. My assignment ended in 1974 and since then I have been working on contract with a Soviet publishing house. But that's another story.

Les Girls

You will have noticed that in these fragments of an autobiography I have said nothing about my adult love affairs. Let women boast of their amorous conquests; a man shouldn't kiss and tell. By and large, all the girls I have loved were worthy of loving. Only a very few female chauvinist pigs treated me as a love object, grabbed at my joystick under the table, zipped open my fly at every opportunity, made me lie down and spread my legs while they examined me. But most of the girls recognized that I was a human being, perhaps not quite up to their intellectual level, but with a mind of my own. "You've come a long way, baby," they would say, to comfort me.

Protest against Spanish dictator Francisco Franco, Toronto, about 1946.
At the end of World War II, progressives worldwide believed that the victory over fascism would also end the largest surviving fascist dictatorship
in Europe—Francisco Franco's regime in Spain. During the Cold War,
however, the United States found Franco a useful ally. Pictured are, among
others, Ben Swankey (far left), Whyte, Edna Ryerson (second row centre),
and Dewar Ferguson (front row right).

Inside the *Canadian Tribune*'s Toronto office about 1947, when it was briefly a daily newspaper. Left to right, Stewart Smith, Leslie Morris (*Tribune* editor), John Boyd (with pipe) and Eva (last name unknown), the secretary of the Communist Party office in Toronto.

A caricature of Whyte, sketched about 1946, by Avrom Yanovsky, who created many cartoons for the *Canadian Tribune* and other leftist publications. Whyte gained considerable weight while in a military hospital after World War II.

Whyte meeting the Vietnamese communist
and national leader Ho Chi Minh in Hanoi
in September 1960

On a second visit to Vietnam in 1961, Whyte interviews people involved in the escalating war to win independence for the entire country.

On holiday in 1961 at Peitaiho (now Beidaihe), 250 km east of Beijing, a popular beach resort for Communist Party leaders and foreign correspondents in the 1960s. Jean Vidal, the correspondent for *L'Humanité* (left), Whyte, and Harry Sichrovsky, of the Vienna *Volksstimme,* soak up the sun.

The Whytes—Bert, Monica and Ricky—and an unidentified Chinese Communist Party official visit the Qing Summer Palace in the winter of 1961.

Whyte's duties as the Beijing correspondent for the *Canadian Tribune* were not so onerous as to exclude sightseeing. The Whytes—Monica, Ricky and Bert—visit the Ming Tombs near Beijing about 1961.

Above: Whyte in 1962 with Pu Yi, the "Last Emperor" of the Qing Dynasty

Left: Whyte at the memorial to Dr. Norman Bethune at Shijiazhuang, China, about 1961. Bethune travelled from Canada in 1938 to aid the Chinese in their campaign to resist the Japanese military takeover of the country. After he died while working with the Eighth Route Army in 1939, Bethune was lionized by Mao Zedong.

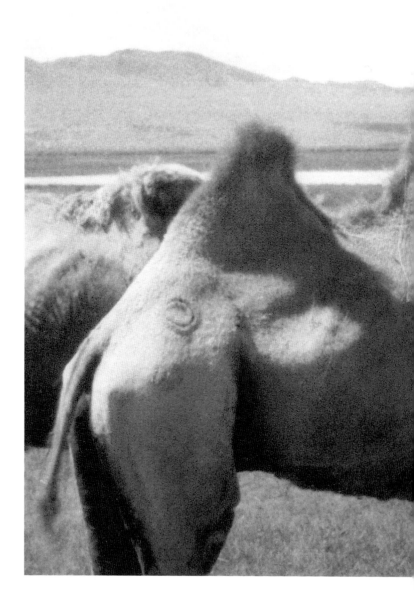

Whyte's last foreign trip before departing Beijing as *Canadian Tribune* correspondent was to Mongolia, where he took in the annual Naadam Festival and, with Monica, toured the country by Jeep.

Whyte's wild side hit the *Tribune* in November 1965 in an article that landed him and editor John Boyd in trouble with party brass and women in the party.

ANN CORIO
Mild version of a famous strip

A nostalgic look at old burlesque

THIS WAS BURLESQUE at the Royal Alexandra in Toronto was like Old Home Week for those patrons of the arts left homeless when Casino ended its striptease era.

The lingering magic of Ann Corio's name brought them out in full force on opening night, including several bald heads in the very front row and a gum-chewing woman in a backless gown sitting regally in a box.

The top bananas were as gamey as ever, the jokes as blue, the skits as ancient, the strippers as bare. It was a trip down mammary lane to see tassel-tossing Marilyn Marshall in action; her exotic specialty brought titters from younger females in the audience.

Steve Mills was billed as top banana but Harry Conley stole the show with his Hotel de France and Sutton Place numbers.

La Corio acted as narrator, took part in many of the skits and wound up doing a mild version of her own famous strip. She went into her routine as the band played A Pretty Girl is Like a Melody and the nostalgia was so thick you could have cut it with a knife.

The baggy-pants comics were lowdown and vulgar: ("Me and the wife drove through Maine last week." "Bangor?" "A couple of times.") Burleycue buffs knew the lines before they were sprung; to much of the distaff side of the audience it was all new and rather startling. ("How I'd love to see my old girl Flo again.") Before the evening ended they relaxed and began to enjoy it.

It wasn't a very good show; it demonstrated, in fact, why burlesque died. Still, its corny approach to sex as fun was refreshing after so many top-priced productions which treat sex solemnly and with an emphasis on its 57 deviations.

—Bert Whyte

With the zeal of an unrepentant pool-shark
still evident at the age of sixty-three, Whyte
attacks the table, to the evident delight of fellow
Communist correspondents visiting the Buryat-
Mongolian Autonomous Soviet Socialist Republic
in the eastern USSR in 1972.

The Whytes at home. The affection between Whyte and Monica is evident in this informal photo taken in 1975 at their Moscow apartment.

CHAPTER FIVE

Letters from China

Foreword

One day Bert came home from the office with a funny expression on his face. "What's wrong?" I asked.

"I've been offered the job of foreign correspondent in Peking for the *Canadian Tribune*. It's for two years minimum. I'll do whatever you decide."

I was gobsmacked, as the Brits say. Now, of all times. Now, when we were finally together. And I thought, if it were me, I'd want to go. I was quite sure he'd refuse the assignment if I said so. But he'd resent it in the weeks and years ahead. What a start to our lives together. And then there were the misgivings at the back of my mind that I had firmly suppressed — that Bert, the political animal, would grow restless in his enforced exclusion from political life.

All this takes time to express in words, but in reality I don't think more than a couple of heartbeats went by before I heard myself say, "Of course you must go. It's the chance of a lifetime."

I saw a flash of relief on Bert's face. "I won't stay a day longer than two years."

And that was that. I informed the party that Roy and I had separated and I needed a full-time job (I was on part-time salary, which was all the Young Communist League (YCL) could afford at the time). We found a new apartment which I expected to share with my grandmother and Ricky for the next two years, and Bert moved his desk and chair and books and personal effects into it.

On a cold, miserable, rainy evening, March 7, 1960, Bert started off on his great adventure.

This is the background against which the following letters were written over a six-month span. (Of well over two hundred letters, excerpts are taken from only a selected few.) It explains the attention to the minutiae of everyday life. Bert felt that by sharing them we could avoid an estrangement over a long period of separation.

It is said that man proposes and God disposes. And so it was with us. As Ricky and I walked off the plane in Peking on September 3, 1960, after the long journey from Vancouver via Toronto, Zurich, Bern, Prague, Moscow, Omsk, Irkutsk, and Ulan Bator, I eagerly scanned the small group waiting to greet the arriving passengers. No Bert! A young Chinese chap came forward: "Comrade Monica? I am Bao Shi-shao." We shook hands.

"Ah. I've heard about you. But where is Bert?"

"Comrade Bert is in Vietnam."

"Ah. Vietnam. And what is he doing in Vietnam?" I felt like adding, "pray tell."

"He is the Canadian delegate to the Congress of the Vietnam Workers' Party."

It was to be another week before Bert, Ricky, and I were reunited.

(Bert later told me that he was fretting about not being there when we arrived and Bao said: "There is nothing to worry about, Comrade Bert. I will meet Comrade Monica.")

A brief run-down. We remained in China until mid-November 1963. It was a wonderful time in our personal lives and an interesting one in a fascinating country. We moved into a flat in the building for foreigners in the eastern section of the city, just above the apartment of Harry and Lotte Sichrovsky [correspondent for the Austrian Communist newspaper] and below that of the Sarzis [from the Italian communist paper *L'Unità*].

Financially there was no need for me to work but I wanted to do more than just go to cocktail parties and embassy dinners. Eventually I was offered a choice of editing work at various Chinese English-language publications, or teaching oral English at the Institute of Diplomacy, which, as the name implies, was a school for future diplomatic staff abroad. I had no formal training as a teacher, but I did have practical experience of teaching classes in the YCL. An interview was arranged and it was agreed that I would start on a three-month trial basis, to be terminated by either party if found unsatisfactory. After one month they asked me to sign a two-year contract, which I said was impractical. If Bert were recalled to Canada I would obviously want to leave. So it was left at that. I stayed with the institute until the week before we left China. I thoroughly enjoyed working with my students, who, while not equally gifted in languages, were all equally eager to learn.

On September 1, 1961, Ricky started his first year at the Russian embassy school.

Bert did quite a bit of travelling around the country, visiting off-the-beaten-path places like Loyang, capital of China for a thousand years, and Xian, the oldest city of the Middle Kingdom, and Yan'an, home base of the Communist Party at the end of the Long March. Unfortunately, I didn't have the opportunity. I did, however, get to go to Vietnam with Bert (he had turned down an invitation to travel around the country following the Congress on the grounds that his wife had just arrived in Peking; in that case, the Vietnamese said, he must come with his wife next year). We also went to Korea the same year and to Mongolia in 1963.

A few weeks every July–August, during what the Chinese called the great heat, we spent at Peitaiho [now Beidaihe] at the seaside.

The people: Roann and Pondoli. Pondoli had one year to go to graduate from Peking University when he was recalled to his home in Albania. No one in our circles doubted the reason: his liaison with a woman from a capitalist country, Sydney Gordon's daughter, Roann.

Dick and Ginny Chen, Jack and Ted Kao. The former and the latter were not related, but in the Chinese fashion, Dick was elder brother, Jack and Ted little brothers. We hit it off and saw a lot of them and learned a great deal from them about the real life and problems of the Chinese people. In 1961 Dick went to Hong Kong to go to a family funeral. He did not return. A few months later Ginny and the children followed. Jack went in 1962. Ted and his mother Kimmie did not get out until years later.

The Sichrovskys left China for Vienna in June 1962. That same year saw the departure of Vidal and Sarzi, the *L'Humanité* and *L'Unità* correspondents.

Over time the Yangs — Xianyi and Gladys — became our closest friends. Restaurants, supper at our place or theirs, bridge, good conversation. My institute was close to their apartment block and on Fridays, when I had a class from 8 a.m. to noon and then a tutorial from 2 to 4 p.m., it became a habit to have lunch with Gladys, who worked at home. In mid-November 1963, the night before we left for Moscow on the first leg of our journey home to Toronto, we spent together, just the four of us. Gladys and I both wept, suspecting we would never see each other again. We were right. Gladys insisted that we correspond. Bert and I thought it was unwise for them; nevertheless we did. Although the Cultural Revolution was three years in the future, there were ominous signs. They paid a heavy price, but survived the ordeal.

On the day of our departure, the whole foreign press corps turned up at the airport. But, as when the Winningtons had left, no Bao. Nor anyone from *Renmin Ribao* (*People's Daily*) or the Foreign Office. However, the dean of the English Department of my institute (a dear man, an Oxford graduate), along with my direct supervisor, appeared. They at once realized their political error. I felt sorry for them as they stood on the fringes of the rather raucous crowd of reporters milling around and suggested that they not wait until boarding was announced. They gratefully escaped.

A final note. We were installed in a Moscow hotel, the Peking, when the three of us went for breakfast in the dining room. The eyes of our waitress were red, she had obviously been crying. There was something wrong, both staff and diners seemed upset, tense, unnatural. I queried her. "Don't you know?" she said. "Kennedy's been killed."

— MONICA WHYTE

March 1960

My darling:

This is a combination of three or four letters — it is now three weeks since I left. It seems more than three weeks, though, probably because I've been on the go so much, and so many things have happened.

I began writing from Irkutsk, in the middle of Soviet Asia, where our Tu-104 was grounded by a storm and I was sleeping three in a room at the airport, but in the middle of my letter we got the word to go and from then on I've been in a whirl. I'd better recap events briefly from the time I left Prague on a Czech jet for Moscow. The plane took off like a hot rod, climbed rapidly, and in a bit over two hours we were sucking candies as we lost altitude and came in to the Moscow airport. The big town looked beautiful from the air — a blaze of lights, and that big red MOCKBA sign produced a thrill, too. My first lesson in Russian — to look for the MY letters to distinguish the men's from the ladies'. The waiting room had a bar, candy counter, etc. and I was dying of thirst but didn't have a kopek. So made friends with the English-speaking announcer and she bought me an orange soft drink. I gave her a deck of Camels I'd bought on the plane, so then she gave me some travel folders of Russia. All very chummy and the exchange might never have ended except that our flight was called. We were scheduled to make stops at Omsk and Irkutsk, reach Peking in eleven hours' flying time. But halfway to Omsk we hit a storm and turned back. Spent another two hours in Moscow airport before starting out again. At Irkutsk grounded for the night.

About half the passengers were Chinese; there was a YCL delegation, which sang songs; a couple of German businessmen, one of whom spoke English; a Russian machine expert who had worked for Amtorg, the old trading outfit, for one year in the US and spoke English not too badly. A couple of the Chinese also spoke English, so I did not lack for conversation. One of the hostesses also spoke English; she sat with me for an hour and we became very friendly — she was training to be an engineer, had been working as a hostess six months, studying at night. When I made her a present of a little Swiss hankie she choked up, went away and came back with some postcards of the plane. (Darling, I am learning to become excessively polite — you will be amazed when we are together again how I'll open doors for you, and light cigarettes, and so on.) At Moscow I had filled out a declaration (the only one on the trip) to give to customs at Irkutsk, saying, among other things, that I was taking no hashish or opium with me. Omsk was snow, twenty below zero, a plunge into Asia, characters straight out of old Russian novels. At Irkutsk saw a long movie of the Moscow Youth Festival, very good. People bundled up in furs, padded coats, etc. sat in easy chairs, on the floor, and stood, crowding the small room. A bench was brought in for the foreign guests — the two Germans and I.

Then over the mountains — and into fabulous China. We were all at the windows as the descent began — the Chinese, many of whom had been working abroad for two or three years, straining to see their homeland — and the curious Russian youth, the Germans and the Canadian.

Modern new airport, and Syd [Gordon] there to greet me, with an interpreter. A long ride to the city — fantastic driving, horn beeping, swinging around bicycles, pedicabs, carts drawn by two horses, one ahead of the other, people walking. Passing units of the People's Army in the fields, working (this never stopped since the 30s — the army maintains its contact with the peasants in this manner), people planting trees, digging ditches, sitting reading and smoking — the "blue ants" the capitalist reporters speak of — and absolutely the happiest looking bunch of people I've ever seen in my life. "Inscrutable Chinese" my foot! They smile and laugh hugely over jokes. And the factories and new buildings! Have to see them going up — by the score, by the hundreds and, in the city, by thousands, alongside the old mud huts and compounds. Then to this hotel, the Hsinchiao, better than the huge and mausoleum-like Peking Hotel, said Syd.

A comfortable room, large, single bed, good-sized desk, two easy chairs and two straight-backed chairs, a small typewriter table, and a tea table. Best feature is the European dining room on sixth floor. I'm on fifth, front room, facing a new hospital across the street. There is also a bar and small billiard room on sixth floor. My room also has sink, toilet, and shower bath; one large clothes closet; big window...

Well, Syd and I had dinner with the interpreter, Bao Shishao. I had creamed chicken soup, an omelet, and Shanghai beer. Bao had consommé, steak and potatoes, tea; Syd had beef stroganov, toast, milk; the whole bill was under five yuan. Then went to Syd's on foot — visited Tungan [Dong'an] Bazaar, a famous couple of blocks of arcade-type stalls, where you can buy everything. There is no shortage of goods of any kind — some things very cheap, others rather expensive. More on this later. And people, people everywhere. And bookstores, with people buying. An international bookstore with English books. A city committee building about the size of the Ford building. Syd, since his wife left, lives at the Peace Hotel — two rooms. His daughter, Roann, sometimes comes from the university to stay a weekend with him. (Had dinner with them and the daughter's boyfriend [Pondoli], an Albanian student, yesterday. The common language of the two lovers is Chinese — which they both speak quite fluently.)

Met some friends of Syd for dinner and drinks — chap named Harry Sichrovsky, also one of Bao's "clients" (he looks after three correspondents: Harry, from the Austrian paper [the *Volksstimme*], Alan Winnington, from the *Daily Worker,* and the *Trib* man). Since then, I've been kept busy getting established. Visit to *Renmin Ribao (People's Daily)*, tea and talk. Visit to information bureau, tea and talk. Attendance as guest at opening of new Press Club for Chinese press workers; drinks, eats, talk, introductions, etc. Met Anna Louise Strong [a US citizen who wrote prolifically and sympathetically about China], invited for dinner tomorrow night. Taken for car trip around part of city by *Renmin Ribao* chap. Dinner with bunch of people, correspondents mostly, at Peking Hotel. Drinks with a Sudanese chap, Achmed Kheir, and his wife Rita, a Viennese, living in the Peace Compound. A long walk by myself, exploring bazaar, new department store, side streets. Visit to jade market with Syd. Tonight, a small dinner to welcome me thrown by *Renmin Ribao* people (I'm warned by Syd to eat lightly, as I'll face fifteen or twenty courses). Still to come — the session with the liaison people, plus a later dinner, etc. Photos taken for press and cable cards. Cards delivered next day. And so on — you can see every beginner gets a fortnight whirl before he has a chance to settle down and do some work.

My confused, general impression of China — fabulous, absolutely fabulous progress — a tremendous leap from the past to the future, with the past and the future evident everywhere side by side. People happy, very much a part of their government in decisions and day-to-day work — youth enthusiasm tremendous. Athletic splurge, right now some hospital workers doing P.T. And morality-conscious population, reaction from former feudal subjugation of women and prostitution. So, today, other extreme.

March 29

You want to know what I've been doing. Well, there were about a dozen at this banquet, held in the famous Peking duck place. One course followed another — I had been warned not to eat much but as guest the host from *Renmin Ribao* seated on my left kept putting stuff on my plate and I was helpless. Luckily I had skipped lunch in preparation for the 7:30 banquet. I had some Shanghai beer, a glass of wine, and some potent 85 per cent white "wine" in front of me, as well as a glass of orange (the popular soft drink here). I drank sparingly, responded to toasts by sipping only. After fifteen or so very nice courses, including cold meats, greens, a soup, asparagus, and so on, the chef brought in the first duck on a platter, held it up, all brown, for inspection, then retired to the side of the room to carve it. This showing of the bird is a ceremony that goes back two hundred years, when the restaurant opened. The ducks are force-fed until they are eighty days old — not less, not more — then killed. Here's how they are eaten: slices are put on the central platter, and two plates of very thin, unleavened pancakes — no thicker than heavy writing paper — are introduced. Two pancakes are placed in one hand (before this starts a waiter hands you a hot, wet washcloth to wipe off your hands and face, as this dish is handled by hand) then choice bits of the roast duck are picked up by chopsticks, dipped in a sauce, and placed on a pancake, along with a few short bits of green onion. Then the business is rolled up, folded closed at one end, and eaten like an ice cream cone. I had three, then the waiter appeared with a second roast duck and we went through the whole business again. While eating the second duck the remains of the first are taken out to make soup (this is the tradition) and by the time we had a couple more dishes the duck soup was ready. The windup is apples and oranges....

Had dinner with Anna Louise Strong — she has three huge rooms in former Italian embassy, which is now part of the Peace Compound. After dinner the old girl talked and talked and talked. She likes mystery stories and science fiction and told us in detail — and very well, I must say — the complete plot to two sci-fic stories, one of which I had read and forgotten. Then she said, as I only live a few blocks away, we must arrange to eat together about once a week. Well ... we shall see.

March 31

... Left at six and went to Polish Embassy — cocktail party for a Polish correspondent returning home. Hungry, no dinner, so kept grabbing bits of sausage and washing it down with Polish vodka. Stood in groups and yakked with people whose names you may be familiar with — Israel Epstein [a US journalist who wrote from China for over forty years], Alan Winnington, etc. The protocol here is to shake hands whenever you meet and when you leave. As you seem to meet almost the same bunch wherever you go, it seems rather silly. Usual newspaper chatter and gentle stiletto work, shoptalk, and boasting. Syd is like Hal [Griffin, former editor of the *Pacific Tribune*], very superior type, and a few others the same. Winnington a bit cynical, after all his years here. (Example: someone commenting on Anna Louise Strong's article in *China Reconstructs*, and the fact that she had gone just a little beyond the official line on something, asking Winnington if he had read it. Alan, "Ah, in China Reeks? No, I haven't seen it.") Winnington is about my age, and at least three people have casually commented that his wife "is quite young, only twenty-five, you know." Etc., etc., meaning that people are the same everywhere, and newspaper types are more so.

April 1
... So I got up, had a light breakfast of toast, jam, and coffee, wrote my first cable for the *Trib* — a straight Congress story — and took a long (three miles) walk to the splendiferous cable office past Tien an Men [Tienanmen Square], then felt tired and didn't feel like trying to cope with a bus conductor (they charge according to the distance you say you are going) so stopped a pedicab and rode part of the way back. Cost me 50 cents [Whyte means fen; one Chinese yuan equals 100 fen]. I don't know about these pedicabs — they will eventually disappear, of course, like the rickshaws, but the Chinese use them today as part of the "walking on two legs" slogan — usually modern methods plus anything at hand to solve a problem, in this case transportation....

I was going to describe the department store. Three floors sell goods, top two or three floors are administration, so far. Lighting rather dim — they save on electricity here — but if you look at something in a glass case a clerk immediately switches on a light in the case, or counter. Swarms of buyers — though no more than in the block rabbit-warren bazaar just across the street. Everyone in everyday clothes — pants and jacket, usually blue, jackets padded; or people's army guys in khaki (very much an ordinary part of the population, you see them working in the fields with the peasants, or in the city helping industrial workers — absolutely no separation — just as the people's police, in blue, are one with the people — more on that later). Children have freedom in the store, as on the streets and everywhere. They run around unmolested, and if tired lie down in a corner and go to sleep. Often a tired mother with an infant will find a comfortable corner to sit down on the floor and nurse her child, or let it have a sleep. Store sells everything, clothes, food (people queue around popular candy counter or food counter, eat right there), liquor (no licensing, any store can sell it, prices of everything the same all over the city, so you don't have to look for "bargains" — fantastic honesty, clerks will chase you a block to give you two cents you forgot on the counter. Mothers and fathers holding up shirts to their chests to find a fit, buying lots of clothing for their kids, and some yard goods, sports equipment, notably fishing poles, footballs, volleyballs, basketballs, sports shirts, pens (which I am told are the best in the world, copies of best Sheaffer ink-filling pens, at cheaper prices, from $3 to $15), writing pads and paper, good supply but rather cheap quality, tricycles and toys for kids, which get a big play — for the first time these people now have money for some luxury goods, though they haven't got around to wearing dresses yet — everything very utilitarian. No elevators or escalators. The store about the same size as Woodward's, or perhaps a bit smaller, and, as I said, only three floors of goods.

April 2
When the wind blows here, it really blows. From my fifth-floor window I see a dust storm swirling over the rooftops. Although it is warm I have closed the windows — and hope

that in half an hour the wind will die down, as it often does. I've just had a hot shower — took advantage of hot water instead of the usual warm water when I happened to wash my hands a few minutes ago and discovered the water was quite hot. So here I am sitting at the typewriter in my dressing gown at 4:30 in the afternoon, debating whether to ring for a glass of hot cocoa (50 cents) — have just decided I will as I'm flush — Bao brought me 300 yuan for the month this morning after I posted your letter....

So after Bao left, after telling me he was working on my visit to a small factory (everything runs in channels — can't be speeded up) I decided to take a walk around the jade market and older sections of the town outside the inner city. Just behind the hotel is the road running through the great wall (the wall around the inner city, not the Great Wall of China, nearest point of which is about twenty miles from Peking). As soon as you pass through the gate and cross a little bridge over a brown stream, you are in old China (an old China all mixed up with the new, however).

A dozen carts carrying bales of rope go past, drawn by little donkeys: one donkey lifts his tail and evacuates — I happen to look at the road and am surprised to see it bare of offal — realize a little bag has caught the droppings, for manure is precious in this country, where the land has been tilled for thousands of years and needs revitalizing.... [A] pedicab driver taking a load to a store somewhere — from producer to buyer via pedicab (these pedicabs carry more freight than people — bags of flour, coal, bales of cotton and rags, personal baggage, lumber, branches (for brooms?), anything and everything. Some have converted into "trucks" with a flat platform on which they pile incredible amounts of goods. Here a bare-bottomed little boy of two squats and pees on the sidewalk, watches with interest his stream flowing down a crack in the cement, gets a stone and tries to block it off. Ancients in long black gowns sit in front of the stores — which are all set back a bit from the street — smoke and ponder....

And so on: I'm trying to get the basis for a first light article, 'Canadian in Peking' stuff — trying it out on you, dear. Now I must go and have dinner with Syd at the Peace Hotel — he's leaving Wednesday for a three-week farewell trip around China — Canton, Wuhan, Chungking, a real trip — then will be back here briefly before going to Germany. And Bao has sounded him out about me taking over his room — 609, Peace Hotel, Peking — while he's gone, and moving in later....

About Chinese girls, a subject you were interested in. Roann, Syd's stepdaughter, told a story. The university has ten thousand Chinese students and four hundred foreigners. It is a romantic setting, made for love. And the students are young. A year or more ago a Chinese girl, one of the campus beauties, and a Hungarian student fell in love. They were together all the time. Finally the Chinese students stepped in, with a critical discussion. They were both sent there to study, etc. etc. Under pressure they agreed not to see each other. But this situation didn't last; soon they were together again, and decided to get married. Approached her parents and got a firm refusal. So decided to create a situation which could not be denied. When she eventually got pregnant, the marriage was agreed to. They were married. But the university authorities had lost face; they expelled the girl. She was married, so moved into a room with her husband. As a wife, she received a certain sum of money. The baby came, they went to Hungary on holidays, then both returned to school this year, and Roann believes she is accepted again as a married student. The case aroused great interest among the students. "Everyone opposed the authorities and backed the lovers"...long pause... "except the Chinese students." We had a little debate on it; consensus of opinion among these old China hands (all have been here seven to twelve years) was that only a very small minority of the Chinese students would actually approve of the conduct of the lovers.

April 7

Here I am in my new and probably permanent quarters. The room is (including bathroom) about the size of our front room, has a fine view of the city from the windows. Can see Tien an Men [Tienanmen Square], south and to the right; the huge Peking Hotel, and other landmarks, plus rooftops of old houses, a number of narrow lanes and compounds, etc. The hotel itself is in a compound, and has a wonderful Chinese restaurant in one of the compound villas. European restaurant is on the eighth floor....

After posting your letter yesterday I went into the barbershop at the Hsinchiao (pronounced Sin-chow, or thereabouts) and darling, you'd love me if you could see me now. The best haircut and shampoo I ever had, and only 70 cents total. My hair was a bit wild and curly; so this hairdresser set out to keep that style.... Anyway, I walked away looking very lovely and adorable and distinguished, yes sirree. And this morning most of the curl is still left. I'm sure you'd go mad about me and run your fingers through my hair like crazy.

Will I get bored with this assignment before two years are up? Of course I will; all the correspondents get bored, just as the lads covering the legislature get bored. This despite the fact that everyone admits China is a very exciting place politically. But with only a handful of foreigners, who meet all the time; and difficulties in breaking through to any close relationships with the people, due to protocol — well, no doubt there will be times I will find the time hanging heavy. Not so yet because I'm still in greenhorn stage, exploring (Syd said I've seen more of Peking in ten days than some correspondents have seen in six months — even prowling around parts he never visited). The trouble is "channels" — you can't just visit a factory, or a gymnasium — it takes days or weeks of negotiations. Even a movie, tickets have to be arranged beforehand, an interpreter assigned to you, etc. Maybe I can break through in time, by a bit of brash Canadianism. But I'll wait awhile and get used to things before trying anything new . . .

April 10
Roann phoned in the afternoon, when I returned to the hotel. She and her wild young Albanian were in the city (university is on outskirts) and coming up for dinner. I invited them to dine with me; we went down to the Chinese restaurant in the compound, had sweet and sour, chicken and greens, an egg dish, pork, steamed bread and finished with soup, as is the local custom. Then they took me over to see some transplanted Canadians — Dick and Ginny — young couple, about twenty-five, two small children, he is Chinese and an adopted son of Jim Endicott, lived in Toronto until six years ago. She is half Chinese and half Irish, lived in Toronto until she married him. He is an engineer or something; she works for Peking Radio. She just returned from her month's summer work in the country — the policy of making all intellectuals learn how workers and peasants live. She lost ten pounds, said she felt wonderful. Was sent to mountains about thirty miles south of city to dig holes and plant trees on barren mountain

top. No meat. Cheapest rice and cabbage for breakfast; for dinner too; and a rice gruel for supper. At first can hardly eat it; later you gobble it up. She said policy very sound, we have no idea the intellectual tradition in China, how students wouldn't lift a finger, but had servants bring the phone, move a chair a foot, etc. When some of these carryovers into government offices had to do manual labour — such as dust a room, sweep a floor — they bound rags around their faces up to their eyebrows, gingerly stretched out broom at arm's length and couldn't even wield it. For Canadians, used to doing some ordinary work — housework or a job — as well as going to school, there was no big problem involved — although she said digging holes with a pick and shovel to plant trees was tough work. Last year she tended pigs, fell in love with them: "Pigs have personalities, you know — and are very sensitive to colds, coughs, flu, etc. We found that traditional Chinese medicine was very effective with our pigs . . ." Think I'll use that bit in an article on pigs I'm writing. If I boar my readers, sow what? (Sorry.) . . .

I learned a lot of things from this couple and want to see them again — it is not easy to meet Chinese who live like Chinese — the officials meet us during work but getting to their homes is another matter, I am told. Expect it is true, but will have to discover for myself.

Are goods harder or easier to obtain than five years ago, I asked. Harder, they said — the demand is greater and it is more difficult to get what you want. "Spoken like a true intellectual," I said, and regretted saying it, so softened and said, "You mean the people have more purchasing power?" Yes, for example, in their compound is an old shack where the lowest of the low, a group of pedicab drivers, live. Imagine, these dirty, illiterate old men now own a radio (a radio costs about $250); they pooled their money and bought it, and play it full blast all day long — Beethoven to Chinese opera, Voice of America, and traditional music — "it makes no difference to them." And the stores are crowded with workers who have some money and buy up all the goods — the new stuff — whenever it appears on the shelves. Even small luxury items.

Had a glass of vermouth and a glass of coffee, and left. As the bus stopped near us, the usual girl conductor got off and began yelling for tickets and rattling along at a good clip. "What is she saying?" I asked Roann. "Give me your tickets here! Don't forget your parcels. Get in the front door, please, comrades! Don't spit on the floor and don't let your children pee on the bus!"

April 12

... After lunch I saw a big Negro chap playing billiards by himself; he looked American, so I got into a game with him; a chiropractor from London — and before that Holland, Cuba, and New York. Over here to begin a four-month course in traditional medicine, particularly (well, the use of needles — I can't remember the right name — puncture is in it). I invited him up for dinner, went home and read *Hsinhua* [New China News Agency]. He came over (Dr. V.J. Holland, calls himself) at six, we went to the Chinese restaurant in the compound, had rice, vegetables, meat balls, prawns, and a bottle of beer. Later took a walk through the department store and along Wangfuching shopping area....

Anna Louise Strong phoned and asked me up for dinner. ... The old girl got to talking — she requires no prodding — told me about her first trip to China from USSR in 1925, how she stayed with [Communist International representative in China Mikhail] Borodin; the next trip in 1927 during the

Kuomintang-Communist split, how she got out of the country, etc. Very interesting. She's an opinionated woman, never learned to speak any Chinese, at seventy-three still does a lot of writing (working on a book on Tibet now), sees not too many people and has swollen legs and can't get around much. I made a date to take her to the Hsinchiao for dinner next Monday. She loaned me a few science-fiction thrillers to read, which will be a pleasure after all the uplifting literature I've been exposed to. . . .

I am still not writing anything about China. Why? I don't know. Like trying to write *Gone with the Wind* on the head of a pin. Only a pinhead would try. (That's not a bad lead.) Too many things I don't know. Why are there no dogs or cats in Peking? Am told, dogs spread infection. Back home, the dog, next to Mother, is Man's Best Friend. And the building boom is fantastic — the people forging ahead — but does such a picture distort? By Vancouver standards, 90 per cent of Peking is one vast slum. Not considered such here, because these have been the homes of the people for scores and hundreds of years. Few sidewalks except on main streets. Dry, worn-out earth everywhere — have to bring in mud to plant saplings — which they are doing. But hardly a sign of GREEN in the city — except for a few special areas, a city without grass. Just brown, dry earth. Cleanliness campaign — brooms sweep the earth sidewalks every day. But playing in the dirt, all children get dirty. No special attention paid to children here — so many of them. The older look after the younger. Coal dumped anywhere. Chickens scratch in it and fluff feathers in coal dust. Babies eat it, experimentally. Everyone works. Hard, but not all-out to exhaustion. A great cheerfulness — the Chinese, unlike inscrutable Westerners, have very expressive faces — laugh a lot, hugely enjoy little jokes. And so on. I know nothing about this country yet.

April 18–19

... At six tonight go back to Great Hall of the People where the Chinese-African Friendship Society is having a cocktail party or buffet supper, I believe, for one hour. These affairs similar; you meet and shake hands again with all the other correspondents and anyone else you happen to know; snatch something to eat and drink; stand around looking pleasant; and then go. . . .

For all I wrote about cocktail parties and buffet suppers turned out to be not so last night — the Great Hall — or a tiny part of it — became transformed into a sort of night club, and I had a nice evening, perhaps the pleasantest since arriving here ... Arrived at Great Hall ... found this was no small affair, we were to go in the great front doors, cars were rolling up driveways, dumping out ambassadors and *chargé d'affaires*, etc. with their ladies all dressed up: Indian girls in saris; Mongolians and Koreans; lots of Vietnamese students from the university; Chinese workers in sweaters and slacks, but a few girls in western skirts and a couple with slit skirts; lots of Negro students from various African countries, etc., etc.

Went across an acre of marble on big carpets, climbed a movie staircase, walked a block down broad-carpeted corridors and came to the reception room where tables filled with food had been set up — long rows down the middle, then scores of small tables, and bars at either side (tables with bartenders and girl waitresses). Going in I happened to meet Guillermo Angelov, the Bulgarian news agency chap whom I sometimes eat with and have taken a sort of liking to; he's a bit dark-complexioned, very sincere; anyway, we looked for press table, knowing protocol would have us somewhere, and found it well in the rear at one side. So, shook hands with Sarzi (*L'Unità*), Jean Vidal (*L'Humanité*)

— they stick around together a lot, Vidal short, sharply dressed, big smile all the time, looks very much alive and with a zest for living; the Italian out of character, larger, very quiet, slow smile, talks very little. And Alan Winnington, another meticulous dresser, blocking what he called "Channel Six," the space between two tables where the waitresses had to pass with their trays of drinks — and urging me to get used to maotai, this vodka-like Chinese drink, powerful, served in very small glasses, taken at a gulp. The German agency chap, a big hulk of a man with wild curly hair, named Eric Henschke, always to be seen with Alan, was at his side. When the girl came with her tray of orange juice, wine, brandy, beer, and maotai, we'd clean up the latter, let her go on her way. Winnington expounded on his worms. He has a three-headed kind. "What are you doing to get rid of them?" "Nothing," he replies, they are a harmless type, and keep all other germs and worms and intestinal animals away. He's had them since Korea, wouldn't part with them. They like maotai, so wouldn't think of leaving him. Everybody everywhere has some sort of germs or worms only in the West it isn't polite to talk about it. Here he is scaring Bert our new colleague.

The speeches began and simultaneously people began eating. I'd say there were about two thousand people at the dinner, but no crowding.... The Chinese workers ate heartily; many of them don't get meat oftener than once or twice a month, if that. But it is interesting that at every big affair there are hundreds of these workers present, from some plant or other that has done good work, or students (lots in this case), or from various organizations.

April 20

You ask what I read. Well, old *Daily Worker* from London and NY; *Peking Review*; *China Reconstructs*; Chinese literature; Soviet literature; science-fiction mags loaned by Anna Louise; weekly overseas edition *Globe & Mail*; *Pacific Tribune* and *Canadian Tribune*; old copies of *New Statesman* and *The Observer*...

Tonight I am taking Anna Louise (don't EVER just call her Anna, I have been warned) to dinner at Hsinchiao.... A.L. very pleased with herself — she was given an honoured seat at the big do the other night because of her age, and seems [veteran Eighth Route Army General] Chu Teh dropped in and spoke to her. She likes celebrities. Told me over the phone that if I had any friends who particularly wanted to meet her at dinner, she didn't mind if I introduced them. This is being very gracious on her part — she seems to like me — I am a good audience. And why not be — she is a damn good storyteller and I can learn a lot from her. Besides, the old gal is obviously a bit lonely.

April 22

... Last night at Winningtons. [Alan and his] good-looking Chinese-Jewish wife [Esther], about your age (Alan is fifty or more) and two children were there. Nice home, by local standards; small courtyard; old building, but several rooms, good bathroom, and a refrigerator. Oldest child about seven, I'd judge, curly hair, dark eyes, handsome as sin, looks a devil too, gleaming smile. He shook hands with his uncles (everyone is an "uncle" in China — or a Big Sister or Elder Brother or Younger Brother, etc.). Other kid is five — a bad one — won't talk English, only Chinese — very big for his age — Esther says, "I think we hatched a monster

—I don't think he's normal, look how big he is." Alan: "Definitely not normal, we've spawned a monstrosity." Well, that's the kind of people and conversation. "I'm sorry, my wife is cooking the supper, I cannot guarantee anything will be edible, but we have plenty of peanuts—have some, they'll kill your appetite." As a matter of fact, we drank beer, ate peanuts, then a big meal. Rice, fish, fried pork ("Try this fried cat; we shot it ourselves—it was going along the fence and I got my .22—Esther used an old Canton cat recipe—not bad—have some more.") Bean curd, greens, soup, coffee. And drank—an expensive rice wine, then maotai, then after supper cracked open a bottle of Johnny Walker (Red Label) straight from Hanoi (a present, like the coffee, from Malcolm [Salmon, the South Asian correspondent of the *Australian Tribune*, who had just been in Vietnam]). Drank half the bottle. Talked a lot of politics—both old party people, also trained journalists. Argued a bit. Lots of satire and some cynicism—but not cynics on any basic things—just things that happen in course of work—like I am. In short, found the company very congenial. And nice to know ALL Chinese kids not perfect; theirs go to normal kindergarten or school—learn the most awful words, all connected with bodily functions—come home and recite praises to Mao all fouled up by the kids—"We try to ignore it, don't let them think it's important," said Esther. At one point...Alan said, "Are you married?" So I said, "Yes and no. Separated. Going to marry a girl I've been in love with a long time. We have a five-year-old. But there are difficulties and neither of us is divorced yet." "We're not married," said Esther. "You should try and bring her over as soon as possible," said Alan. "It only costs 10 cents to get married here, and they don't give a damn what the situation is back home. I had a girl who was going to wait for me, and when I went back in six months she was married and living in the United States." "THANK YOU for your comforting words," I said.

April 25–30

Spring has come to Peking. Now it is possible to tell the boys from the girls without looking at the hairdos. What I mean, the padded jackets have been discarded; the pedicab drivers are rolling up their pant legs to the knee; the girls have taken off two or three shirts and a sweater, thus peeling down to only a couple of shirts and a sweater.... How they stand even this amount of clothing I don't know — it was 25 degrees yesterday or 78 by our measurement — plenty hot! And in July and August it hits 40 — which I make out to be 115–125. Maybe that's when the people here strip down? I've already shot my bolt — only wear thin sports shirt in the afternoons....

Sunday morning tried to sleep in — rolled over at seven and closed my eyes and drifted off — BOOM BOOM went the drum, and cymbals banged, and it was a long parade down the street in front of the compound, then around the back of the hotel — banners and kids and their parents and old people — undoubtedly a call to set up — or join — an urban commune in this district. [Was eating breakfast in the dining room] then a very nice thing happened. I watched eight new little girls being hired. They had all been selected before, of course, and were all dressed the same, in neat light grey pants and jackets, hair in two long braids with ribbons. They were led in and seated around a big table; a waitress brought them tea, they all rose and bowed slightly to her, shook hands; the chief bartender, who is also in overall charge of the dining room, came over; they all got up and were introduced; then sipped their tea and waited; in came a party secretary from somewhere (probably street or district, or perhaps just of the hotel) and an assistant, with briefcase. More smiles, bowing, shaking hands, but the girls were nervous. He sat down at head of table, shot some quick questions (my guess, questions on addition — could they add up a bill properly, give right change, etc.). After about three minutes he seemed satisfied, rose, smiled, shook hands with each girl again, headed for the elevator. Out came the kitchen staff then, and all the waitresses, more chairs found, everyone introduced to everyone else, too many to shake hands, but rose, bowed, smiled. The cook said a few words. The head waitress spoke briefly. The bartender spoke a bit longer, then ended the meeting, led the new girls around the dining room, and on a tour through the kitchen. Then more handshakes and smiles and the girls were relieved to go on a later shift — I saw them in the courtyard later. But I thought — my, what a nice way to be hired for a job! ...

Walked up to department store, a madhouse on Sunday; everybody buying shoes, it seemed; you sit on floor to try them on, or hop around on one leg, or plunk the little kids right on glass counters nearby and try on tiny shoes (they have lovely colourful clothes for babies, in contrast to limited selection for grownups). There are some chairs in shoe department, but not enough and many are taken by women who sit down to feed their babies; or by country cousins who put the babies in the chairs to sleep an hour or so (no one here would wake a child who is tired). So the customers make do as best they can. Saw one family moved, though — real peasant types, with all their bundles. Mother looked for a good spot to have a rest and feed her youngest; decided the foot of marble stairs was most comfortable; arranged her bundles and children around her, pulled out a breast and shoved nipple in junior's mouth. Only thing was, she completely blocked the stairs — and was asked to move a bit to the side. Outside the store, Red Army men, peasants, women with babies, children, lay or squatted in sun. The tea vendors did a good business; also the popsicle sellers, who can never meet the demand....

Re your comments on stories — well, difficulties. Congress, like legislature in Victoria, boring as hell if you want to know truth. And all we get is half an hour listening to speeches — then escape for translation and tea. We are expected to cable straight reportage on political stuff — not brought here to record personal impressions. Nelson [Clarke] writes [from the *Canadian Tribune*]: "We are well pleased with your cables so far, and congratulate you on their brevity, as well as on their clarity....We'll be looking forward to receiving some stories on your impressions of the life of the people." Now as to latter, I am well aware that regardless of Nelson, what READERS think of my stuff will depend almost entirely on personal features. I sent one early piece on urban communes, not too good and now out of date; one quite good but rather flippant piece which I wonder if Nelson will run, called Dateline, Peking, and dealing with kids, pigs, pedicabs, absence of dogs in city, sparrows, and bedbugs; and one piece of straight reportage, but with a personal tie-in of a visit to a factory. The question is, will they be used? As for the Chinese, they will neither understand nor appreciate the flippant piece; they are very pleased with the political cables. ALL their papers consist of politics; though there is some human interest writing about innovators, etc., it is also in a serious vein.

April 26

... Well, what I've been doing. Yesterday morning went to see the new Peking railway station. Most correspondents get a guide for this trip. It means tea with the party director and a conducted tour. I tried it on my own; spent two hours wandering around. Vast marble halls, etc., and hundreds of people coming and going; families packing their belongings in shawls and a few cardboard suitcases; shoes off, peasants stretched out having a sleep on the leather couches; women sitting on the marble floors, feeding babies — you know, I think I told you, half the Chinese are babies. Also, women wear half the pants in China (a new slogan for our women's commission?). One peasant girl, dirty face, sitting at the doorway of a waiting room, sweater pulled up and both breasts bare, baby sucking one nipple and hanging onto the other with his hand. Mama's breasts need a wash, baby needed a bath too; but I guess the milk was clean enough. Soldiers with their guns catching catnaps, waiting for a train. (You also see PEOPLE on the streets with guns — boys and girls — members of the millions-strong people's militia.) ... Four escalators (only one running at a time, though) to second floor. Two more huge waiting rooms crammed with people — you know, not only do they have a lot of Chinese food in China, as Charlie Caron remarked, but they also have a lot of Chinese people. And two rest rooms and playrooms for mothers with babies: cradles, cots, swinging cots, playpens. Many counters — dozens — selling literature (a lot of people read here, too), postcards, handkerchiefs, sox, soap (several big washrooms for men and women together — separate toilets, though) — scarves, powders, etc. Also an eager crowd of country cousins staring in awe, counting their yuan, buying purple ties, etc. Reading rooms. A YCLer reading aloud, with dramatic gestures, a heroic tale to a bunch of peasants. Glasses, the earnest crusading type. Luggage room — with clerks helping people to tie up their cardboard crates so that there is a slight hope their belongings will stay intact. A few women with babies slung on their backs — the old style. And some old women with broken feet — from binding. They take tiny, mincing steps. Guess you know the story — an emperor's daughter born with deformed feet. But that couldn't be, so edict was ALL girl children have arches broken, four toes bent back and bound to heel, making a tiny, pointed foot, not much good to walk on.

May 1

... I agree fully with you, that if I don't inject the personal angle I'll soon lose a lot of readers. So in the May Day story — a short cable sent an hour ago — I did just that ...

When Alan Winnington went to Tibet last trip, with Gordon and dozen or so other correspondents, he wrote highly personal story (I think I used a bit of his in *Pacific Tribune*) about "Today I spent 12 hours with the Panchen Lama [the second-highest–ranking Tibetan Buddhist lama, after the Dalai Lama], ate dinner with him, walked out in the fields to admire his thoroughbred horses," etc. etc. Told what he asked Panchen Lama, what PL said to him, etc. Other correspondents were furious — it had all been mass interview, dinner, etc. and Alan's story sounded like a personal scoop. Even the Chinese, who rarely criticize openly, raised question. Alan, with aplomb (this is Syd's version of story, he does not love Winnington) answered, "That's what my paper wants." Alan, by the way, is off to Korea on short notice — he covered the war from this side, and can sometimes arrange these things that would take others months.

May 2

As you must know by now, no big parade here this year. Leaders went down to the people instead — and there were hundreds of small parades, plus celebrations in every park, school, factory, and so on. Syd and I walked to Tienanmen Square — only about forty thousand there, but as little groups came in it swelled to maybe two hundred thousand or more. Sturdy girls marching in shorts, shouting slogans, holding banners aloft. Other girls in filmy green skirts (worn OVER their rolled-up blue overalls, as we noticed when they hitched up the skirts to sit down in the square). Dance groups. Commune groups with charts and pictures of achievements. Students. And so on.

The morning celebrations (estimated to have involved three million) lasted from 9 to 12 noon. Walked to Peking Hotel and had dinner with Chen Si-lan, the dance director (Syd tells me she was quite a famous dancer in Soviet Union some years ago) and from listening to them talk I learned that Rita had sort of walked out on Syd in huff and taken passage back to Canada . . . they have a hectic marriage. . . .

About May Day slogans . . . at foreign office conference I asked the question: "Will there be political slogans this year on May Day and what will they be — can you tell us?" Now here is something in China. This should have been answered: "We are not releasing slogans in advance." Or, more brutally, "No comment." But in China the answer is: "There will be no political slogans this year. Of course, as the CC [Central Committee] statement on May Day pointed out, the THEME will be international friendship, fulfillment of our plan, and world peace — but there will be NO SLOGANS." A few weeks ago I would have taken that to mean there would be no slogans — as I reported there were no actual urban communes in Peking, after a direct answer had stated, "No,

there are NO ACTUAL COMMUNES YET IN PEKING."
Now, three weeks later, I'm much smarter. The day after the
NPC [National Party Congress] speech it was announced
there were FIVE communes in the city, had been operating
nearly two years. That was two days after the press conference. Next day there were NINE communes. At last count,
a week or so ago, there were thirty-eight urban communes
— all started in 1958, the press stories say. So, I did NOT
cable there would be no slogans, I understood they simply
did not wish to announce them. Today press reports the
slogans: unity of socialist camp, etc. Americans get out of
Taiwan; oppose American war drive . . .

Alan Winnington says: "You get used to it. This is the
only party I know of that comrades will look you straight
in the eye, tell you an absolute lie, then a few days later
when the truth is revealed, calmly say it had not been offi-
cially decided to announce such-and-such at the time you
inquired, and feel no sense of anything wrong." So — you
live and learn.

[*The same evening in Bert's hotel room: Syd, his stepdaughter, Roann, and her Albanian boyfriend, Pondoli, and
Dick and Ginny.*]

So we had a couple of beers and Ginny working early tomorrow and had to go get some sleep. Told one funny story
which led to another from Syd. I can't resist telling both,
because you'll get yet another insight on China.

When she arrived from Canada, Ginny knew only one
Chinese word, "Bu" or "No." Don't forget she is half Chinese, and looks Chinese. Well, one day in a place waiting
for Dick to phone her, she needed a pee, so went behind a
little swinging door where they had a cuspidor (relic from
foreign occupation) for women to pee into. "I was squatting
over this thing when the telephone rang and I heard a man

shouting into it, like everyone does," said Ginny. "Well, you know I was sure it was Dick, so I called out something, 'Is that for me?' or something like that. So the man puts down the phone and opens the door to discuss it with me. There I was with my pants down and trying to stop and yelling 'Bu! Bu!' at him, and he looked puzzled, and what did I want, and goes out and closes the door, then comes back in again and says something, goes out again, comes in again . . . and me trying to pull my things together . . . and he's puzzled why I'm so excited about, after all, nothing."

Syd tells of an incident in his trip. His interpreter was a Shanghai intellectual, than which there is no whicher. And the funniest part of the story—unconscious to Syd—is that his own high-faluting English manner caused the trouble in the first place. But the story. They had just finished a long official luncheon and were due to start an exhausting afternoon trip around the city. Syd tells the interpreter, I would like to have a wash. "A wash?" "Yes," says Syd, rubbing his hands together, "a washroom, understand?" Yes, he understood, he would go and see. Away he went, didn't come back for ten minutes. When he sat down, he assured Syd, "It is being arranged." "Arranged?" said Syd, who was needing a crap badly by this time. "Are you sure you know what I want? Washroom, bathroom, toilet." "Yes, yes, they were arranging everything — things backward here, you understand." Another five minutes passes, Syd says, look, let's go, and gets up. "This way," says the interpreter. They cross from the restaurant into another building, climb to the third floor, at each floor two women usher them onward and upward. Finally, a room, women rushing around erecting a screen, carrying tubs and pails of hot water. The interpreter beams, "A wash, yes?" Syd spies a swinging door cubicle, points to it, angrily tells the interpreter, "I want to go THERE — get these women out of here." He goes over and squats down, as he does, the door slowly swings open, he can't reach it, and it's one of those hole-in-floor squatting toilets. Meanwhile, interpreter in a tizzy. Can't possibly admit he made a blunder, would lose face. So people walk back and forth, taking look at Syd to see how he is progressing, and wondering why he spoke so angrily — did the bath they were fixing not suit him? Poor Syd, with all this attention his bowels freeze up, he can't do anything. Finally, he comes out, saves face of the interpreter by going behind screen, noisily splashing water around, using three towels to dry hands and face — happy interpreter explains foreign custom to wash after meals, besides, guest is hot and tired, appreciated wash-up very much, etc.

Well, of course these things are funny, they also smack a bit of the "funny stories on my travels" approach, but these things DO happen ... and Chinese must have a fund of tales about Canadians and Americans even funnier than these.

May 8

[*The night before Syd Gordon left for Berlin, a number of friends turned up in Bert's hotel room.*]

... Then the phone rang again, it was Dick and Ginny, they also had been invited by Syd to come over. So up they came. Then Roann and her Albanian dropped in. Then Gladys and her husband Yang Xianyi. Gladys was brought up in this country by missionary parents, sent to London so she wouldn't marry a Chinese, met Yang at university and later married him in China — they have lived here since before liberation — work as a team of translators and polishers at Foreign Languages press — she is considered best translator of poetry into English in China, I am told.

May 9

...Syd phoned, his plane had been delayed from early morning to later, now a hurry-up call from Bao to be ready in half an hour. I went down to Syd's room, he wasn't half packed... finally we got in the car, sped to the airport which is quite a long distance from town — again I saw the Chinese countryside as if for the first time...the big factories and some apartments to house factory workers going up simultaneously a few miles from city — then the peasants, the little villages, everyone living like one family in the clay huts behind the village walls — you can understand when you SEE why communes are logical here, although they would be not only impractical but impossible in any other socialist country.

A short wait at the airport, Syd's luggage three kg. overweight, but finally sent through. Then at 11:30 the call to board the plane, unlike Canada, we could walk part way on tarmac, then stopped at a red line. I thanked Syd for his kindness to me. Syd WAS very kind to me, took me everywhere, introduced me to all his friends, did not pass judgment on anyone, said he had likes and dislikes as I would undoubtedly have, but would make my own circle of friends in time. He resented what he thought was bad treatment by *Canadian Tribune* — had he wanted to, he could have been unco-operative, instead he did his best to make things easier for me and displayed a certain generosity and kindheartedness on a number of occasions. So, you know, I felt a little lump at seeing him go — "I just can't believe I am leaving China," said Syd. "I know that someday I must come back, I will come back." And I was thinking, here I was waving goodbye, and only five or six weeks before he was waving hello when I stepped off the plane on my arrival. Roann cried a little, the plane took off at noon, we headed back to town in the car. Bao told me that with Syd gone, Alan and

Harry in Korea, he was being sent to the countryside to work a couple of weeks at manual labour....

Late in afternoon Esther Winnington phoned, reminded me that I had accepted invitation to go to Yangs for dinner, suggested I come up to her place as she had asked Gavin Greenleigh and his newly arrived wife over, and as they lived in (place we hear Dorise [Nielsen] is) consequently had car at their disposal. So I had a bath and shave and had to put on my good suit (because sent coat and pants to cleaners Sat.) and took pedicab and arrived at her place about five — we didn't go to the Yangs till six. Esther told us about her children's problem. Joe, seven, is the handsome dark devil I described to you before . . . at least foreigners think he is handsome, so he likes foreigners like us, calls me "Uncle Bert" as soon as I come in. But the Chinese don't like dark skins, so they make a fuss over Didi, age 5, who is big and has a light skin. So Didi likes Chinese and hates foreigners (who make a fuss over his brother) and carries it to point where he refuses to speak a word of English at home or to anyone, though he understands it. And Joe, on the other hand, dislikes Chinese, who favour his young brother....

We went to Gladys's place, her husband not home yet, his Sunday (one a month) to go and work on a plot of ground. We had a drink, just started supper when he came home, a bit tired. Main dish was a sort of dumpling, stuffed with greens. I ate fifteen or twenty. Poor Gavin, his wife doesn't like it here, it is so obvious, she's afraid of the food — and hasn't been out alone in city yet — or rather, once in car, but afraid of getting out of car — a woman of, say, sixty or so, he's about the same, works for Hsinhua news agency; she has lived all her life in Australia, touched a bit of ham (rare delicacy), two pieces of tomato with sugar, tried but didn't finish a pickle; told us about terrible blasting going on near their swank apartment. ("You'd think if people complained they would have to stop it.") She came with Gavin a year or so ago when he first came — didn't like it and after a week or so returned home — he's been trying to get her to return ever since . . . and now she's here but food does not agree with her, also the loudspeaker comes on early in the morning, plays anthem, etc. ("Oh, we have one that starts at 5:45 a.m.," says Esther, "but the Chinese people LIKE noise, you must understand.") . . . .

Invitation to Tienanmen this afternoon, 3 p.m., there is to be a demonstration of one million against Japan-US treaty. So when I finish this I will post it, walk down to Peking Hotel for lunch and then stroll through the hundreds of thousands (at least they keep a path open to stands) to our section. What do you do at a meeting of a million people? Listen to speeches. And not worth the cable. (In the courtyard below, hotel workers putting finishing touches to their banners.) To insure the million, all schools will be closed, and all government buildings. Urban communes will send big delegations. But factories will continue working.

8:30 p.m. Friday, May 13

. . . Speaking of buying, I bought a pair of pants yesterday. Told you Bao had been sent to work in country for a fortnight, but Chang Chi-hsin, the other English interpreter, came around — found note Bao left saying I wanted pants, so he got coupons (not for cloth but for cotton lining — need coupons to buy cotton, nothing else). First we went to market — I want to do a little story on market for my byline: "Peking light" material (how did you like first one?) and saw the "pay by the minute" theatre. What you do is get a ticket with time punched on it, and go in. There were maybe seventy-five people there. Tea can be bought. On stage continuous vaudeville acts (that is, monologues, "cross-talk," songs, recitations, storytellers) perform from 2 to 8 p.m. and as you go out you pay—at rate, I believe, of 2 cents for every five minutes. We saw a girl do a sing-song story, accompanied by a three-piece Chinese orchestra, and she also beat time on a drum herself, then a couple of young "cross-talk" comedians—then we left, tried a new ice-cream machine "parlour" in an alleyway, the ice cream was very poor, then had a "soda" at another place, at 60 cents a shot.

May 28

Yesterday, went to new [train] station watched people for a long time using the escalator, probably the only one in town —there are four in station, but only one used at a time, for economy ... reactions of people, most of them using it for first time, very interesting...two guards at bottom and one at top, or rather assistants, not guards...woman and five-year-old approach, she loses nerve, child steps on moving thing and is rapidly drawn away, mother gives a little cry and pulls her back by the hand, off this dangerous contraption...then looks ashamed and laughs, an assistant grabs her by elbow and pushes her on, why it was nothing at all, it now has become a moving stairs, that's all, and they stand on the same step and look around—only suddenly a new crisis, the stairs are disappearing, become a flat line and going into the floor again, you might get sucked in, what to do...JUMP...so they jump, mother dragging daughter, and there they are, safe and sound, way up on second floor, so they turn and look at the contraption again, why, it isn't so frightening when you examine how it works, next time it'll be easy... and a Red Army man from the south, obviously, it would never do for him to show fear when hundreds of peasants are using the thing, so he steps on without looking down, his feet squarely over a crack — suddenly the crack separates and one end goes up and he's thrown off balance, he grabs handrail and recovers, looks sheepish...mother and baby and an old pair in seventies are turned away by the attendant, who points to elevator thirty feet away, tells them to take it to second floor...but the old couple bewildered...get lost on way to elevator...elevator, what's that, something like an elephant? What does she mean, those two little doors in the wall? We'll watch the doors and see — they open and it's only a little room, some people come out some go in — but there's no sense in that, we want to go upstairs, and she won't let us use the moving stairway; we'll ask this sweeper — get in elevator, the box, she says ... all right, these young people must know what they are doing, let us hold hands and take a chance, depending on the party and Chairman Mao — well, what a funny sensation ... I stand at the top, watching them come out — looking bewildered, then dawning comprehension — look where we are, away up where we wanted to go, as high as the top of the moving stairs!!...

The official stories of this station don't tell true story at all — for example, waiting rooms can seat fifteen thousand — ah yes, if people just SAT — three or four sitting people ... and hundreds stretch out on floor, their luggage piled around them.... Many peasants with dirt-encrusted feet and ankles ... two peasant girls, one with bow in hair, her friend examining her head carefully and cracking lice. (In Rewi Alley's book I read of campaign to convince some young peasant lads that lice are not an essential part of your body, needed to maintain your health, but that vermin must be destroyed.) ...

Well, darling, I'll have to go now.... Wish I could write

some of above stuff in columns but you know it would never be understood, either here or at home . . . they would think I was "making fun" of these wonderful people.

May 30

I guess I'd better tell you more about the W[innington] party. First, Alan, as a Britisher, was invited to [Chinese Premier] Chou [En-lai]'s party for Monty [British Field Marshal Bernard Montgomery]. It was FANTASTIC — a weird collection of people (clever selection) including the former [Chinese] emperor, several former Kuomintang generals and the Red Army generals who defeated them, girl parachutists who jumped for Monty in a display before — just ordinary kids in ordinary clothes among all the brass. Monty slightly befuddled by it all. Chou (with Alan at elbow scribbling — all very informal and he got a thousand words to cable out of it) introduces Montgomery to the former Emperor. "And what do you do now," says Monty. "I'm a botanist," says Pu Yi. "Ah yes," says Monty, "that's like a gardener, isn't it? A very healthy occupation — but I see you are smoking, you shouldn't smoke, very bad for the health." And Chou introduced him to famous ex-Kuomintang general and, alongside him, "the general who defeated him." Monty says to K. man, "And how many troops did you have?" "A million." "A million," says Monty, "and how, then, were you defeated?" "They all crossed over [to the communists]," explains the general. Anyway, Monty broke a long-standing rule [since he was an uncompromising health faddist who opposed tobacco and alcohol], drank a toast, and as you know, invited Chou for personal visit. Next day he went to Shanghai, met Mao. Probably more to this story than just "informal" visit — long talks with Chou, five or six hours. But the fantastic set-up party

— "The only one missing was Chiang Kai-shek [the defeated former president of China who had established the Republic of China in Taiwan after the revolution in 1949]," said Alan....

After mailing letter to you at noon I went to Peking for my usual club sandwich and beer. Then sat down for dessert with Angelov, the Bulgarian, and a Czech correspondent who is leaving for home in couple of days and very glad about it all. You see all the correspondents here — and especially those trying to service dailies or news agencies — get very fed up with Peking methods (slow, slow, slow) which give absolutely no scope for a reporter to get a story on his own. The old joke here is:

Patient to doctor: I don't know what's the matter with me. I feel frustrated all the time, stifled, sort of smothered...

Doctor: Ah, another Peking newspaper correspondent...

Well, not a very good joke, but expresses a feeling. I haven't got it yet — 1st I work on a weekly 2nd *Trib* doesn't seem to give a damn about keeping up with China news 3rd I get relief writing my human interest stuff — most of the boys want to be "foreign correspondents." My frustration will come from the other end — if CT doesn't use my stories of visit to factory & urban commune.

June 3

... I was in Peking Hotel for lunch Thursday ... spotted Reuters man and the, pardon me, THE Times man from London, so sat down with them — Times man a real cold fish, he's "expert" on Far East for his paper, here to reacquaint himself with China, was here last in 1954 with British delegation ([Clement] Attlee, etc.) and before that in 1948 at Liberation, and before that, well, I gather he is a missionary's son, born and brought up here — there are quite a few of that breed around, some good, most bad — I think he's the latter, in fact, no doubt about it. I suppose it doesn't do my reputation any good to be seen hobnobbing with riff-raff from the capitalist press, but I'm a liberal-minded fell … hey, stop shoving snow down my neck, I'm only kidding.

June 6

Here it is June 6, sixteen years ago the Second Front opened, I was stationed in a camp near Dover, living in tents, went to medical tent that morning and then heard the announcement … a few weeks later we were driving north in our carriers through London and down to the mouth of the Thames, where we embarked … sweating it out in Channel as they closed the hatches over us and we zig-zagged to escape submarines, knowing that if we were hit we'd had it … then over the side, down the rope ladders onto big landing barges, where we sat in our carriers for an hour as barges lined up; and a radio playing American jazz music, who had it I forget … then in to the beach, all de-mined and marked off, we rolled ashore and hardly got our treads wet — well, not more than two feet of water — despite weeks of building up sides of carriers, etc. … two minutes to tear down all our waterproofing … then into an assembly yard, where we broke all the rules of years of training, with vehicles hub to hub and us sleeping under them … a few Jerry planes could have knocked out the whole Second Division that night … then into a field a mile on (our troops only held a strip about four or five miles deep, Caen had not yet been taken) and on his first reccy trip our major got slightly wounded jumping into a ditch (a bit of shrapnel in knee they said) and flown back to England … and then into action, nineteen solid days of it, and the runs from the canned food, and hives, and my mortar knocked out of action and #2 man wounded — seventeen pieces of shrapnel . . . and our lieutenant killed . . . and another of crew wounded . . . and Nick and Hersch joined crew . . . second mortar knocked out before it fired a bomb . . . and so on and so on . . .

June 8

Dear Ricky:

Yes, I remember the fun we both had making the snowman, and how we rolled a big ball of snow up to the corner, it was so heavy we both had to push on it. But that was away back in the wintertime, and now it is summer and very hot here in China. You ask me how the Chinese say thank you. They say "hen hao" which sounds something like "he haw" and when they say hello they say "nin hao" which sounds like "Knee Haw" but I do not speak very much Chinese. I'll bet you could learn it quicker than me, because you already speak two languages, English and Russian. . . .

On my way home [from dinner with Anna Louise Strong] I was hit up by first beggar I've run into, a ten-year-old boy, in the dark he walked along, touching my hand . . . thought I was just brushing against someone and sort of withdrew my hand . . . felt his hand again . . . looked down, he was just following me, touching me with a cupped hand, looked up at me . . . now, dammit, I only had change and roll of $5 bills . . . a bill far too much, anyway, kid would likely get in trouble trying to change it . . . so I gave him all my change, about 30 cents, I think, enough for a bowl of noodles or some kind of a meal . . . it kind of shook me, though I pass people sleeping on sidewalk almost every night, sometimes whole families in from country, with their bedrolls and everything . . .

wondered after if the kid was alone, or more likely with a grandfather or someone.

June 16

China: Hawking and spitting publicly have always been considered normal procedure in this very dry and dusty climate. But sometimes it still comes as a bit of a shock when a well-groomed, pretty girl clears her throat, HHHWWWKKK, and spits — even when she carefully lifts the lid of a spittoon pot to get rid of her phlegm in a sanitary manner. Sanitary mothers also pee in the pots, which are scattered around in the stores, and some on the streets. That's fine for little boys, who can aim, but more difficult for little girls. They usually find a grating, squat in the traditional Chinese manner — just as their dads and mommies squat to rest or wait for buses — and pee in a forward arc, hitting the grating a foot and a half ahead of them, because of their squatting position. (Try it, dear.)

June 26

... Well, at 3 p.m. Sat. a meeting in the Great Hall. This is anti-imperialism week (what week isn't?) so there were speeches — it was anniversary of Korean War, which began a decade ago, June 25, 1950. Then dances, a sort of play with some ballet and tumbling thrown in, kicking around the US flag on stage, etc. etc. by members of PLA troupe. I forgot to tell you that Thursday afternoon, in 95°F or so, Harry [Sichrovsky] and Lottie and Bao and I went to visit new PLA Museum outside city, covered third floor, story of war in Korea, including captured documents, etc. I suppose history will decide how the thing started; there is pretty solid evidence US tried some germ warfare (Alan was there, saw bunches of contaminated flies, etc. in winter, dropped in snow from containers, etc.) Among souvenirs showing Yankee degeneracy — deck of poker cards, with nudes on back. By the way, you'd better bring some cards when you come — shop around and get a good hot deck.

June 27

. . . Felix [Greene, cousin of the novelist Graham Greene] told me an amusing story: the other night he went to a dance at the British Embassy . . . "they assume because you are there that you are one of THEM, and against the Chinese, whom they always refer to as THEY" and one lady said to him, "The Chinese are a very LAZY people, and this government has made them more lazy" . . . well, said Felix, NEVER have I heard anyone call the Chinese lazy, they have been called toiling blue ants, and regimented slaves, and too industrious to compete on a fair basis with westerners . . . but NEVER before had I ever heard anyone characterize them as lazy, so I asked why, and she said, "The other day I was shopping and called a pedicab driver to take me home, and he refused because it was his LUNCHTIME." Well, said Felix (or so he told me) I said to her, you misunderstand the significance of what happened, for never before was a pedicab driver in a position to say NO to a foreigner — he never had that independence — and seldom was he able to eat a LUNCH, he usually ate a bit of rice in the morning and some rice and greens at night, but nothing at noon. So the lady, says Felix, looked at him oddly and walked away.

June 29

[I've been approached about taking holidays at Beidaihe, 250 kilometres east of Beijing, which is the Communist Party leadership's summer beachside resort.] Would I like some? The interpreter today was not Bao but Chang. I knew he had my room and everything all worked out. I said, yes, very nice, but not alone, probably same time as Harry and Lottie. He drew out floor plan, this family here, that one there, in house owned by paper [*Renmin Ribao*], and room for myself alone. We thought you would probably want a room alone — laugh, your wife not here yet — and it is six hours by train, twenty minutes by car to village, but we have a car from the paper here — laugh, but you can walk it if you like . . . you will eat at restaurant run by International Club, a ten-minute walk, but food not too good, not as much variety as at your hotel (so what? I said) well, said Chang, grinning, this is just being fair, comrade, to give you a warning; beach about five minutes' walk from room.

July 4

The important news first — you will be able to come over around the end of August. A peculiar letter from Nelson [Clarke, from the *Tribune*] this morning, all he said about our problem [of whether or not, and how, Monica and Ricky could join Whyte] was: "Following up on my last letter, particularly with respect to the request which you made. We consider this to be a personal, family matter. We see no reason why we should raise any objection to you carrying through the plan you outline."

Period. That's all. He then went on to discuss other matters. . . .

Cheers. I think this calls for a drink. I have half a tumbler of vermouth left, and a good shot of gin. I'll make a W. cocktail and toast you "bottoms up"...GAMBEI!

And finally, Nelson has become aware of some developments at last. So he tells ME about them, thusly: "There are some rather lively discussions going on these days. Suggest you try to follow them...as closely as you can. I'll just mention the next issue of our Marxist Review, which I've arranged that you receive regularly by airmail. The main point I want to make at the moment is the importance of keeping abreast of developments."

July 17, Peitaiho

"Peitaiho [Beidaihe] (282 m. from Mukden) is chiefly known on account of the summer resort for Europeans on Mt. Lienfeng-shan, 5 m. to the S. of the station. On this hill, which is washed on two sides by the Sea of Po-hai and the River Tai-shui and commands a delightful prospect, are found villas and hotels for the accommodation of summer visitors. One may reach the place on a donkey, the hire of which is 50 cents."

— From *An Official Guide to China,* prepared by the Imperial Japanese Government Railways, Tokyo, 1915

Sarzi brought along the above book and I have been enjoying it; it helps one understand the changes, too. For instance, in those days visitors usually used "rikishas" with "2 pullers, 30 cents per hour; $1 per ½ day; with 1 puller, 20 cents per hour."

The hotel names told the story too: Grand Hotel des Wagon Lits; Astor House; Bristol Hotel; Acropole; Metropole; Hotel du Nord; Hayashi; Fusokwan.

The traveller had problems. For instance, Peking had its

customs house outside the city wall, levied duties on all merchandise brought into Peking. As other cities did the same, a travelling businessman paid over and over again. Also, Peking — like most cities — issued its own currency.

July 22, Peidaiho

Hello darling —

... Yesterday was a busy day. Visited a miners' sanitarium in the village in the afternoon, got a short story for future writing (time copy). In evening went to Peking Opera (troupe here for four days) and saw *The Monkey King* — 8 p.m. to 11:30 p.m. Would have left at 10:30 intermission, but Alex was enthralled by the Monkey King, his friend Pig, the Sea King, the Monk, etc. — he had read the story so followed the action — and refused to leave. We had seats in the front row — 70 cents — and enjoyed the performance, though it was a bit tedious in spots. Said Alex [Sichrovsky] afterwards, with nine-year-old wisdom "That Monkey King would make a fortune in a capitalist country." But even here, where there is quite a levelling of wages, the highest paid people are the old, established stars of Peking Opera. Some get 1000–1500–2000 yuan a month, I was told. Not the members of the chorus, etc. but the stars.

July 29, Peking

Well now, my darling: so you ridicule my well-meant efforts to help you pack; you resort to feeble satire and imply that my suggestion to perhaps consider buying a one-burner hotplate which could almost fit into your purse is the same as bringing along a kitchen STOVE. You suspect that I will next ask you to bring along the kitchen sink. You wonder aloud if I am turning into a replica of the proverbial Englishman who requires all the comforts of home when he travels abroad — and you heroically infer that YOU need none of these bourgeois comforts, YOU can face the realities of life, YOU haven't lost contact with reality, etc. etc. ad nauseam.

All right, smarty pants. Bring yourself and Ricky, some cigars and pipe tobacco, a couple of pairs of panties and some nylons. If you find you have an extra forty pounds on your luggage ticket, bring more cigars. Satisfied?...

Anyway, you can get stockings here. In the summer everyone goes bare-legged, but in the fall the girls buy nice purple and pink cotton stockings, so you might as well live like the masses, DARLING!...

Well, not another word from me on this subject — I fear you will begin taking me apart again if I dare give you any more "tips."...

Well, dear, I'll end this. The plan calls for Harry and I to return to the seaside sometime next week, and that will likely mean the end of my writing to you. But don't be lonesome, keep busy packing, and write me lots of short notes if you haven't time for long letters, keep writing from Toronto and until you are on your way.

August 2

At 7:30 went to Hsin chao, had my usual favorite dinner, beef à la stroganoff on toast (that is, the way they make it, shredded beef and mushrooms in mushroom sauce), ice cream, and tea. The Negro chiropractor [Dr. V.J. Holland] sat down with me — he is leaving today for Moscow and then London — told me his tale of woe — got slightly involved with a bus conductor, he says she was warned to stay away from him and transferred to another bus after she had visited his hotel room with a girlfriend once — he found out her new bus line, she seemed distressed and "afraid" to talk to him, he sent her a letter with an elaborate plan to meet him, not recognize him, follow him to park — he thinks "security" got hold of letter (I think she probably turned it over) and when his course ended he was politely asked when he intended leaving — he says his hotel clerk told him he was a "security risk" — and of course he puts it down to some discrimination against Negroes — he tells me that a certain Negro university student who got in trouble through affair with Chinese girl student, which had unfortunate consequences for her, was sent home (this I know is true) and before he left called him up for advice — his advice was to tell off the authorities, tell them it was discrimination, etc.... but, I said, you know the rules here, students are told them very plainly, they know that they are here to study and return to work at home, and that Chinese girl students, even if they wished to marry them, cannot leave their own country, where they are needed in the work of construction — maybe someday these rules will be relaxed, but right now everyone knows these are the rules, so where is the discrimination? Ah, he said, but we Negroes, Bert, we know discrimination everywhere, how did they know I wanted to go to bed with the girl, maybe I wanted to marry her, isn't that discrimination? ... but, I said, you talk of going back to your girl in London, and looking forward to making love to her again — so it's logical that you DIDN'T intend to marry this Chinese girl, after all, you only met her on the bus, persuaded her to take a walk, talked the few words you know and then had her up and tried to talk with the aid of dictionary, now is it logical that you would fall in love, or are Chinese more logical in their assumption that you wanted to go to bed with her? ... not at all, he says, how can any man know anyone else's mind — I might quite well have decided to marry her.... Well, I left it at that ... but the "discrimination" angle — phooey!

August 9, Peitaiho

So, goody goody gumdrops! I expect to see you and Ricky stepping off the plane here in three weeks. If you are shy about kissing me in public — why, we'll behave like Chinese husband and wife — shake hands — and save the intimacies until later. (I think, though, I'll be bold and put my arms around you.) ...

Well, you know, I can't think of another blessed thing to tell you to bring — you've intimidated me ever since the STOVE episode. You mention wearing shorts — you'll be able to wear them here through September, I understand. October is also a nice fall month — it gets cold about middle of November and lasts until March. Sunshine — no rain — but dust storms blow up, I am told....

Darling, bye now — I'll paste this together and mail at supper tonight.

August 12, Peitaiho

Barring unforeseen news from you or Nelson [Clarke at the *Canadian Tribune*] today, this will be my last letter — but please keep writing to me. As this will be posted in the village at noon it will likely go to Peking tonight and so should reach you about the 20th or 21st....

Oh darling, I've said all these things many times. You know I'll be fretting until you are on your way. As Hollywood war movies say: "This is it." ...

Bye, bye, I'm impatient. Can't resist this: I'll see you in the suite by and by ...

Appendix

Seamen Aiming to Build Union
Plan to Establish Offices in All Great Lakes Ports
by BERT WHYTE

This morning we covered the waterfront in order to discover the reaction of the seamen to the latest organization formed to unite the Great Lakes seamen, the Marine Workers' Union of the Great Lakes. The general consensus of opinion was:

A union was urgently needed: the men are eager and ready to organize; that the Marine Workers' Union offers them the kind of a union they have long fought for, but the aforementioned union is as yet little known to the majority of the sailors.

Our next step was to approach D. Ferguson, Toronto organizer for the Marine Workers' Union, and to interview him concerning the immediate and ultimate aims of the union.

"Our immediate aim," stated Mr. Ferguson, "is to enroll members and build up our organization. Our ultimate aim is to establish shipping offices at Toronto, Montreal, Port Colborne, Fort William and other points on the Great Lakes, and to help our members both to secure jobs through us and to establish better working conditions through united effort."

Get Members
When questioned as to definite plans of action, Mr. Ferguson stated that at present his efforts are directed towards securing members and that the members themselves will formulate the policy of the unions. "We have no room for dictatorship methods such as existed in the last union," declared Ferguson emphatically. "Who is better able to determine the policy of a union than the members themselves?"

Assisting Mr. Ferguson, who has had seven years' experience on the Great Lakes, are several prominent trade union leader[s], which is in itself a guarantee of the sincerity of the union.

"Such steps as ultimate affiliation with the A. F. of L. will be decided later on by the union members," said the Toronto organizer, again stressing the democratic nature of the association. Officers and organizers will be recruited from the ranks of the seamen.

"Just what, in your opinion, are the chief grievances of the men on the Great Lakes boats today?" we asked.

Wages

"First, the question of wages," replied Mr. Ferguson. "Although a raise of 10 per cent in wages has taken effect on some boats this year, Canadian seamen are still receiving only approximately half the wages paid to American sailors.

"Second, the practice of paying off in ports. As soon as a boat strikes port, it is the custom of a great many of the boats to lay off the crew for the few days the ship may be in port, during which time the men work three hours a day in return for their board.

"Third, the system of carrying skeleton crews. During the past few years, some of the canal boats have been in the habit of paying off deckhands at Port Colborne while on the trip to the head of the lakes and reengaging these men on the down trip when they are again urgently needed. This policy leaves the skeleton crew to do extra work without extra pay while on the upper lakes."

Questioned for further details about organizational activities, Mr. Ferguson replied that over 700 letters announcing the birth of the union had been distributed among the working seamen with gratifying results. The drive for members is producing spendid returns, and an office will shortly be opened in Toronto.

"In the meanwhiile, any readers who wish further details may receive same by writing to the Marine Workers' Union of the Great Lakes, Box 174, G.P.O. Toronto," concluded Mr. Ferguson.

{This article appeared in the *Daily Clarion* on May 29, 1936. It offers a sample of Whyte's journalism at the time.}

Notes

1. *Pacific Tribune*, February 24, 1950.
2. Earle Birney, *Down the Long Table*, rev. ed., with an introduction by Bruce Nesbitt (Toronto: New Canadian Library, McClelland and Stewart, 1975 [1955]), 64.
3. Franz Mehring and Edward Fitzgerald, *Karl Marx: The Story of His Life* (London: John Lane, 1936), xii. Viewed online at http://www.questia.com/PM.qst? a=o&docId=74031391.
4. Maurice Isserman, review of *Red Chicago: American Communism at Its Grassroots, 1928–35*, by Randi Storch, H-HOAC book review, May 1, 2008.
5. Monica Whyte reveals that even in the 1980s, when the couple considered returning to Canada from the Soviet Union, Bert still expected to take up with the Communist Party of Canada. Whyte died in Moscow before he could return (interview with Monica Whyte, March 28, 2010).
6. Library and Archives Canada (hereafter LAC), Bert Whyte file, MG10 K2 545/6/575.
7. See Larry Hannant, ed., *The Politics of Passion: Norman Bethune's Writing and Art* (Toronto: University of Toronto

Press, 1998), 122–26; Michael Petrou, *Renegades: Canadians in the Spanish Civil War* (Vancouver: University of British Columbia Press, 2008), 42–45.

8. Norman Penner, *Canadian Communism: The Stalin Years and Beyond* (Toronto: Methuen, 1988), 254.

9. LAC, Access to Information and Privacy (ATIP) Request A 2006 00545, Bert Whyte, RCMP memo for file, March 16, 1970.

10. For a discussion of other narratives of the road, see Todd McCallum, "*Vancouver Through the Eyes of a Hobo*: Experience, Identity, and Value in the Writing of Canada's Depression-Era Tramps," *Labour/Le travail* 59 (Spring 2007): 43–68.

11. Interview with Monica Whyte, December 20, 2006. Victor Hoar, *The Mackenzie-Papineau Battalion: Canadian Participation in the Spanish Civil War* (n.p.: Copp Clark, 1969), 146, and Michael Petrou, *Renegades: Canadians in the Spanish Civil War* (Vancouver: University of British Columbia Press, 2008), 77, also offer accounts of Black's bravery in Spain.

12. In 1936 the Party changed the name of its paper from *The Worker* to the *Daily Clarion*. Whyte refers to an article he wrote for *The Worker* in 1936, which was likely near the end of its life.

13. By the late 1970s, the RCMP Security Service had opened files on more than 800,000 individuals and organizations. In 1984, when the RCMP SS was transformed into the Canadian Security Intelligence Service, some half a million of these records were still intact. Of those, CSIS kept 30,000 because they related to ongoing security matters. Library and Archives Canada acquired another 30,000, which archivists there considered to be of historical value.

However, the disposition agreement between CSIS and LAC that accompanied the files required LAC to consult with CSIS before releasing any record under the Access to Information Act. Under this agreement, CSIS reviews every file before release. In the Bert Whyte file, hundreds of pages are entirely blank and many more have significant deletions.

14. LAC, ATIP Request A 2006 00545, Bert Whyte, RCMP report, October 22, 1940. In 1939–40, Whyte attended a party school of the Communist Party of the United States of America in Cleveland, Ohio, before returning to Canada, where he became CPC organizer in Ottawa.

15. Ben Swankey, *What's New: Memoirs of a Socialist Idealist* (Victoria: Trafford, 2008), 88–89. Another CPC activist, John Boyd, recounted a similar story of the party's haphazard effort to organize underground in Manitoba during World War II. See John Boyd, "A Noble Cause Betrayed . . . but Hope Lives On: Pages from a Political Life," which is reproduced on the Socialist History Project website, at http://www2.cddc.vt.edu/marxists/history/canada/socialisthistory/Remember/Reminiscences/Boyd/B1.htm. Boyd's memoir was originally published in 1999 as a Canadian Institute of Ukrainian Studies Research Report (no. 64; ISBN 1-894301-64-1). The print edition is available from CIUS Press at http://www.utoronto.ca/cius/publications/rr/rr64.htm.

16. Interview with Monica Whyte, December 20, 2006.

17. *Globe and Mail*, March 14, 1940, and January 18, 1941; *Clarion*, February 1, 1941. Norman Penner asserts that "many Party members [in World War II] found reading the [Canadian] *Tribune* a relief, much easier to accept than the clandestine publications from the underground,

with their exhortations to revolution and civil war" (*Canadian Communism*, 168). Whyte's work proves that not all the notes from the underground were tiresome diatribes.

18. It should be noted that Frank Scott, a prominent intellectual force within the Co-operative Common-wealth Federation, also argued, during that party's early-September 1939 debate about whether the war had an anti-fascist or an imperialist character, that it was an imperialist war. See Sandra Djwa, *The Politics of the Imagination: A Life of F.R. Scott* (Vancouver and Toronto: Douglas and McIntyre, 1987), 185.

19. Penner, *Canadian Communism*, 161.

20. Clement Liebovitz and Alvin Finkel, *In Our Time: The Chamberlain-Hitler Collusion* (New York: Monthly Review Press, 1998), 132 and passim. The authors set out in detail the complicated tactical shifts of the Western countries, especially Britain and France — some of them breathtaking in their brazenness. The Munich agreement of September 1938, for instance, appears to have been intended to facilitate a rapprochement between fascist Germany and capitalist Britain and France, to lay the groundwork for a German attack on communism in the USSR, while the Western European countries would remain out of German hands. From this perspective, Hitler was untrustworthy not because he was an aggressor but because he could not be counted on to abide by the agreement made with British Prime Minister Neville Chamberlain and French Prime Minister Édouard Daladier at Munich.

21. *Clarion*, February 1, 1941.

22. On the military's wariness about communists, see Larry Hannant, *The Infernal Machine: Investigating the Loyalty of Canadian Citizens* (Toronto: University of Toronto Press, 1995), 119–20, and Swankey, *What's New*, 109.

23. Unfortunately, despite inquiries, it has been impossible to identify Rita's full name.

24. Interview with Monica Whyte, December 20, 2006.

25. LAC ATIP Request A 2006 00545, Bert Whyte, report of February 16, 1946, by Captain E.B. Morgan.

26. Frank K. Clarke writes about the Cold War campaign to oust progressives from the Toronto Board of Education: see "'Keep Communism Out of Our Schools': Cold War Anti-Communism at the Toronto Board of Education, 1948–1951," *Labour/Le travail* 49 (Spring 2002): 93–120. In the Board of Education, the anti-communist campaign was less successful than in the city council. In the Ontario legislature, two communists, A.A. MacLeod and J.B. Salsberg, were elected in the 1943 contest. Both were Red-baited, but MacLeod held his seat until defeated in the 1951 election, while Salsberg was voted out only in 1955.

27. LAC ATIP Request A 2006 00545 Bert Whyte, RCMP memorandum of November 6, 1945; RCMP memo to Inspector Parsons, September 12, 1946; John Boyd, personal communication, August 20, 2008. Whyte's election to the party's national committee also made him the target of a public campaign by the Canadian Chamber of Commerce, which named him in its publication *The Communist Threat to Canada*, published in 1947. Whyte's tenure in the central committee likely ended in 1948, when he decamped for the west coast.

28. *Pacific Tribune*, August 8, 15, and 22, September 12, 19, and 26, October 17 and 24, November 21, and December 12, 1952, and January 9, 16, and 23 and April 24, 1953. Ross Lambertson examines this case in detail in "The Black, Brown, White, and Red Blues: The Beating of Clarence Clemons," *Canadian Historical Review* 85(4) (December 2004): 755–76.

29. University of British Columbia Rare Books and Special Collections, Lily Greene fonds, Box 1, File 1-9, McEwen to Lily et al., February 9, 1953.

30. *Pacific Tribune*, March 25, 1955. An article typical of his campaign against the violent NHL brand of hockey, in contrast to the quicker and less violent game played in the USSR, can be seen in the April 10, 1953, *Pacific Tribune*.

31. Interview with Monica Whyte, March 18, 2008.

32. *Pacific Tribune*, April 1, 1955.

33. Interview with Monica Whyte, August 20, 2008. Whyte's reaction might have been typical of Anglo-Canadian opinion, while the party leadership was intent on a higher ideological purpose that transcended Anglo "prejudices." Whyte and other writers were part of a pioneering communist effort to show that sports were far from an apolitical aspect of life. Communist sports writers in the United States and South Africa, for instance, fought the racial bias of the sports establishment. Two important figures in this group died within a week of one another in December 2009. One was Lester Rodney, who, as a reporter, columnist, and sports editor for the US communist paper the *Daily Worker*, campaigned against the colour bar in professional baseball in the 1930s and 1940s. See his obituary in the *San*

Francisco Chronicle, December 25, 2009. Another was South African Dennis Brutus, whose campaign against apartheid in that country and its manifestations in sports led to him being imprisoned at Robben Island with Nelson Mandela. See Amy Goodman, "The Poetic Justice of Dennis Brutus," *Truthdig*, December 29, 2009; available at http://www.truthdig.com/report/item/the_poetic_ justice_of_dennis_brutus_20091229/.

34. *Pacific Tribune*, September (no date), 1951. Whyte's view of women should not be distorted. Concerning their full participation in sports, for instance, he argued that "the emancipation of women in the field of sports pro- ceeds apace, and mossback males who try to throw up roadblocks will dwindle in numbers until they eventually wind up in museums, right next to brontosaurus" (*Pacific Tribune*, March 5, 1954).

35. *Canadian Tribune*, November 1, 1965; interview with Monica Whyte, August 20, 2008.

36. Interview with Monica Whyte, December 20, 2006.

37. Ibid.

38. Ibid.

39. Hugh Deane, *Good Deeds and Gunboats: Two Centuries of American-Chinese Encounters* (San Francisco: China Books and Periodicals, 1990), 161.

40. *U.S. News and World Report*, January 27, 1950.

41. In the early twenty-first century, the strategic outlook of the US elite towards China is still framed by words echoing from the 1960s — "good," "bad," and "commu- nist" — but they have acquired a new meaning. China after 1979 qualified as "good" by quickly and decisively becoming integrated into the global capitalist system.

But in a world marked by inter-imperialist competition, even capitalist countries can be rivals, which the US and China increasingly seem to be. Thus, condemning China as "communist" allows the US to portray China as "bad," even though the fundamental US complaints are over matters such as trade and currency disputes and geopolitical zones of control.

42. Interview with Monica Whyte, December 20, 2006.

43. Ibid. See also Faith Johnston, *A Great Restlessness: The Life and Politics of Dorise Nielsen* (Winnipeg: University of Manitoba Press, 2006), 255–57.

44. *Canadian Tribune*, August 12, 1963.

45. Editorial Department of *Renmin Ribao, The Historical Experience of the War Against Fascism* (Beijing: Foreign Languages Press, 1965), 12–13. As the experience of the decades to follow would make abundantly clear, imperialism had not abandoned war as a means to impose itself on the people of the world. Events also quickly overturned the idea that nuclear weapons had fundamentally altered the nature of war. In March and August 1969, for the first time, armed conflict broke out between countries that possessed nuclear arms — China and the USSR. Yet these border clashes featured conventional weapons only. Thus it is evident that in some ways nuclearweapons are, as Mao insisted, paper tigers. Just because countries *possess* nuclear weapons doesn't mean that they will use them. Of course, this is no guarantee that they won't use such weapons in the future. Clearly, prevailing political and military conditions influence the choice of weapons to be used in a war. The development of a particular weapon doesn't render war impossible. The Chinese Communist Party saw well the danger of the revisionist argument that the massive scale of the weaponry now in the hands of imperialists would make war between imperial powers impossible. Another point of contention was the impact of national liberation movements. The struggle of the Vietnamese people against US aggression illustrated Mao's idea that a popular national liberation war could be successfully waged against a country possessing nuclear weapons, one whose political and military elite included some (Douglas MacArthur and Curtis "Bombs Away" LeMay, among others) who hankered to launch a nuclear war.

46. The timing of the People's Republic's decision to invite and pay for Western correspondents from communist newspapers in the late 1950s suggests that the initiative was likely part of the jockeying in the early days of the Sino-Soviet split, as China attempted to cultivate more favourable media attention in the West, particularly among active communists there.

47. *Workers Vanguard*, March 31, 1964.

48. Interview with Monica Whyte, December 20, 2006; LAC, MG 30 (Ted Allan Papers), D388, vol. 68, file 68-20, Kastner to Allan, n.d.

49. Charles Taylor writes, for instance, that in the autumn of 1959 the *Globe and Mail*'s Frederick Nossal arrived in Beijing "to open *the first Western* newspaper bureau since the Communist victory a decade earlier" (my emphasis): Charles Taylor, ed., *China Hands: The Globe and Mail in Peking* (Toronto: McClelland and Stewart, 1984), 7. Fifty years later the *Globe and Mail* was still claiming to be "the first Western newspaper allowed to open a Peking [*sic*] bureau" (*Globe and Mail*, October 3, 2009). Taylor and his latter-day counterparts seem to be unaware of the fact that

Agence France-Presse opened a Beijing bureau in 1958 and Reuters also had a correspondent there in the 1950s. In addition, correspondents from communist newspapers in Canada, Australia, Italy, and Britain had long preceded the *Globe*'s representative in China. Perhaps to Taylor they forfeited their Western status by being communist.

50. *Tribune*, July 22, 1966.

51. Interview with Monica Whyte, December 20, 2006.

52. Ibid.

53. Inner-party strife was the subject of a lengthy RCMP report of March 16, 1970, in the Bert Whyte file. In it, an RCMP source inside the party described the CPC as "facing a very real crisis" because of the Soviet suppression of the reform movement in Czechoslovakia. Even the long-standing core members of the CPC, the Ukrainians, were overwhelmingly opposed to the Soviet Union's action in Czechoslovakia (LAC, ATIP Request A 2006 00545, Bert Whyte, report of March 16, 1970). On June 24, 1970, an RCMP report pointed out that Whyte still supported the party line, although he did not like William Kashtan, who had become secretary general in 1964, when Leslie Morris died.

54. LAC, ATIP Request A 2006 00545, Bert Whyte, report of March 20, 1967.

55. *Canadian Tribune*, February 9, 1973.

56. Interview with Monica Whyte, December 20, 2006.

57. Ibid.

58. The Canadian Committee on Labour History has been one of the most active publishers of such works. A list of them can be found on the CCLH website at http://www.cclh.ca/books/index.php.

Index

Chorley Park Military Hospital, 77, 237
church, 38–39, 72–76; Baptist, 42, 72; Methodist, 42; Presbyterian, 38, 42; United, 72
Churchill, Winston, 17, 203, 227, 234
Chu Teh, 291
CKMO Radio (Vancouver), 247
Clarke, Nelson, 28, 295, 313, 318
Clemons, Clarence, 22–23, 326n28
Cobalt (Ontario), 38, 45–46, 50–52, 58, 64–68, 94
Colby, Mel, 222
Cold War, 3, 21, 36, 160, 239–40, 251, 325n26
Communist International (Comintern), 8–9, 16, 18, 287
Communist Party of Canada (CPC), 4, 6–10, 13, 15–16, 18, 26–27, 31–32, 34, 36, 177, 179–80, 194, 321n5, 330n53
Conroyal Mine, 46–48, 84–85, 101
Co-operative Commonwealth Federation (CCF), 7, 108, 162, 244, 247, 324n18
Copper Cliff (Ontario), 38
Corio, Ann, 25
Cornwall (Ontario), 177, 184
Cranbrook (British Columbia), 120
Creston (British Columbia), 122
Czechoslovakia, 8–9, 17, 33, 330n53

d
Daily Clarion, 12, 15, 18, 156, 168, 177, 179–84, 186, 322n12
Daily Worker (Britain), 27, 291
Darrow, Clarence, 73–74
Davis, Jim, 167
De Leon, Daniel, 167–68
Dempsey, Jack, 56–57, 60, 87
Dent, Wally, 200–201
Dong'an Bazaar, 276
Doukhobors, 5, 124
Dutch resistance, 231

e
Eaton's stores, 101, 134
Elko (British Columbia), 119
Endicott, James, 285
Engels, Friedrich, 27
En-Lai, Chou, 307
Epstein, Israel, 279
Erlich, Muni, 166, 229
Estevan (Saskatchewan), 145

f
Falaise (France), 210–11
Ferguson, Claude Dewar, 26, 140, 152–53, 160, 168, 207, 239–40, 251
Finkel, Alvin, 17, 324n20
Ford strike in Windsor, 237
Fort Macleod (Alberta), 118
Freed, Norman, 239

g
Gananoque (Ontario), 58–59
General Montgomery, 204, 209, 220, 307
German-Soviet Non-Aggression Pact, 8
Globe and Mail, 15, 21, 110, 180–81, 329n49
Goatfell (British Columbia), 120–22
Gordon, Roann, 272, 276, 283, 285, 287, 299, 301–2
Gordon, Sydney, 31, 272, 301
Gorodetsky, Reuben, 199–200, 225, 229
Gouzenko, Igor, 21
Gowganda (Ontario), 47, 94–95
Grand Forks (British Columbia), 124
Great Depression, 7, 11, 16, 107, 134
Greene, Felix, 312
Greenleigh, Gavin, 303–4
Griffin, Hal, 248, 279

h
Haileybury (Ontario), 38–39, 42, 44, 46, 52, 58, 61–62, 64–66, 98
Half-moon Bay (British Columbia), 135
Haywood, Big Bill, 142, 148

Henschke, Eric, 290
Hibou, 159
Hirschfeld, Harry, 213–14
Hitler, Adolph, 12, 16–17, 186, 188, 210, 219, 229, 324n20
Hoar, Victor, 141
Ho Chi Minh (Vietnam), 255
Holland, 50, 214, 221, 223–27, 229, 231, 233, 287, 316
Housewives' League of British Columbia, 245

i

Imperial Optical Company, 237
Industrial Workers of the World (Wobblies), 7, 138, 142–43, 145, 147, 159, 163, 281
Irkutsk (USSR), 270, 274–75

j

Jeffries, Jim, 47, 73
Jews, 41, 43, 71, 76, 89–90
Johnson, Ernest George ("Black Mac"), 198
Jones, Effie, 244–46

k

Kao, Jack, 272
Kao, Ted, 272
Kardash, Mary, 5
Kastner, Rose, 31
Katinen, Leo, 111
Kenny, Bert, 146
Khrushchev, Nikita, 8, 28
King, William Lyon Mackenzie, 14
Kingston (Ontario), 45, 47, 58, 60, 68–69, 71–72, 80 81, 84, 89, 99–101, 108, 33, 151–52, 177, 184, 194–95
Kingston Whig-Standard, 59–60, 82
Kirkland Lake (Ontario), 43, 46–47, 52, 65, 84–85, 101, 191
Korean War, 28, 311
Ku Klux Klan, 71–72

l

Labour-Progressive Party, 21, 160, 238, 244
Lac Seul (Ontario), 137
Lake Timiskaming (Ontario), 38, 50, 52, 64
LaRose, Alfred, 50–51
Lee Tong, Harry, 39–40
Leopold, (Jack Esselwein) John, 194–95
Leniszek, May, 244
Lethbridge (Alberta), 118
Levitt, Joe, 199–200
Library and Archives Canada (LAC), 13, 322n13
Liebovitz, Clement, 324n20
Lipman, Barney, 89–94, 99–100
London (England), 56–57, 194–95, 197–98, 202, 208, 225, 233, 287, 291, 301, 308–9, 316–17

m

MacBrien, James, 107
Mackenzie-Papineau Battalion, 9, 12, 141, 192, 206
MacLeod, A.A., 325n26
Malone, Dick, 210
Maltin, Sam, 242
Mann, Tom, 144
Mao Zedong, 28, 30, 261, 292, 306–7, 328–29n45
Maple Leaf, 222, 224, 231, 234
Maple Leaf Gardens, 108, 111
Marx, Groucho, 32
Marx, Karl, 6
McEwen, Tom, 23, 165, 248
McLaughlin, James, 76–77, 94, 101, 134–35
Medicine Hat (Alberta), 117
Millionaires' Row, 52, 61, 64–66
Montgomery, Bernard, 204, 210, 216, 227, 307
Montreal (Quebec), 23, 51, 94, 107, 140, 154–55, 163, 186, 195, 242
Montreal Canadiens, 23
Morgan, E.B., 20

Morris, Leslie, 10, 30, 185, 241, 252, 330n53
Moscow, 4–5, 9–10, 21, 29, 32–35, 147–48, 150, 161, 249, 268, 270, 272–75, 316, 321n5
Munich Agreement, 324n20
Murphy, Harvey, 26, 85, 146, 148–52
Murray, Jim, 45
Mussolini, Benito, 12

n

National Federation of Labour Youth, 26
National Hockey League (NHL), 23–24
Nelson Gaol (British Columbia), 122–23, 318
Nevin, Johnny, 194
New Democratic Party, 244
Nichol, Dave, 214
Nielsen, Dorise, 29–30, 303
Nixon, Richard, 29
Non-Partisan Association, 244, 247
Noranda (Quebec), 7–8, 48–49, 102–3, 110–12, 119–20, 139, 161, 164–66
North Bay (Ontario), 130, 189

o

Oldenburg, 232–33
Olynyk, Mike, 192, 200, 208
One Big Union, 142–44, 148
Orange Order, 42
Ottawa (Ontario), 13–15, 18, 21, 49–50, 65, 68, 82, 108, 177–82, 184–85, 188, 194, 199, 323n14
Ottawa Citizen, 15, 180
Ottawa Clarion, 14, 18
Ottawa Journal, 21

p

Pacific Tribune, 22–24, 248, 279, 291, 297
Paine, Thomas, 75–76
Panchen Lama, 297
Peace Arch Park (Washington), 248
Pembroke (Ontario), 43, 65–66, 72, 109, 169, 177, 183

Penner, Norman, 9, 16, 323n17
Penticton (British Columbia), 124–25
Petawawa Internment Camp, 183
Phillips, Paul, 141, 166–67
Poland, 17, 89, 177
Pople, Jim, 184–85
Prague Spring, 33
Princeton (British Columbia), 125–26
Pu Yi, 261, 307

q

Queen Elizabeth, 234
Queen's University, 45, 60, 68, 77, 82, 95, 184

r

Ralston, James, 204
Reader's Digest, 33
Red Lake (Ontario), 45
Regina (Saskatchewan), 115
relief camps, 4, 118, 120, 124–26, 129, 136–37, 161, 168
Relief Camp Workers' Union, 108, 162–63
Renmin Ribao (People's Daily), 273, 277–78, 313, 328n45
Richard, Maurice ("the Rocket"), 23
Rita (Bert Whyte's first wife), 19, 25, 206, 221, 298, 325n23
Robeson, Paul, 248
Rose, Fred, 26
Rouyn (Quebec), 101–3, 111, 114
Royal Alexandra Theatre, 25
Royal Canadian Mounted Police (RCMP), 6, 9–10, 12–13, 24, 34, 177–78, 185–86, 188
Ruddell, Elgin, 244
Russian slave labourers, 231

s

Salmon, Malcolm, 292
Salsberg, J.B., 155–56, 239, 325n26
Samuelson, Roy, 26
Sanderson, M.A., 21
Sanderson, R.A., 247
Sand Merchant, 154, 159

ℓℓℓℓℓℓ

This book was printed on 60 lb Rolland Opaque50 with photo inserts on 80 lb Sappi Flo Gloss. The text face is ITC Cheltenham, designed by Tony Stan. The sanserif face is Trade Gothic, designed by Jackson Burke. The display face is Stephen Rapp's Raniscript.